AVRIL LAVIGNE'S

MAKE 5 WISHES

VOLUME 1

Starring Avril Lavigne
Concept by Camilla d'Errico
Story by Camilla d'Errico
and Joshua Dysart
Script by Joshua Dysart
Art by Camilla d'Errico

D1424576

Avril Lavigne's Make 5 Wishes Volume 1
ISBN-10: 1 84576 683 0
ISBN-13: 9781845766832

Published by Titan Books,
A division of Titan Publishing Group Ltd.
144 Southwark Street
London SE1 0UP.

This edition published by arrangement with Ballantine Books, an imprint of Random House Publishing Group, a division of Random House, Inc.

Some of the artwork contained in this work is preexisting.

Printed in Spain.

A CIP catalogue record for this book is available from the British Library.

This edition first published: September 2007
10 9 8 7 6 5 4 3 2 1

Project direction by House of Parlance Media, www.houseofparlance.com
Coloring: Dave McCaig
Background Art and Additional Coloring: Sunder Raj
Lettering: Ed Brisson
Cover Art: Camilla d'Errico
Cover Design: Dreu Pennington-McNeil

What did you think of this book? We love to hear from our readers. Please email us at readerfeedback@titanemail.com, or write to us at the above address.
To subscribe to our regular newsletter for up-to-the-minute news, great offers and competitions, email booksezine@titanemail.com

www.titanbooks.com

CONTENTS

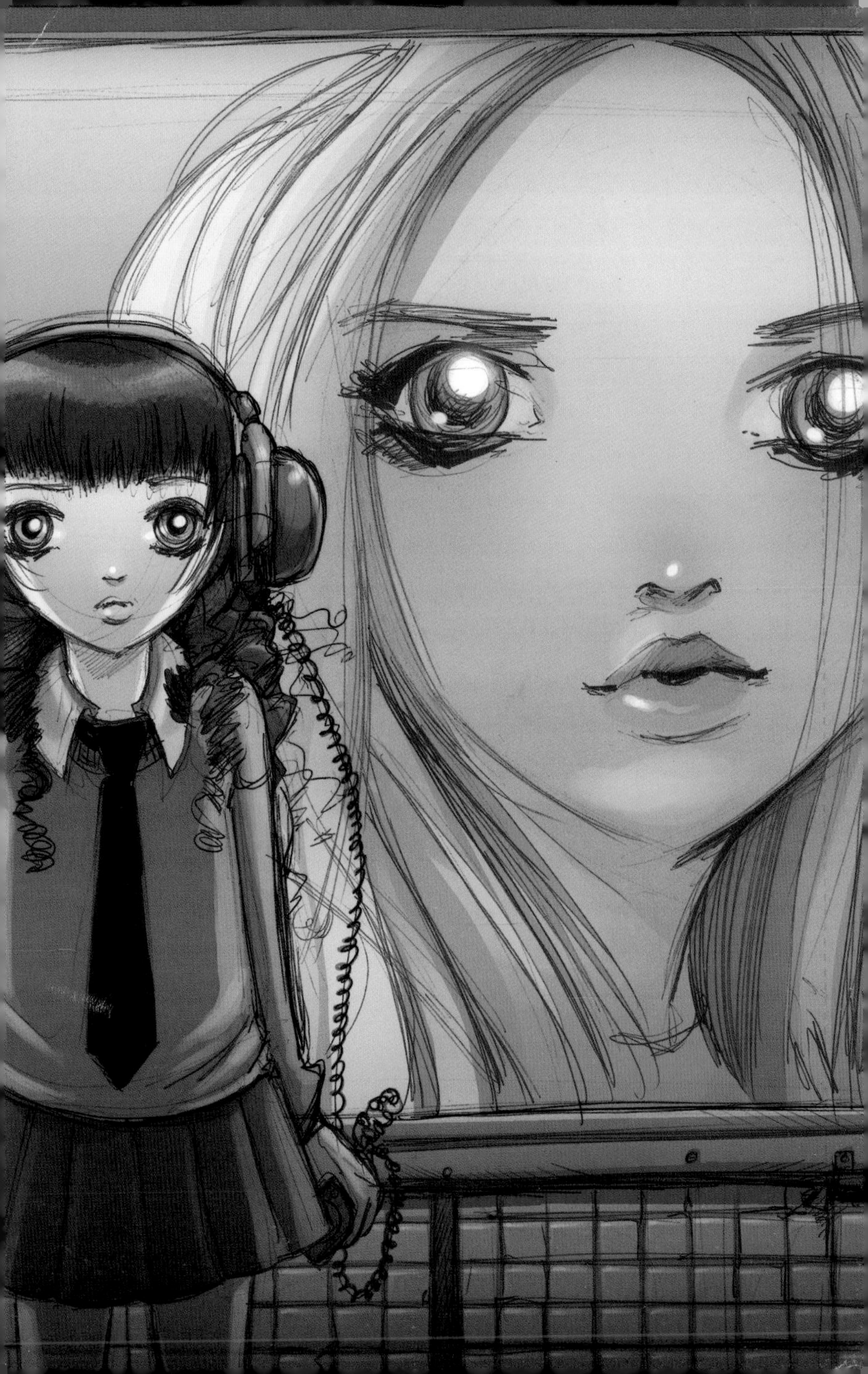

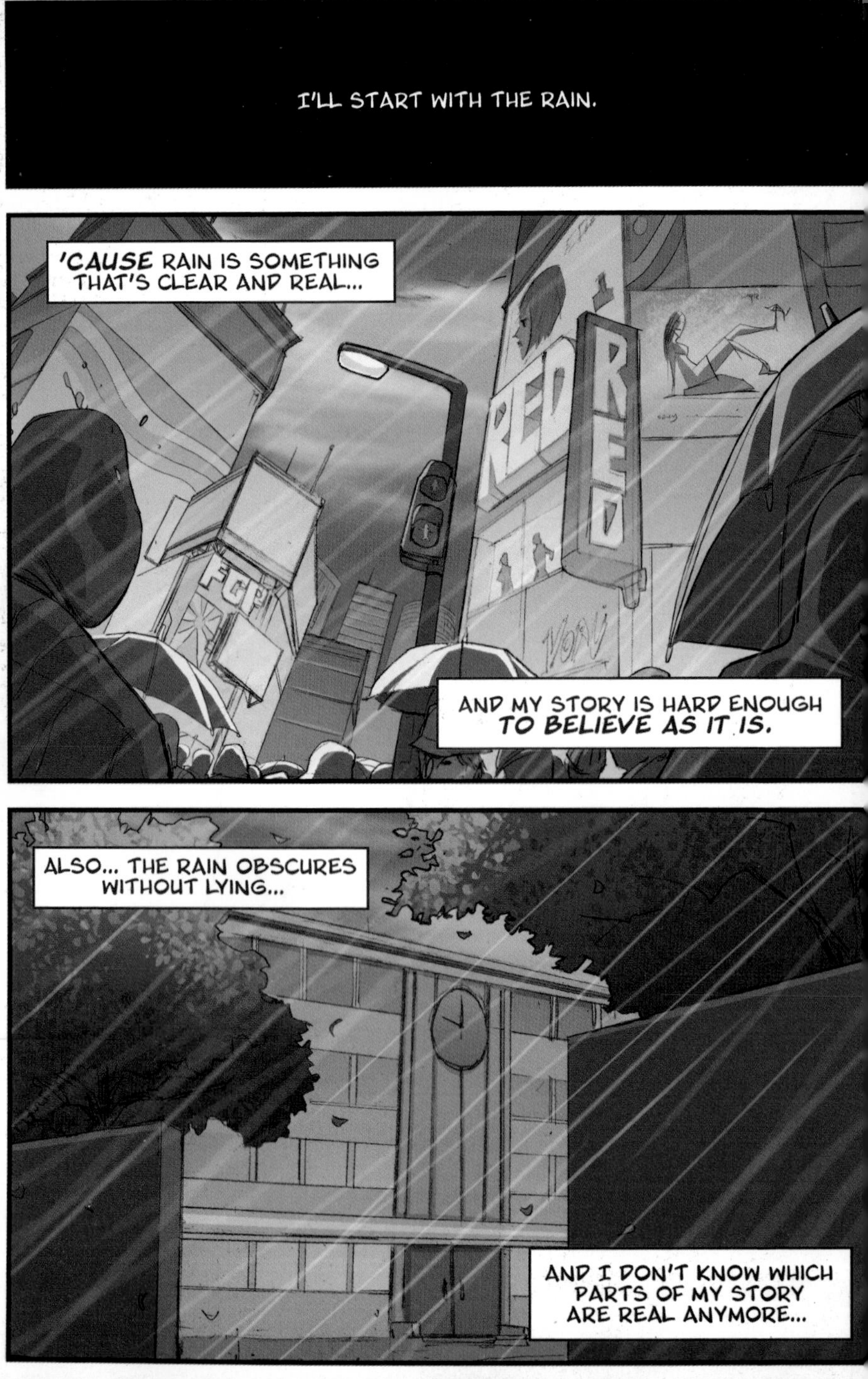
I'LL START WITH THE RAIN.
'CAUSE RAIN IS SOMETHING THAT'S CLEAR AND REAL...
RED
RED
AND MY STORY IS HARD ENOUGH TO BELIEVE AS IT IS.
ALSO... THE RAIN OBSCURES WITHOUT LYING...
AND I DON'T KNOW WHICH PARTS OF MY STORY ARE REAL ANYMORE...

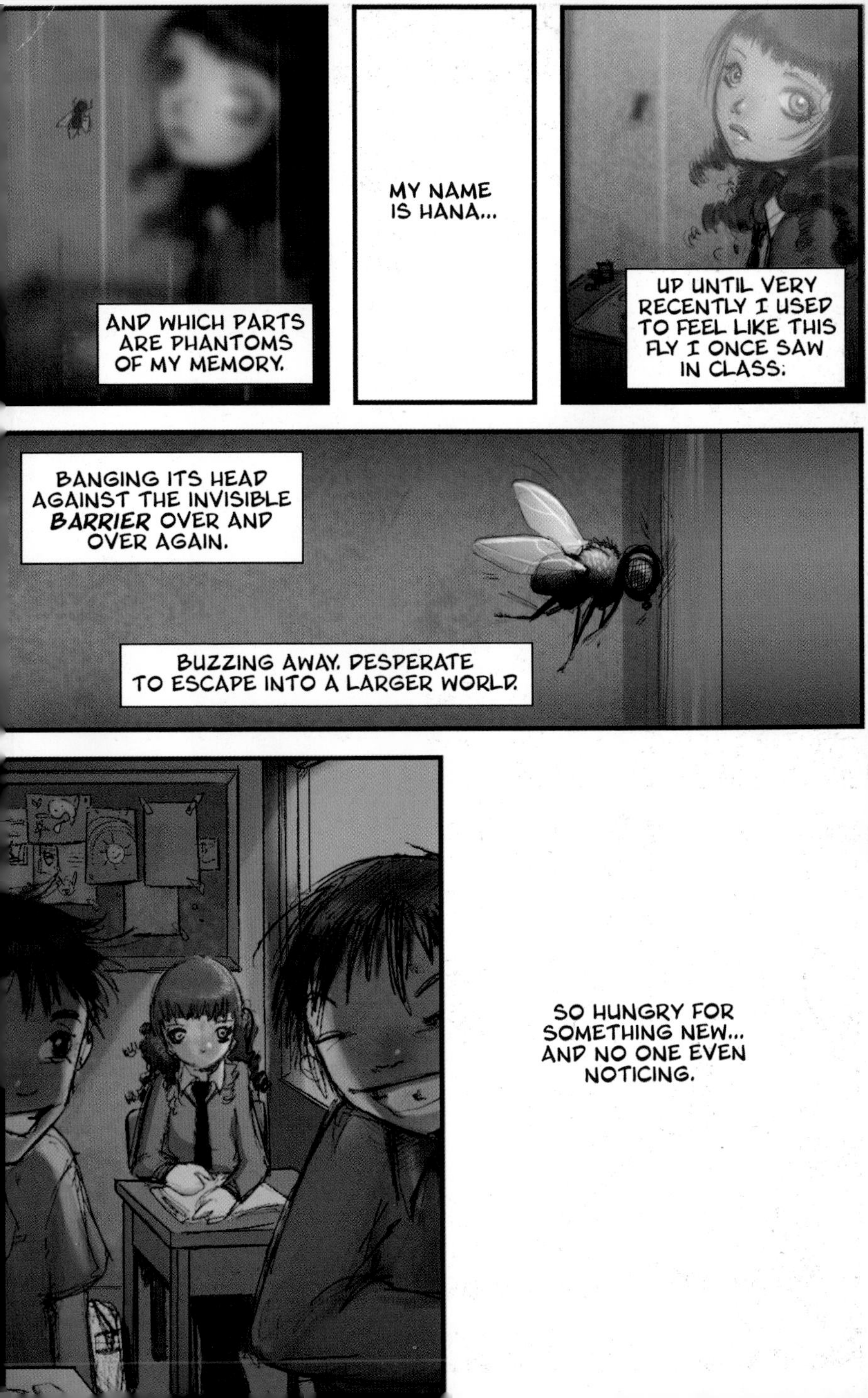
AND WHICH PARTS ARE PHANTOMS OF MY MEMORY.
MY NAME IS HANA...
UP UNTIL VERY RECENTLY I USED TO FEEL LIKE THIS FLY I ONCE SAW IN CLASS:
BANGING ITS HEAD AGAINST THE INVISIBLE *BARRIER* OVER AND OVER AGAIN.
BUZZING AWAY. DESPERATE TO ESCAPE INTO A LARGER WORLD.
SO HUNGRY FOR SOMETHING NEW... AND NO ONE EVEN NOTICING.

I WAS SMALL, TOO. INVISIBLE.

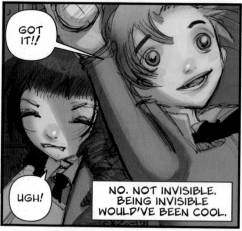

GOT IT!!

UGH!

NO. NOT INVISIBLE. BEING INVISIBLE WOULD'VE BEEN COOL.

I JUST WASN'T WORTH NOTICING.

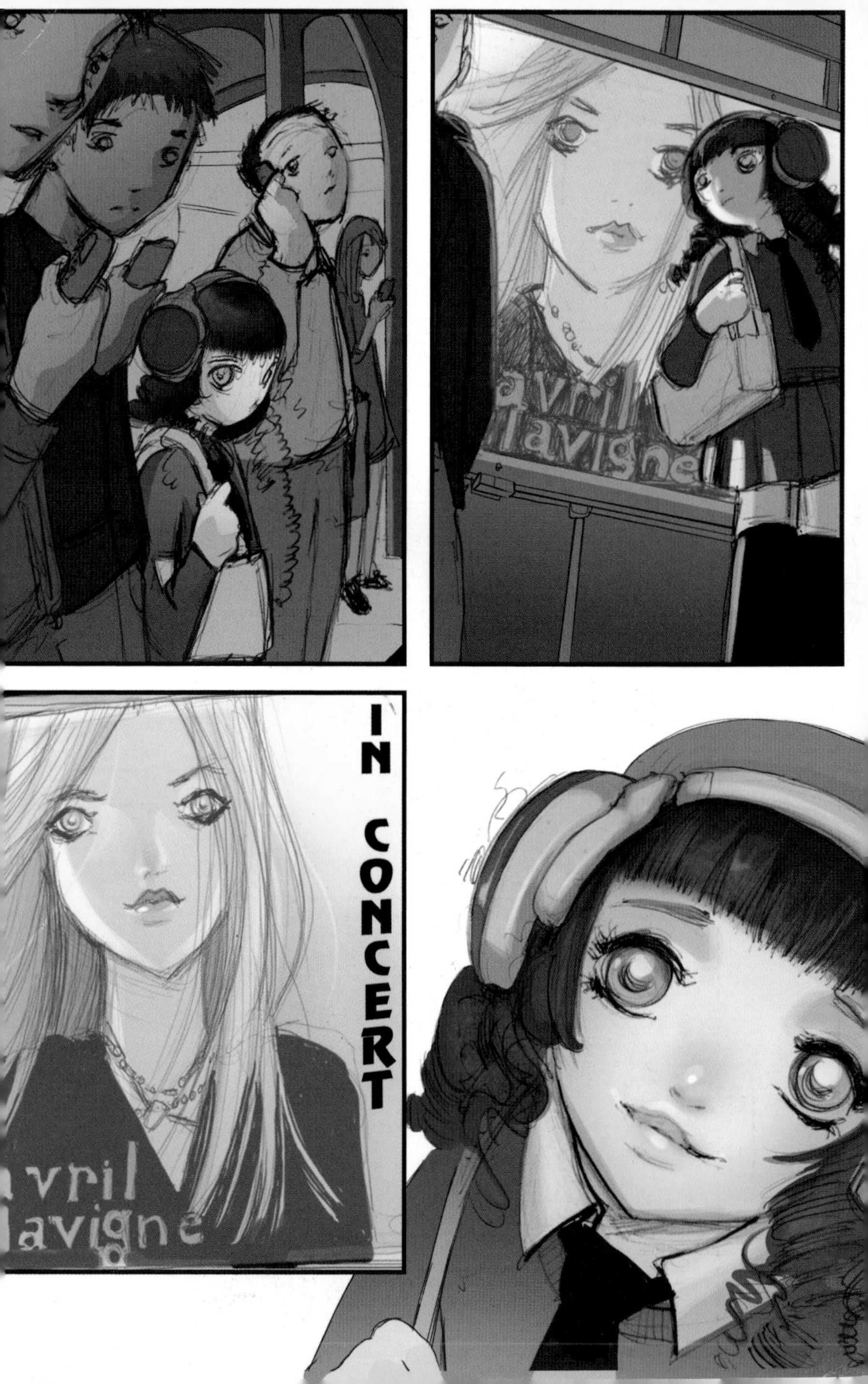
avril lavigne
avril lavigne
IN CONCERT

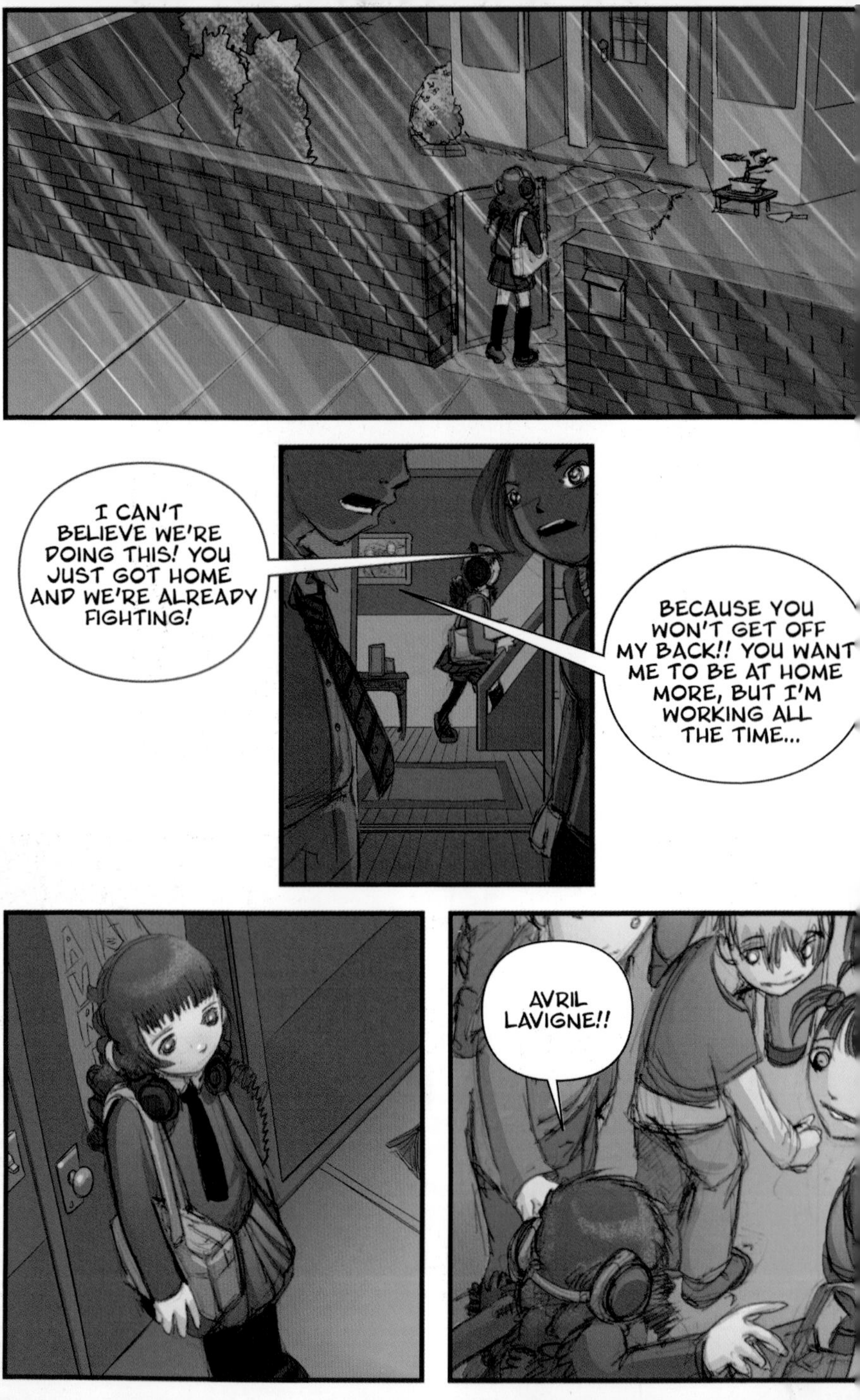
I CAN'T BELIEVE WE'RE DOING THIS! YOU JUST GOT HOME AND WE'RE ALREADY FIGHTING!
BECAUSE YOU WON'T GET OFF MY BACK!! YOU WANT ME TO BE AT HOME MORE, BUT I'M WORKING ALL THE TIME...
AVRIL LAVIGNE!!

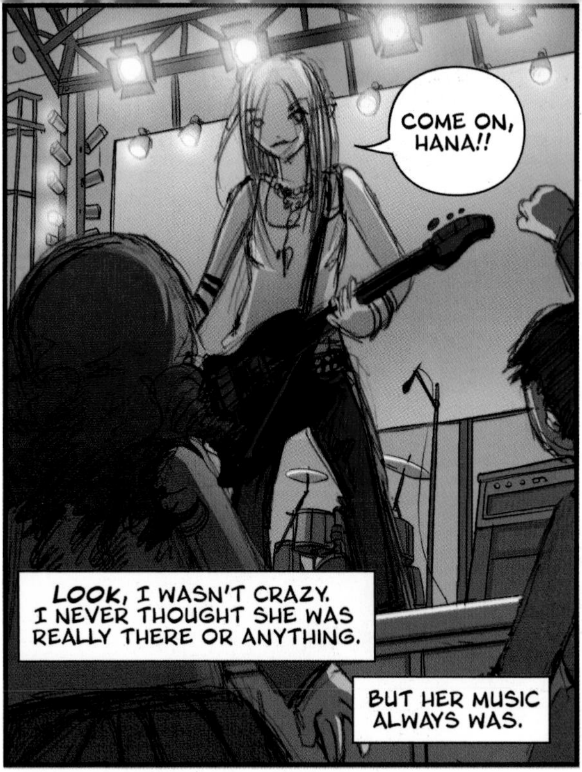
COME ON, HANA!!
LOOK, I WASN'T CRAZY. I NEVER THOUGHT SHE WAS REALLY THERE OR ANYTHING.
BUT HER MUSIC ALWAYS WAS.

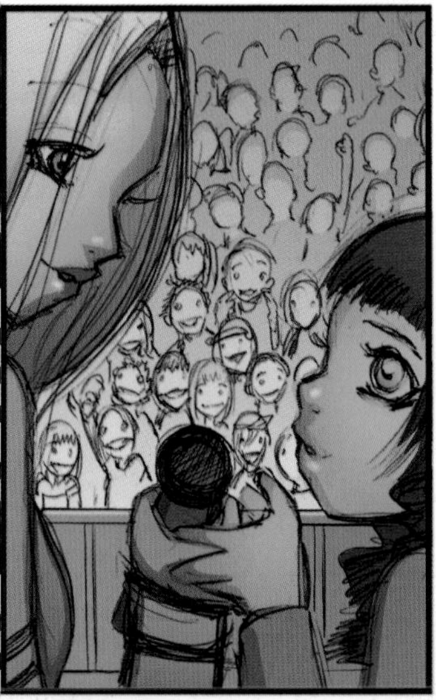

IT WAS IN EVERY PART OF MY LIFE. AND EVEN THOUGH IT SEEMED TO COME FROM SO FAR AWAY...

IT STILL FELT LIKE IT WAS AIMED RIGHT AT ME...

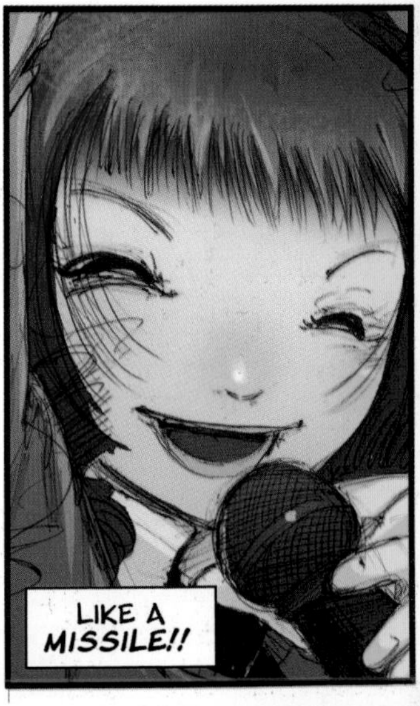
LIKE A *MISSILE!!*

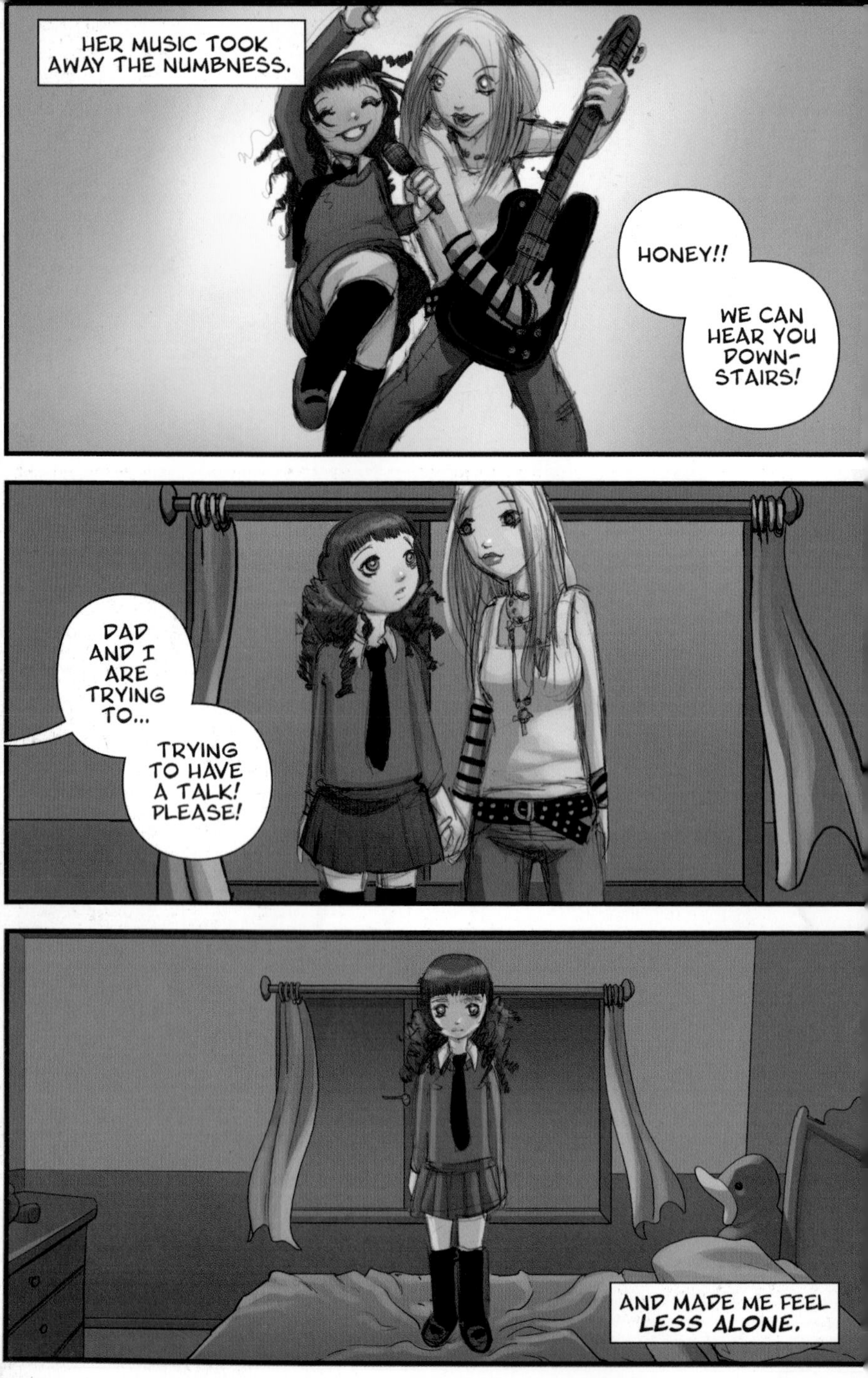
HER MUSIC TOOK AWAY THE NUMBNESS.
HONEY!!
WE CAN HEAR YOU DOWN-STAIRS!
DAD AND I ARE TRYING TO...
TRYING TO HAVE A TALK! PLEASE!
AND MADE ME FEEL LESS ALONE.

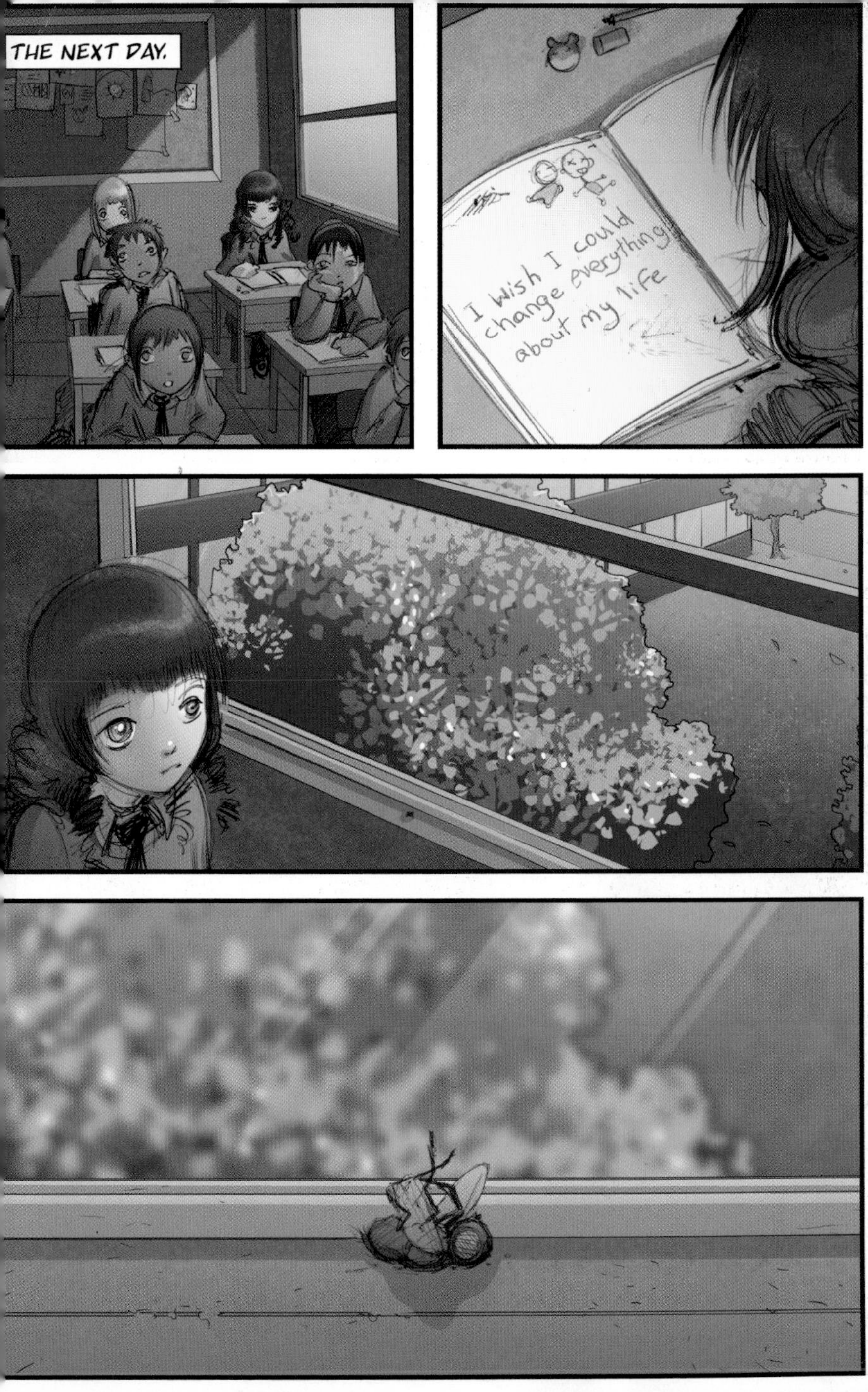
THE NEXT DAY.
I wish I could change everything about my life

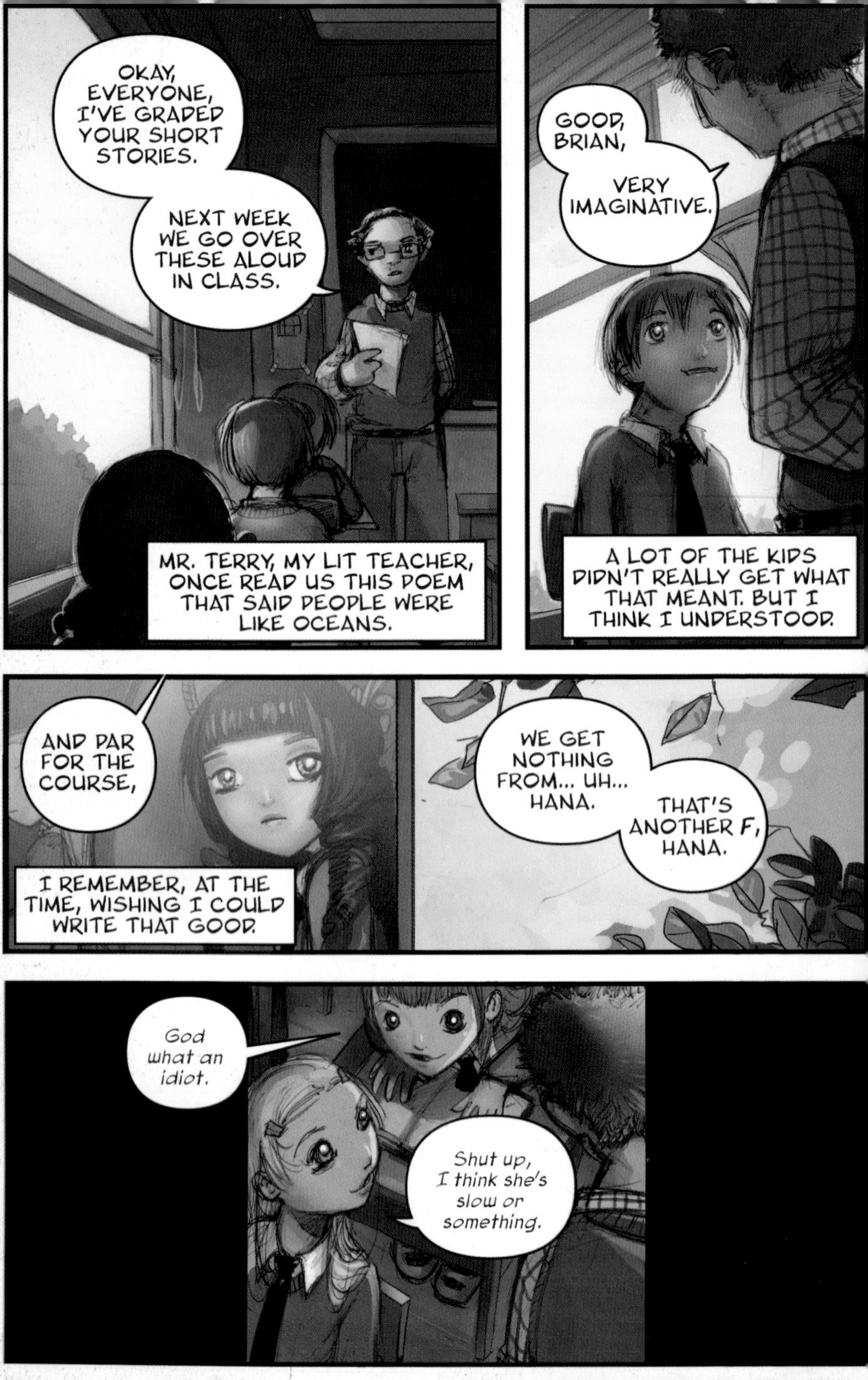
OKAY, EVERYONE, I'VE GRADED YOUR SHORT STORIES.
NEXT WEEK WE GO OVER THESE ALOUD IN CLASS.
MR. TERRY, MY LIT TEACHER, ONCE READ US THIS POEM THAT SAID PEOPLE WERE LIKE OCEANS.
GOOD, BRIAN,
VERY IMAGINATIVE.
A LOT OF THE KIDS DIDN'T REALLY GET WHAT THAT MEANT. BUT I THINK I UNDERSTOOD.
AND PAR FOR THE COURSE,
I REMEMBER, AT THE TIME, WISHING I COULD WRITE THAT GOOD.
WE GET NOTHING FROM... UH... HANA.
THAT'S ANOTHER F, HANA.
God what an idiot.
Shut up, I think she's slow or something.

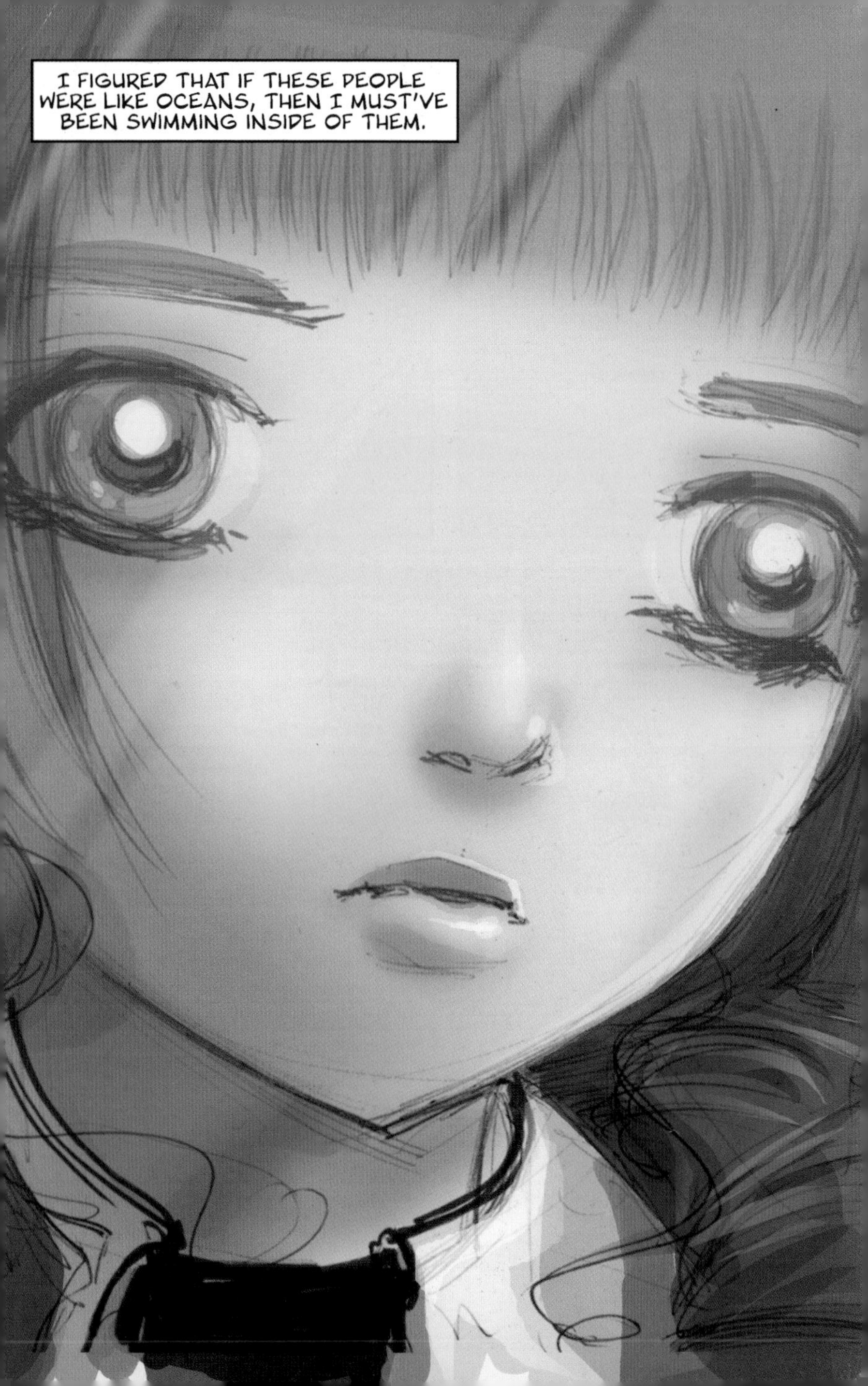
I FIGURED THAT IF THESE PEOPLE WERE LIKE OCEANS, THEN I MUST'VE BEEN SWIMMING INSIDE OF THEM.

I FOUND MR. TERRY ON A LOCAL FREE DATING SITE AND ANSWERED HIS AD.

I SENT A PICTURE OF MY AUNT, AND TOLD HIM I LOVED TO READ THE CLASSICS.

THE PICTURE HE SENT BACK OF HIMSELF WAS FROM, LIKE, 10 YEARS AGO OR SOMETHING.

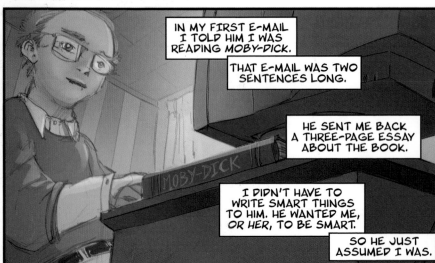

IN MY FIRST E-MAIL I TOLD HIM I WAS READING MOBY-DICK.

THAT E-MAIL WAS TWO SENTENCES LONG.

HE SENT ME BACK A THREE-PAGE ESSAY ABOUT THE BOOK.

I DIDN'T HAVE TO WRITE SMART THINGS TO HIM. HE WANTED ME, OR HER, TO BE SMART.

SO HE JUST ASSUMED I WAS.

LONELY PEOPLE ARE THE EASIEST TO FOOL.

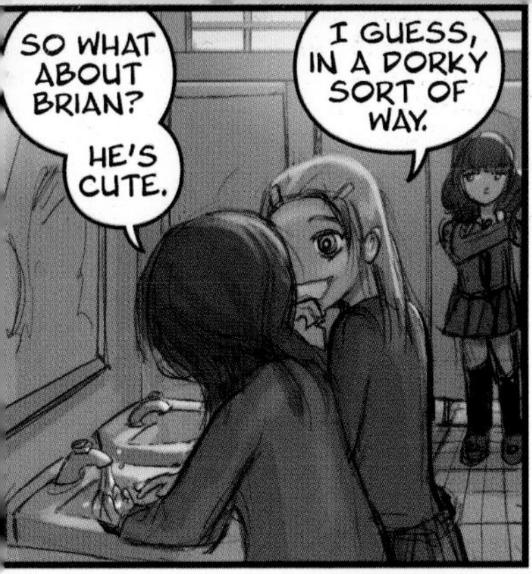
SO WHAT ABOUT BRIAN?
HE'S CUTE.
I GUESS, IN A DORKY SORT OF WAY.

ROSE I FOUND ON A HIP-HOP CULTURE BLOG, BUT IT TOOK SOME DIGGING ON SEARCH ENGINES.

SHE CALLED HERSELF DJ PLASTIC TAGS.

HER PROFILE SAID SHE WAS A 25-YEAR-OLD BRAZILIAN GIRL.

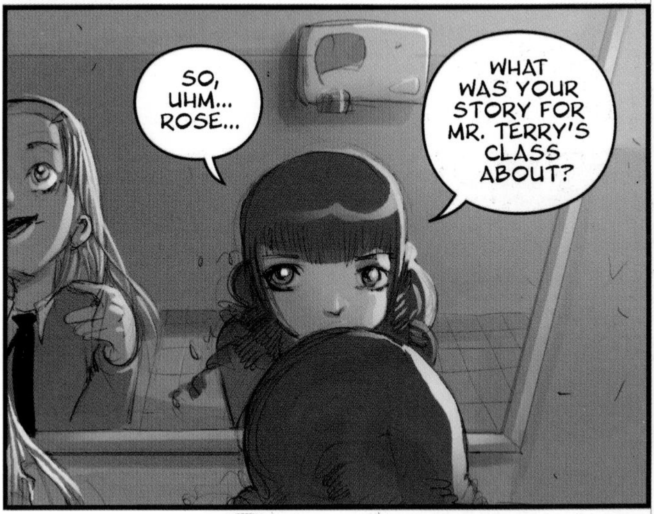
SO, UHM... ROSE...
WHAT WAS YOUR STORY FOR MR. TERRY'S CLASS ABOUT?

WE E-MAILED EACH OTHER ALL THE TIME TO TALK ABOUT MUSIC.

SHE THOUGHT I WAS SOMEONE OLDER, TOO.

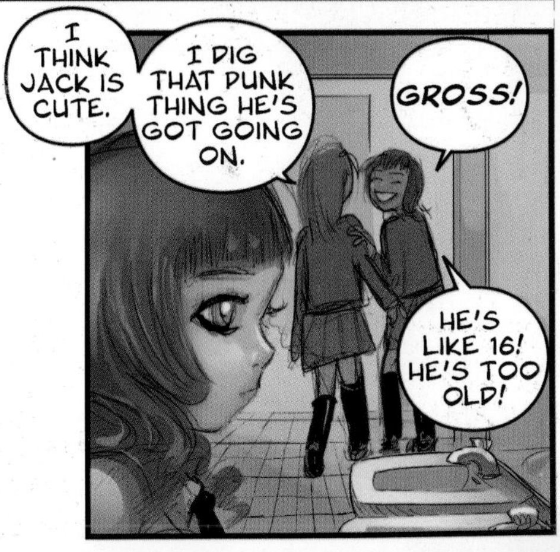
I THINK JACK IS CUTE.
I DIG THAT PUNK THING HE'S GOT GOING ON.
GROSS!
HE'S LIKE 16! HE'S TOO OLD!

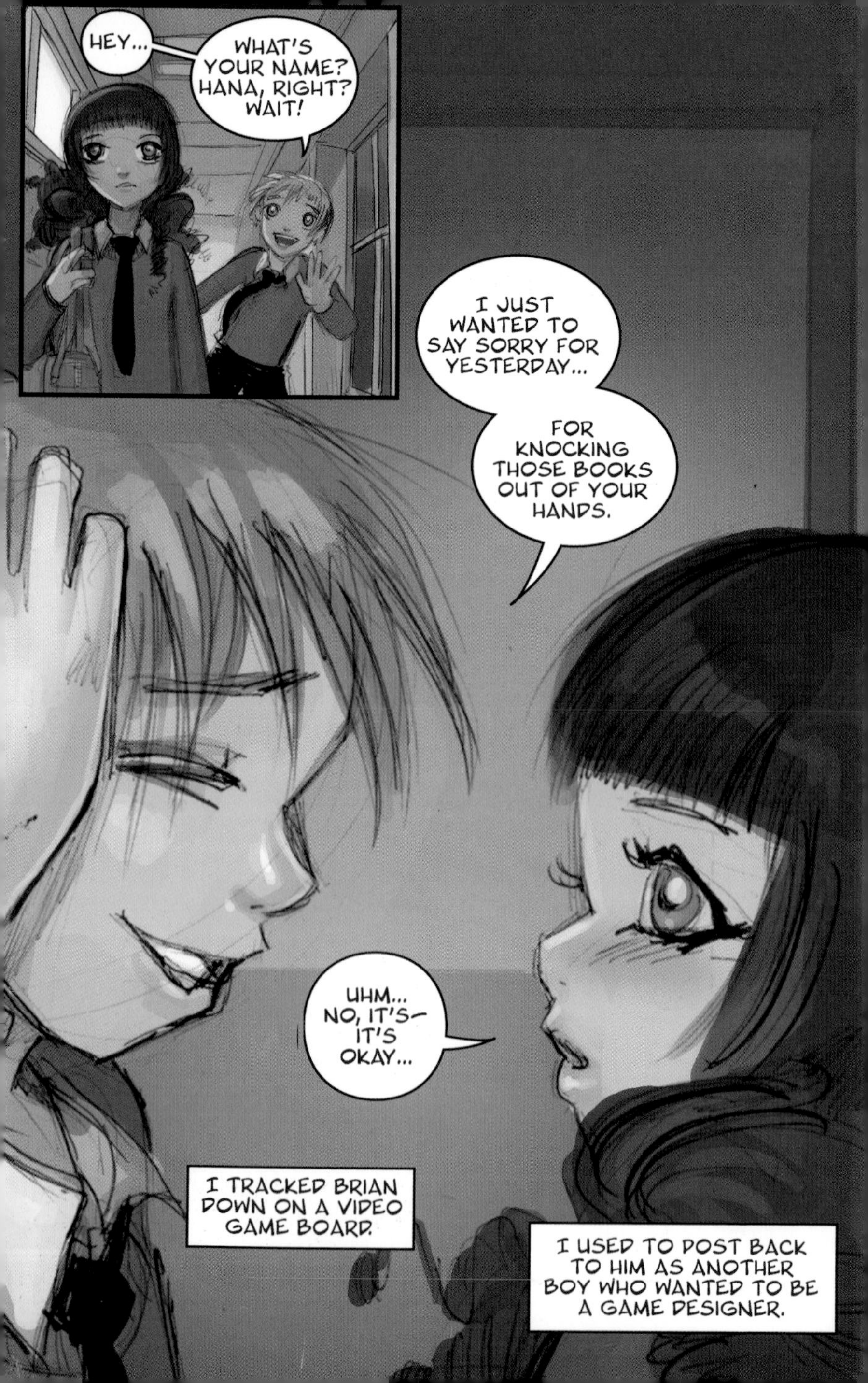
HEY...
WHAT'S YOUR NAME? HANA, RIGHT? WAIT!
I JUST WANTED TO SAY SORRY FOR YESTERDAY...
FOR KNOCKING THOSE BOOKS OUT OF YOUR HANDS.
UHM... NO, IT'S- IT'S OKAY...
I TRACKED BRIAN DOWN ON A VIDEO GAME BOARD.
I USED TO POST BACK TO HIM AS ANOTHER BOY WHO WANTED TO BE A GAME DESIGNER.

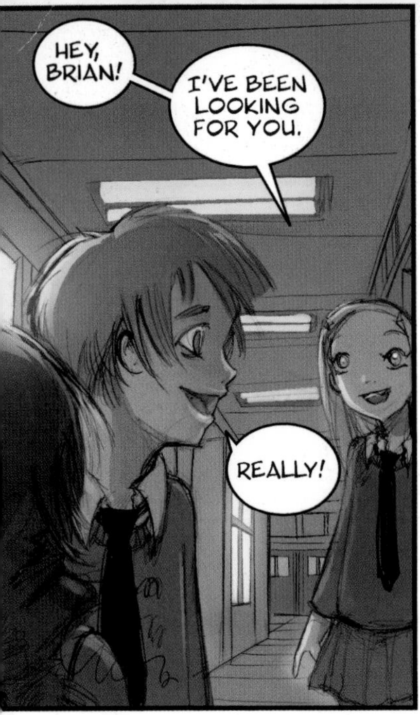
HEY, BRIAN!
I'VE BEEN LOOKING FOR YOU.
REALLY!

THEN THERE WAS JESSICA.

I FOUND JESSICA IN A RELIGIOUS CHAT ROOM AFTER SEEING HER PRAY BEFORE EATING LUNCH ONE DAY.

SHE THINKS I'M AN OLDER MAN WITH LOTS OF MONEY WHO'S LOST FAITH IN GOD AND IS CONTEMPLATING SUICIDE.

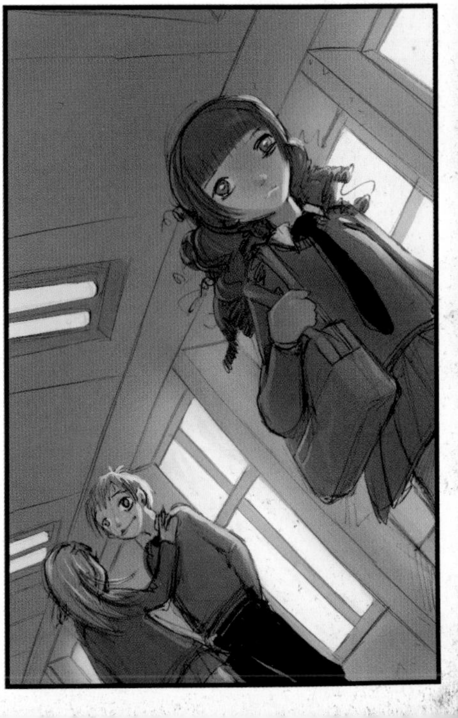

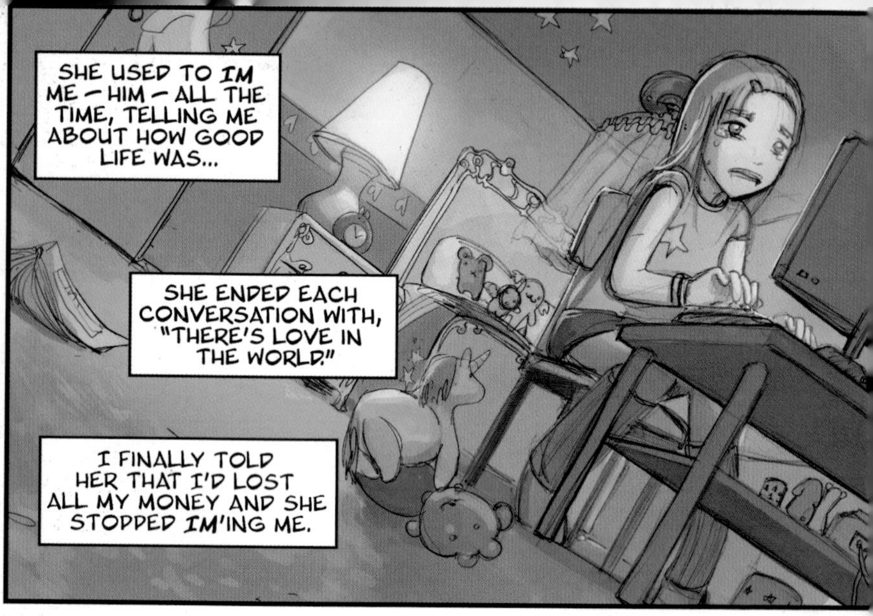
SHE USED TO IM ME — HIM — ALL THE TIME, TELLING ME ABOUT HOW GOOD LIFE WAS...
SHE ENDED EACH CONVERSATION WITH, "THERE'S LOVE IN THE WORLD."
I FINALLY TOLD HER THAT I'D LOST ALL MY MONEY AND SHE STOPPED IM'ING ME.

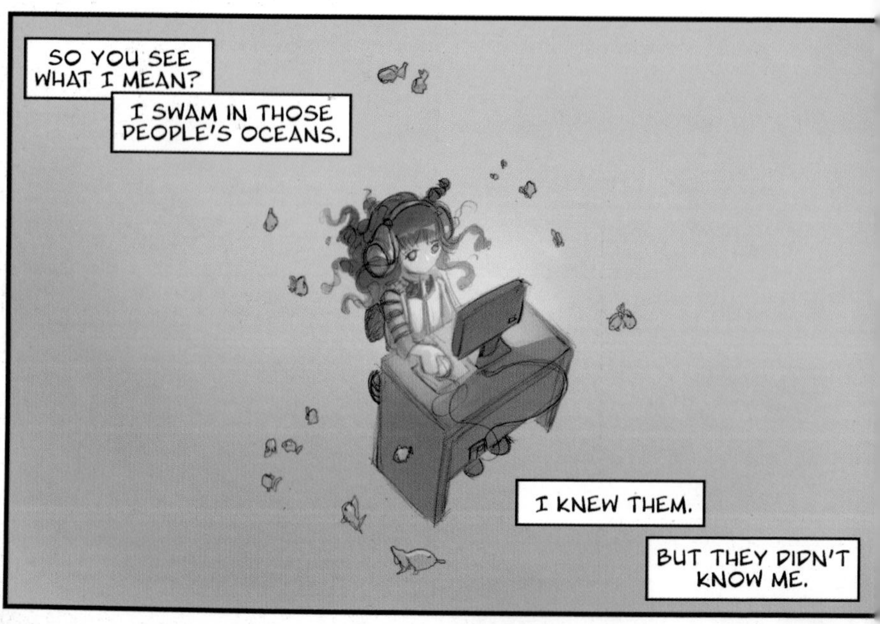
SO YOU SEE WHAT I MEAN?
I SWAM IN THOSE PEOPLE'S OCEANS.
I KNEW THEM.
BUT THEY DIDN'T KNOW ME.

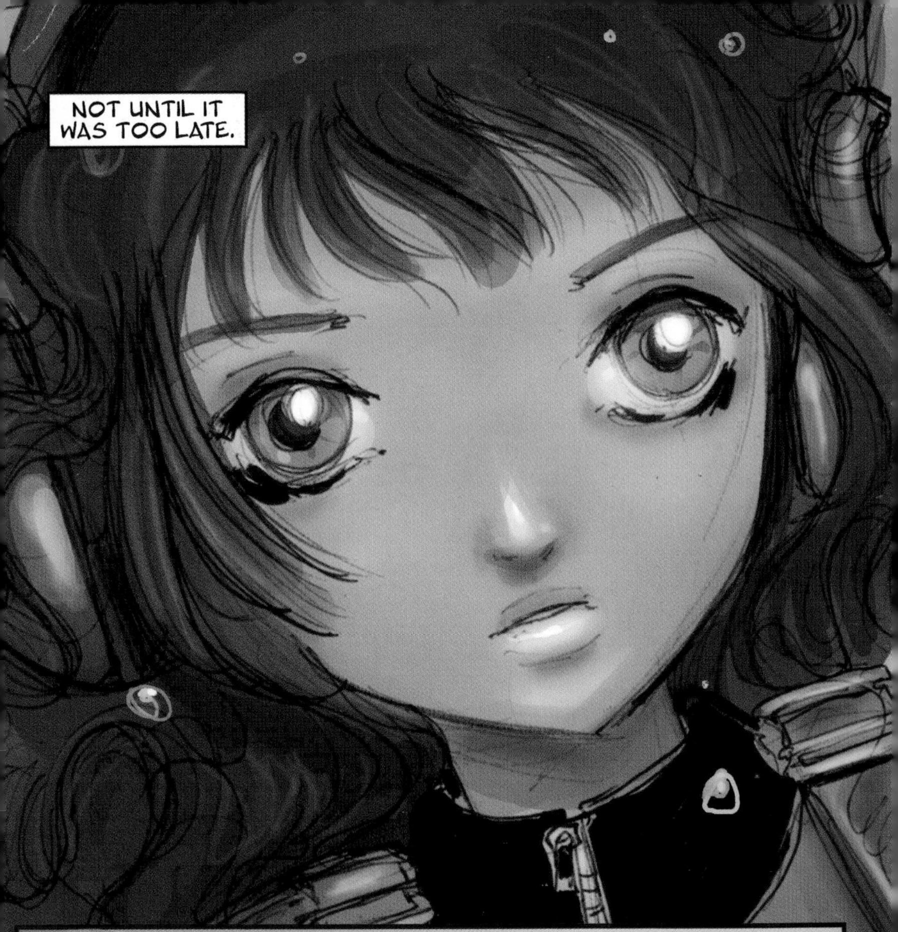
NOT UNTIL IT WAS TOO LATE.

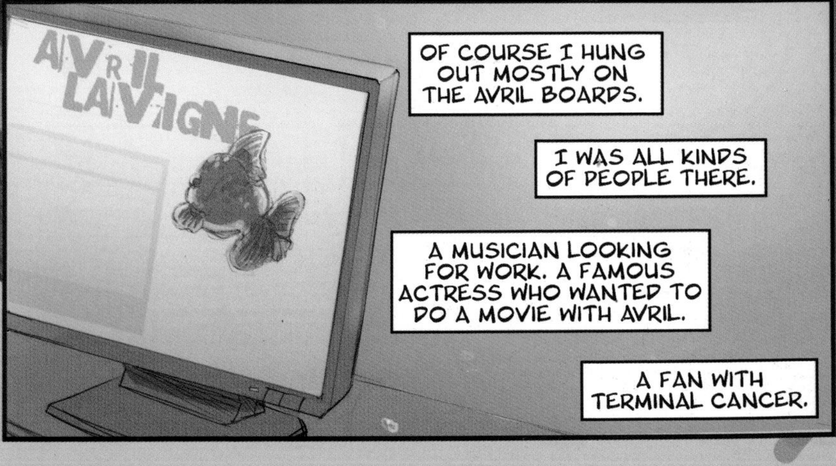
AVRIL LAVIGNE
OF COURSE I HUNG OUT MOSTLY ON THE AVRIL BOARDS.
I WAS ALL KINDS OF PEOPLE THERE.
A MUSICIAN LOOKING FOR WORK. A FAMOUS ACTRESS WHO WANTED TO DO A MOVIE WITH AVRIL.
A FAN WITH TERMINAL CANCER.

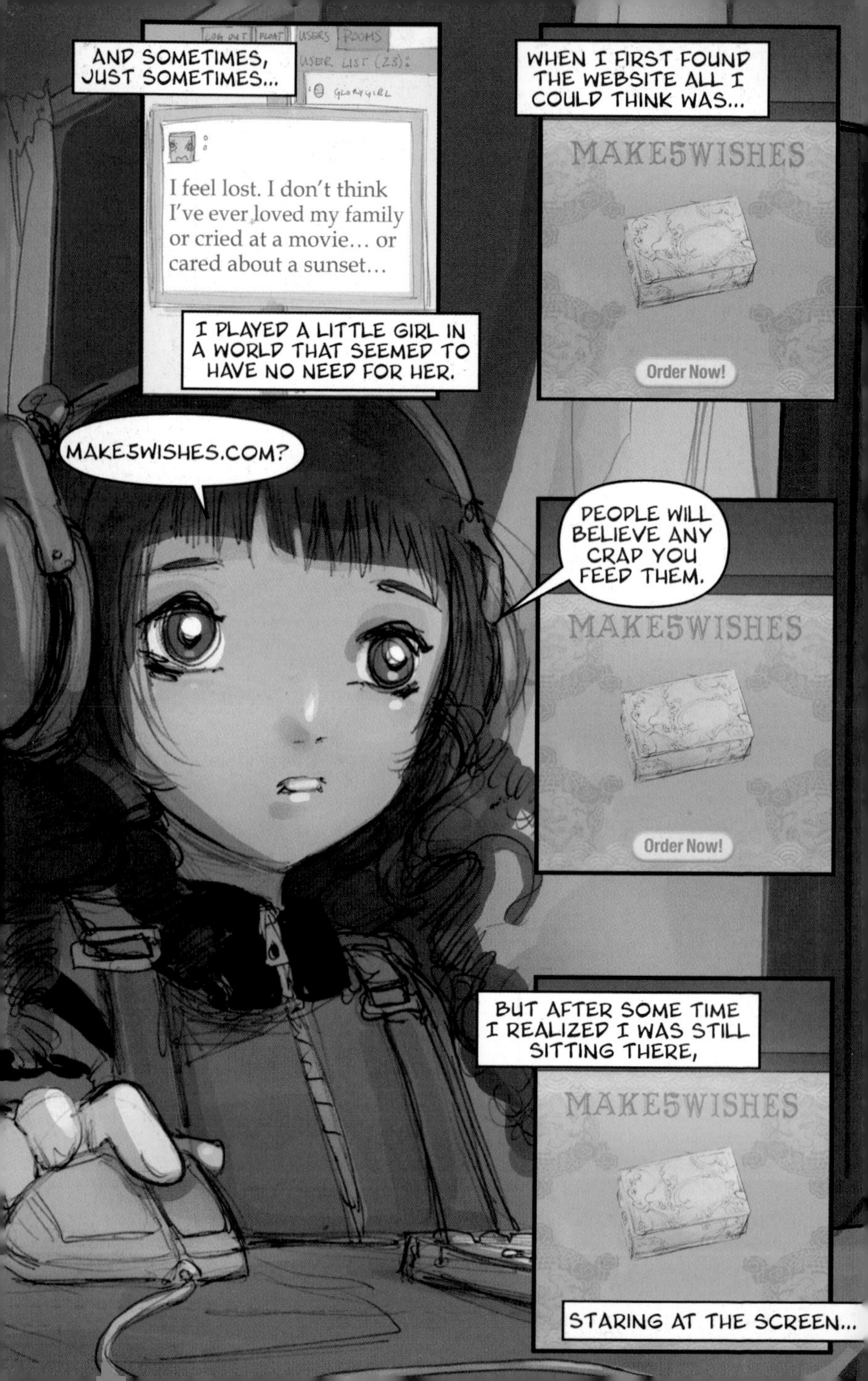
AND SOMETIMES, JUST SOMETIMES...
LOG OUT
FLOAT
USERS
ROOMS
USER LIST (23):
GLORYGIRL
I feel lost. I don't think I've ever loved my family or cried at a movie... or cared about a sunset...
I PLAYED A LITTLE GIRL IN A WORLD THAT SEEMED TO HAVE NO NEED FOR HER.
WHEN I FIRST FOUND THE WEBSITE ALL I COULD THINK WAS...
MAKE5WISHES
Order Now!
MAKE5WISHES.COM?
PEOPLE WILL BELIEVE ANY CRAP YOU FEED THEM.
MAKE5WISHES
Order Now!
BUT AFTER SOME TIME I REALIZED I WAS STILL SITTING THERE,
MAKE5WISHES
STARING AT THE SCREEN...

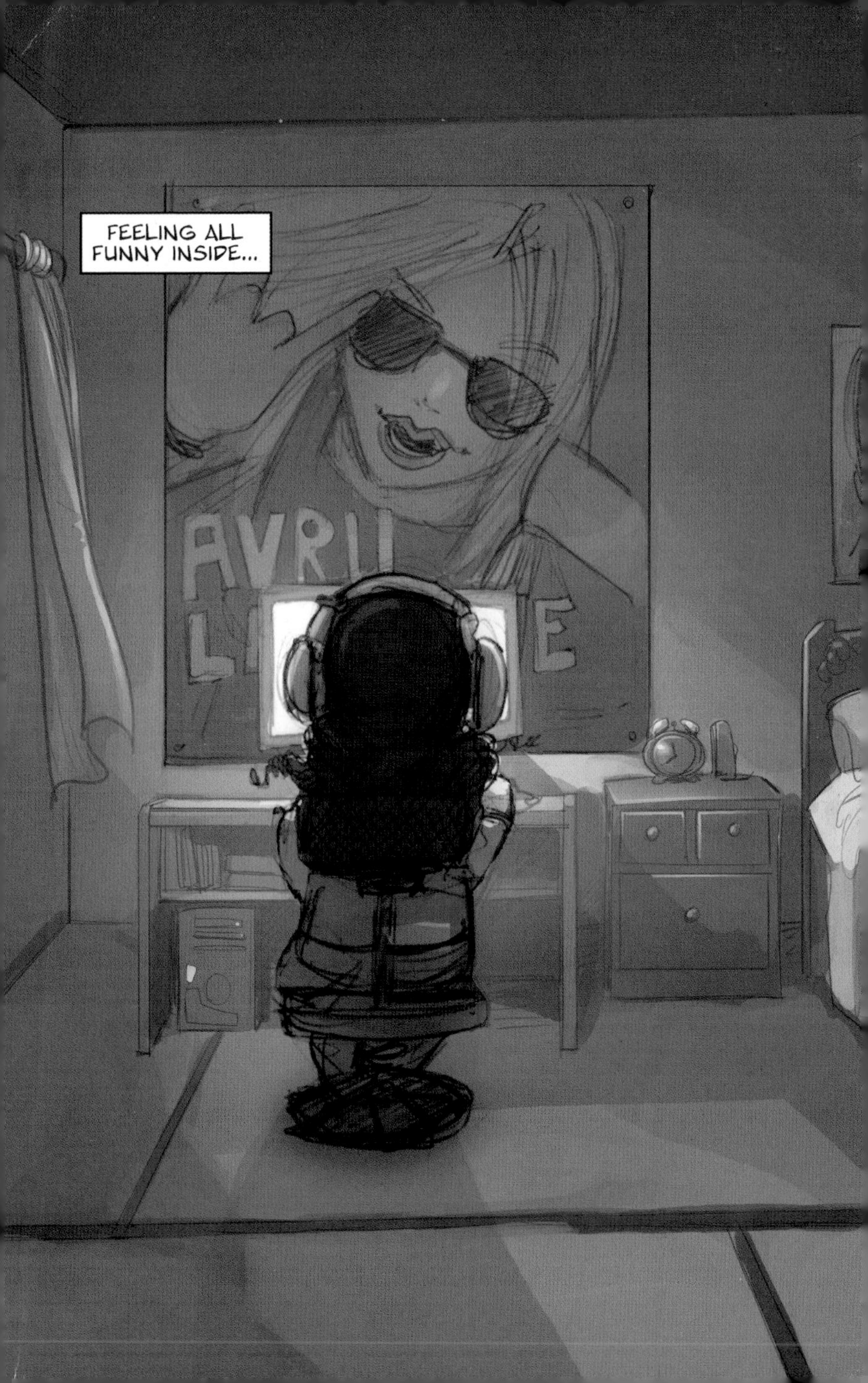
FEELING ALL FUNNY INSIDE...

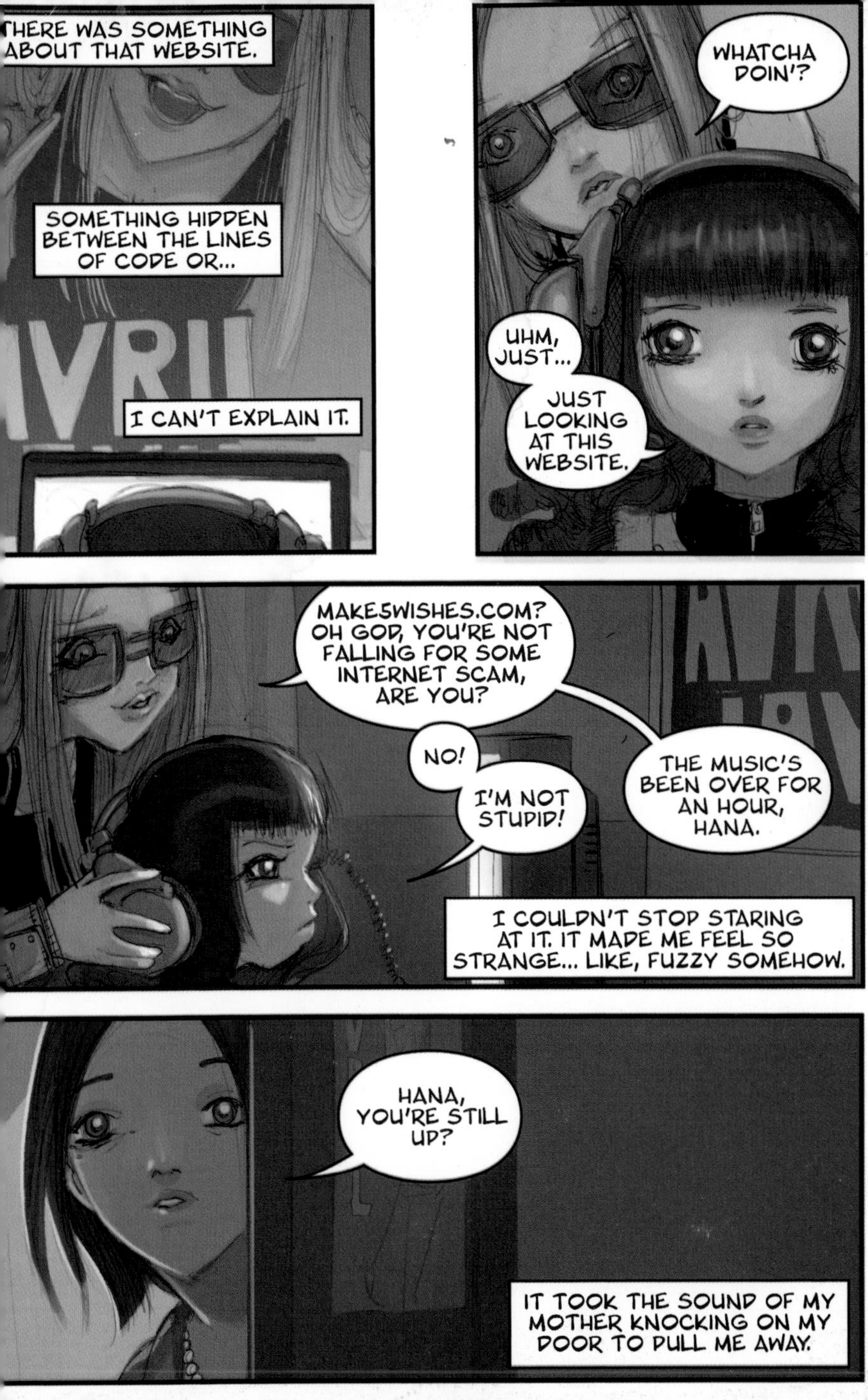
THERE WAS SOMETHING ABOUT THAT WEBSITE.
SOMETHING HIDDEN BETWEEN THE LINES OF CODE OR...
I CAN'T EXPLAIN IT.
WHATCHA DOIN'?
UHM, JUST...
JUST LOOKING AT THIS WEBSITE.
MAKE5WISHES.COM? OH GOD, YOU'RE NOT FALLING FOR SOME INTERNET SCAM, ARE YOU?
NO!
I'M NOT STUPID!
THE MUSIC'S BEEN OVER FOR AN HOUR, HANA.
I COULDN'T STOP STARING AT IT. IT MADE ME FEEL SO STRANGE... LIKE, FUZZY SOMEHOW.
HANA, YOU'RE STILL UP?
IT TOOK THE SOUND OF MY MOTHER KNOCKING ON MY DOOR TO PULL ME AWAY.

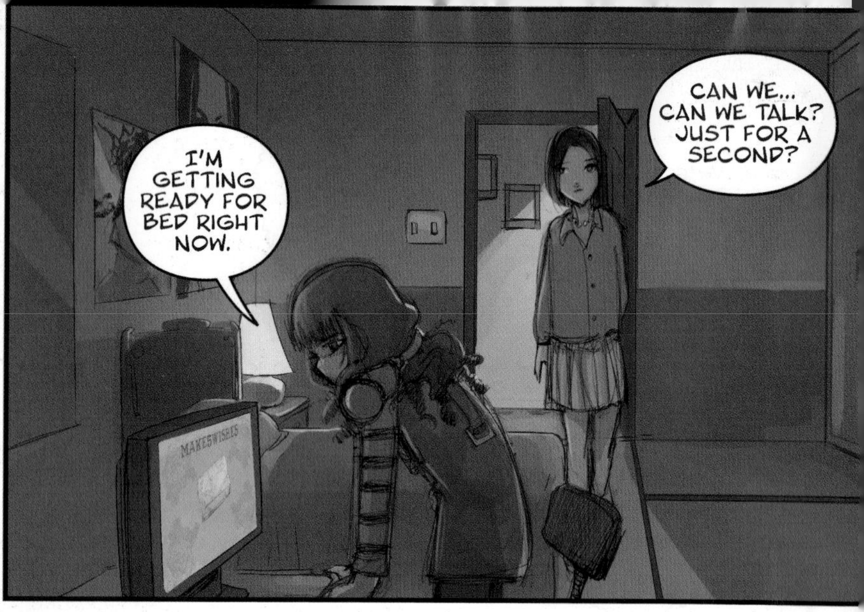
CAN WE... CAN WE TALK? JUST FOR A SECOND?
I'M GETTING READY FOR BED RIGHT NOW.

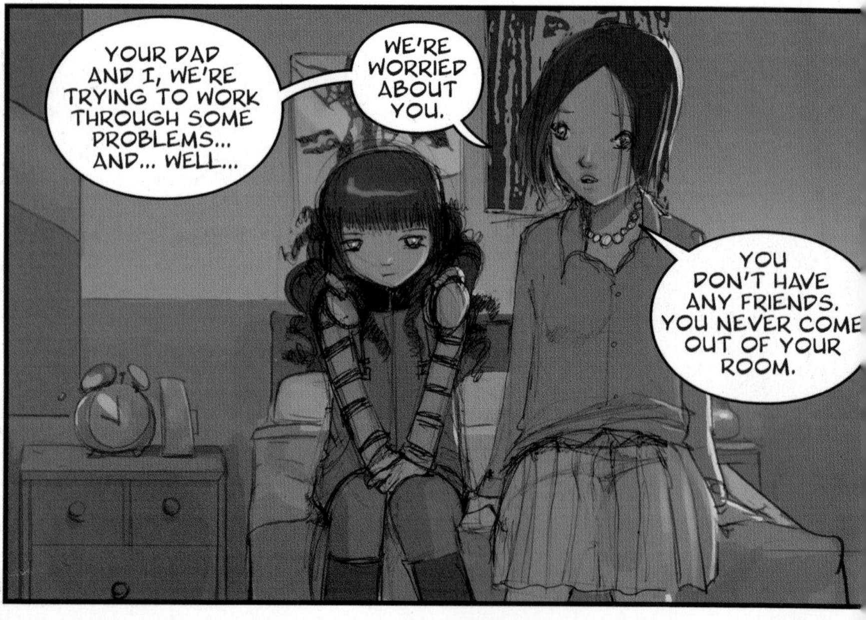
YOUR DAD AND I, WE'RE TRYING TO WORK THROUGH SOME PROBLEMS... AND... WELL...
WE'RE WORRIED ABOUT YOU.
YOU DON'T HAVE ANY FRIENDS. YOU NEVER COME OUT OF YOUR ROOM.

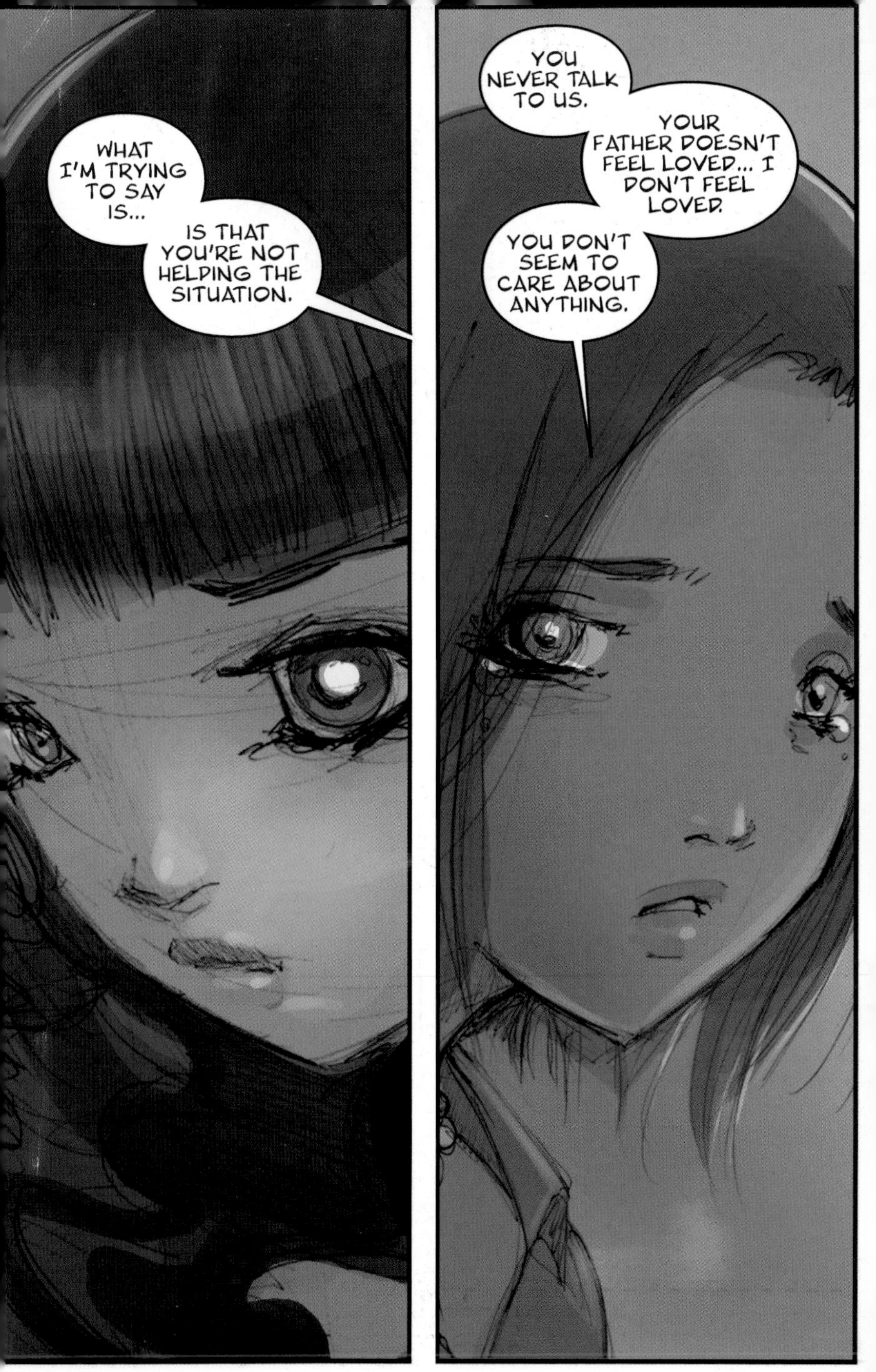
WHAT I'M TRYING TO SAY IS...
IS THAT YOU'RE NOT HELPING THE SITUATION.
YOU NEVER TALK TO US.
YOUR FATHER DOESN'T FEEL LOVED... I DON'T FEEL LOVED.
YOU DON'T SEEM TO CARE ABOUT ANYTHING.

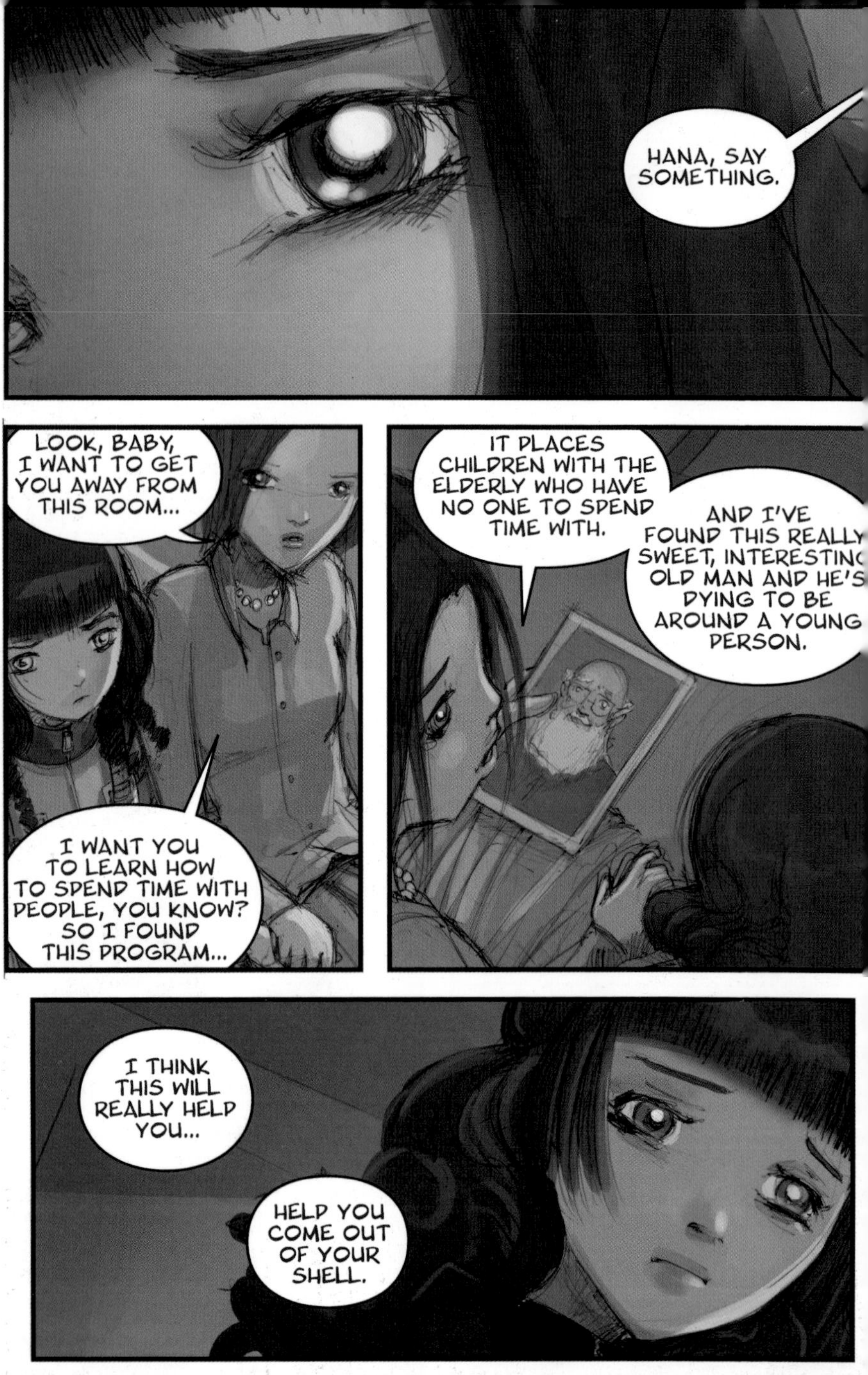
HANA, SAY SOMETHING.
LOOK, BABY, I WANT TO GET YOU AWAY FROM THIS ROOM...
I WANT YOU TO LEARN HOW TO SPEND TIME WITH PEOPLE, YOU KNOW? SO I FOUND THIS PROGRAM...
IT PLACES CHILDREN WITH THE ELDERLY WHO HAVE NO ONE TO SPEND TIME WITH.
AND I'VE FOUND THIS REALLY SWEET, INTERESTING OLD MAN AND HE'S DYING TO BE AROUND A YOUNG PERSON.
I THINK THIS WILL REALLY HELP YOU...
HELP YOU COME OUT OF YOUR SHELL.

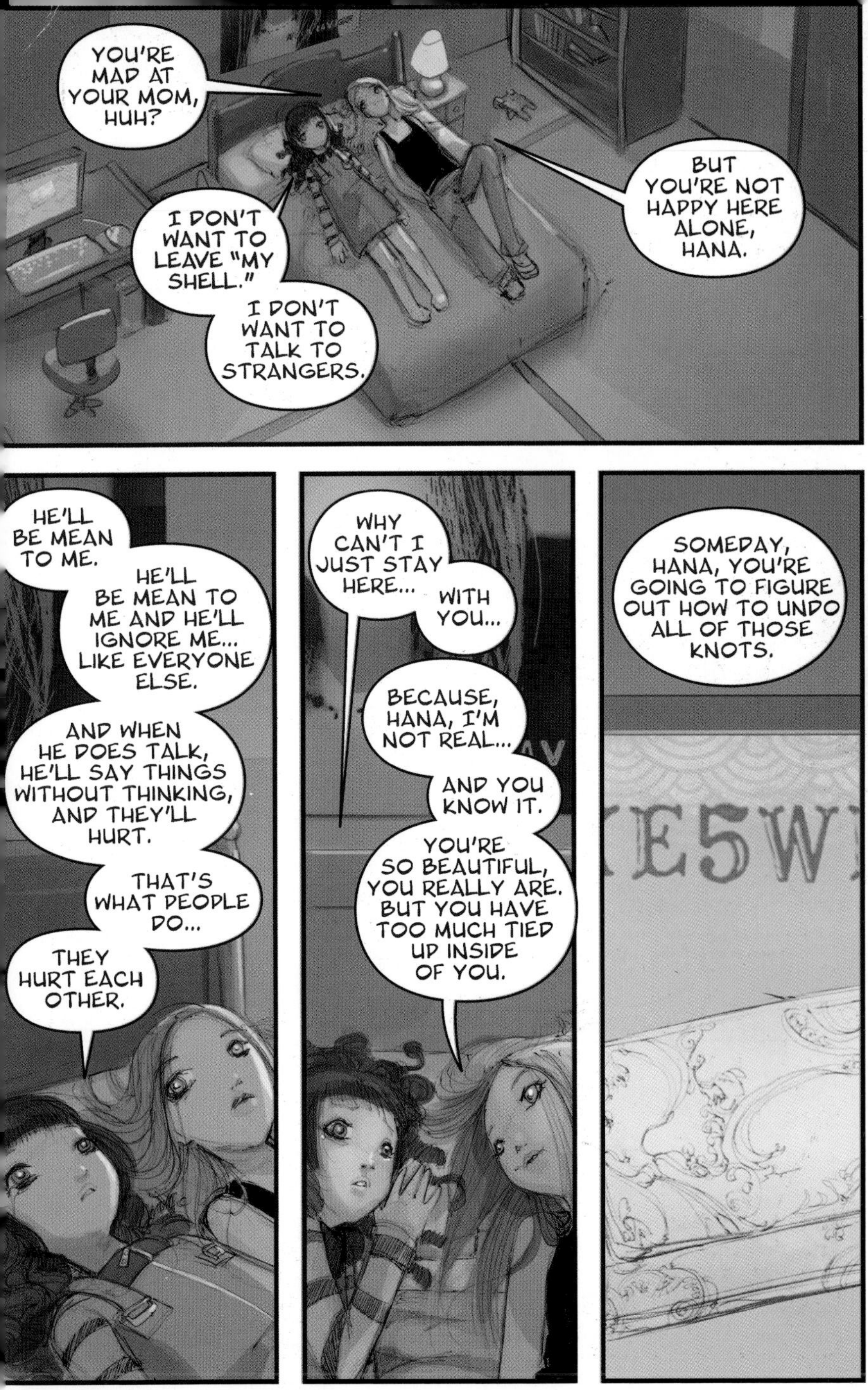
YOU'RE MAD AT YOUR MOM, HUH?
I DON'T WANT TO LEAVE "MY SHELL."
I DON'T WANT TO TALK TO STRANGERS.
BUT YOU'RE NOT HAPPY HERE ALONE, HANA.
HE'LL BE MEAN TO ME.
HE'LL BE MEAN TO ME AND HE'LL IGNORE ME... LIKE EVERYONE ELSE.
AND WHEN HE DOES TALK, HE'LL SAY THINGS WITHOUT THINKING, AND THEY'LL HURT.
THAT'S WHAT PEOPLE DO...
THEY HURT EACH OTHER.
WHY CAN'T I JUST STAY HERE...
WITH YOU...
BECAUSE, HANA, I'M NOT REAL...
AND YOU KNOW IT.
YOU'RE SO BEAUTIFUL, YOU REALLY ARE. BUT YOU HAVE TOO MUCH TIED UP INSIDE OF YOU.
SOMEDAY, HANA, YOU'RE GOING TO FIGURE OUT HOW TO UNDO ALL OF THOSE KNOTS.

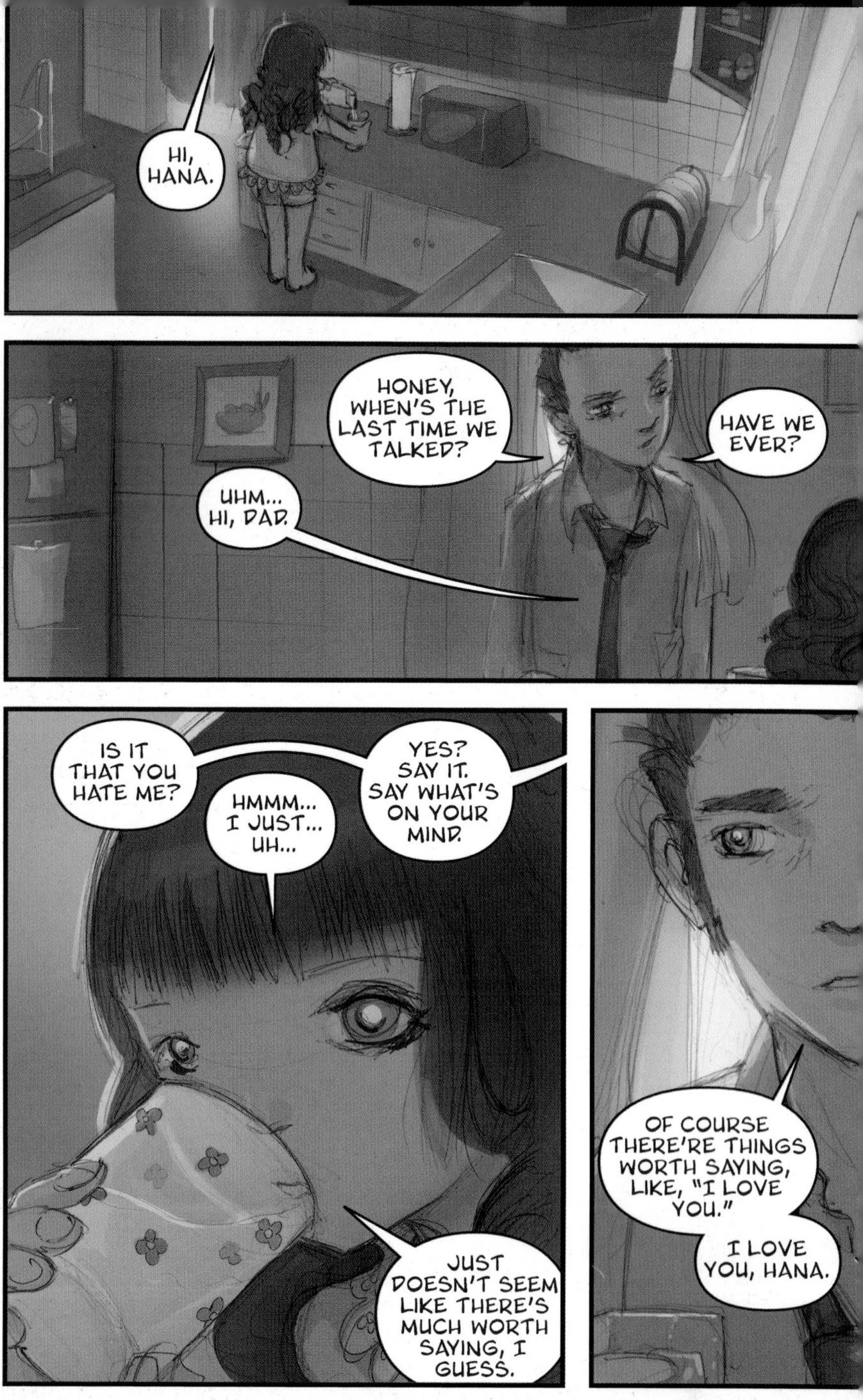
HI, HANA.
UHM... HI, DAD.
HONEY, WHEN'S THE LAST TIME WE TALKED?
HAVE WE EVER?
IS IT THAT YOU HATE ME?
HMMM... I JUST... UH...
YES? SAY IT. SAY WHAT'S ON YOUR MIND.
JUST DOESN'T SEEM LIKE THERE'S MUCH WORTH SAYING, I GUESS.
OF COURSE THERE'RE THINGS WORTH SAYING, LIKE, "I LOVE YOU."
I LOVE YOU, HANA.

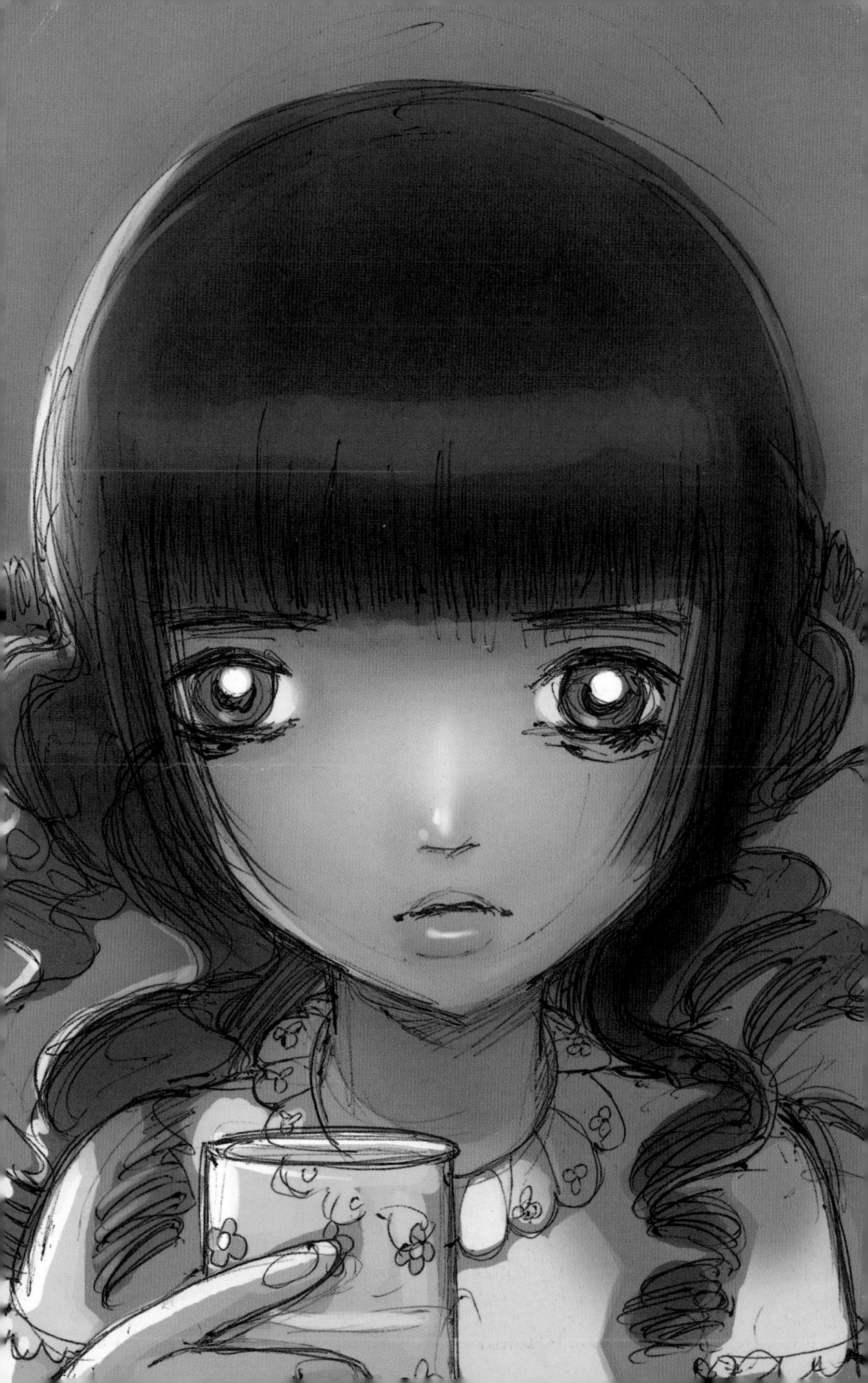

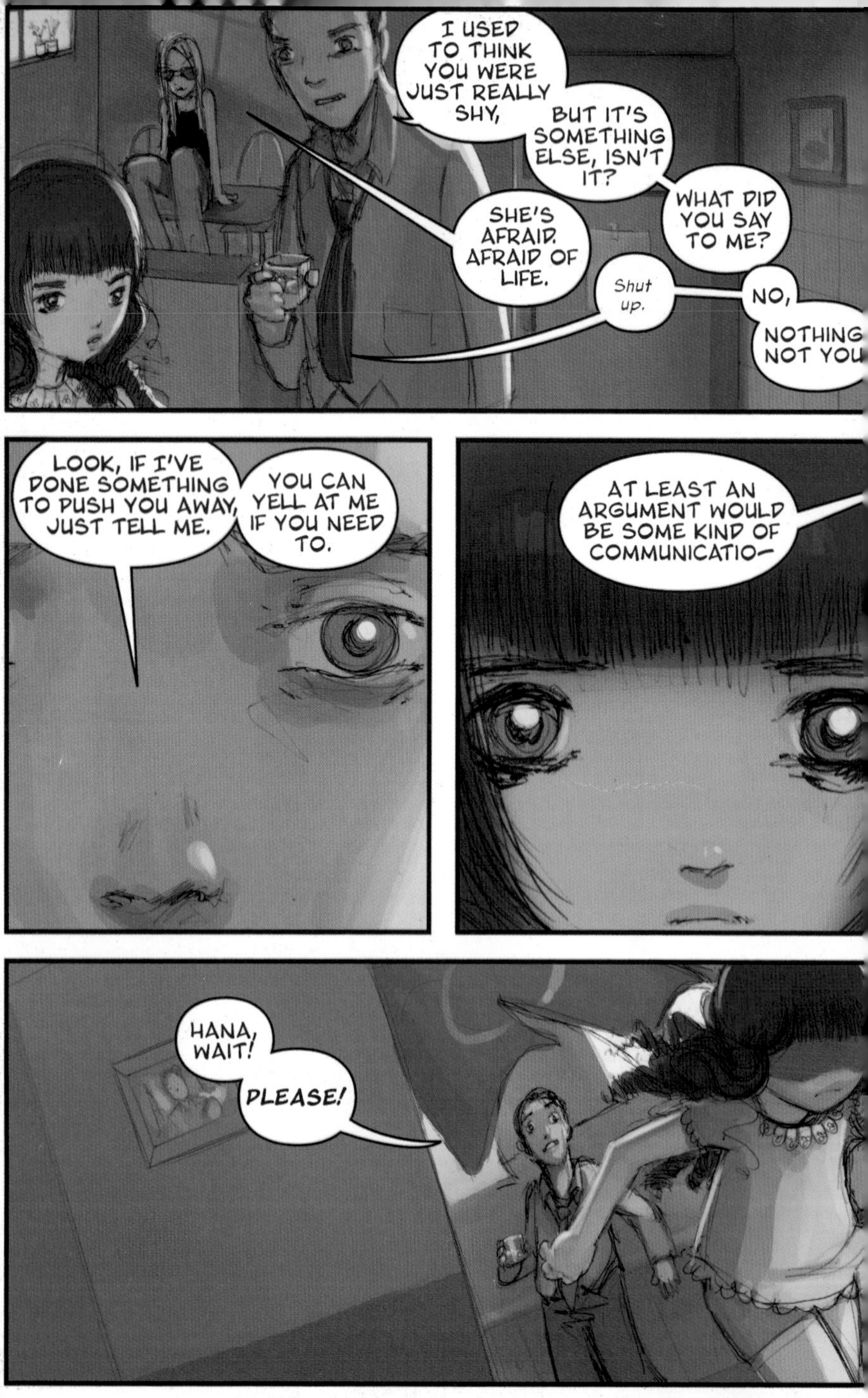
I USED TO THINK YOU WERE JUST REALLY SHY,
BUT IT'S SOMETHING ELSE, ISN'T IT?
WHAT DID YOU SAY TO ME?
SHE'S AFRAID. AFRAID OF LIFE.
Shut up.
NO,
NOTHING NOT YOU
LOOK, IF I'VE DONE SOMETHING TO PUSH YOU AWAY, JUST TELL ME.
YOU CAN YELL AT ME IF YOU NEED TO.
AT LEAST AN ARGUMENT WOULD BE SOME KIND OF COMMUNICATIO—
HANA, WAIT!
PLEASE!

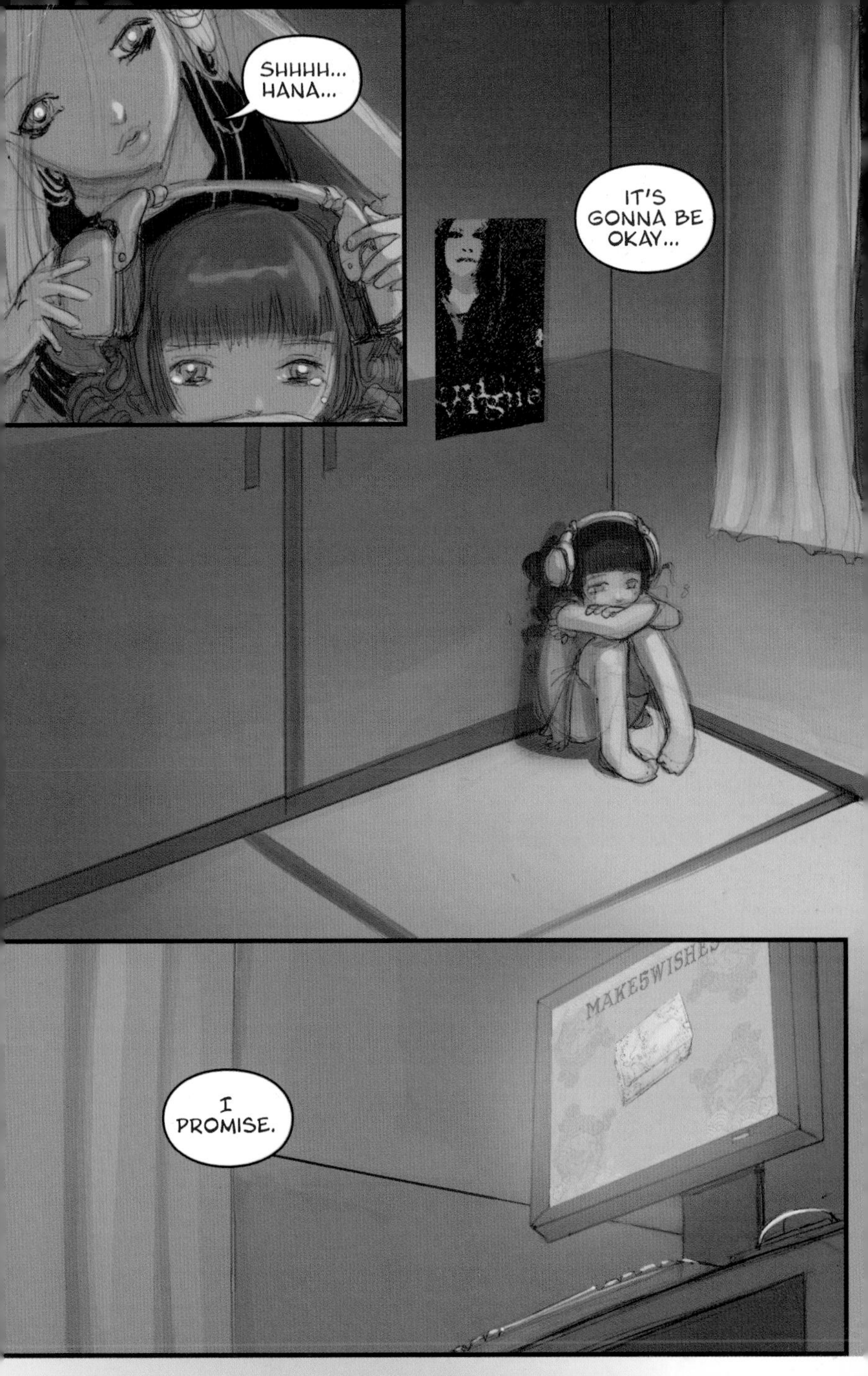
SHHHH... HANA...
IT'S GONNA BE OKAY...
I PROMISE.
MAKE5WISHES

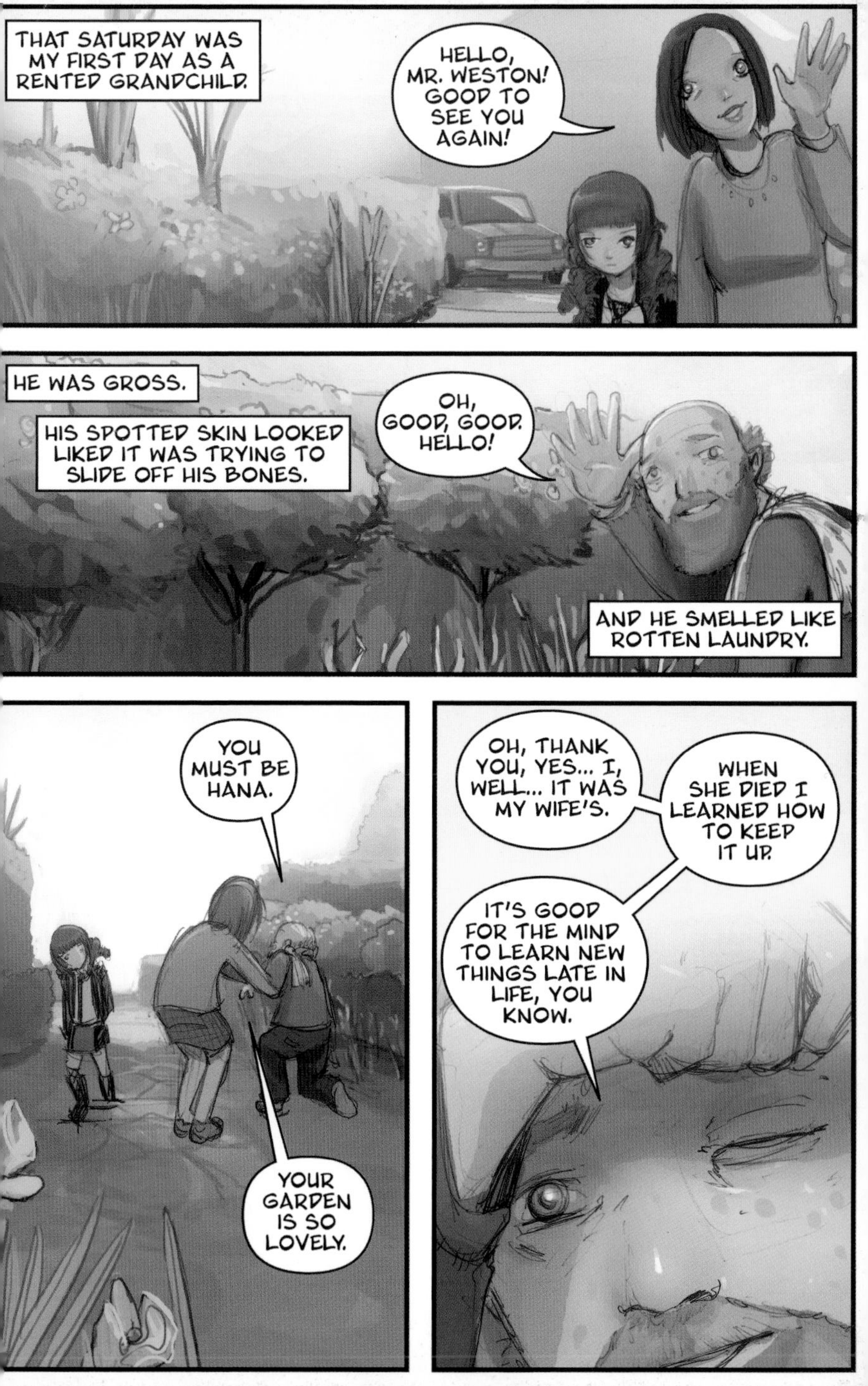
THAT SATURDAY WAS MY FIRST DAY AS A RENTED GRANDCHILD.
HELLO, MR. WESTON! GOOD TO SEE YOU AGAIN!
HE WAS GROSS.
HIS SPOTTED SKIN LOOKED LIKED IT WAS TRYING TO SLIDE OFF HIS BONES.
OH, GOOD, GOOD. HELLO!
AND HE SMELLED LIKE ROTTEN LAUNDRY.
YOU MUST BE HANA.
YOUR GARDEN IS SO LOVELY.
OH, THANK YOU, YES... I, WELL... IT WAS MY WIFE'S.
WHEN SHE DIED I LEARNED HOW TO KEEP IT UP.
IT'S GOOD FOR THE MIND TO LEARN NEW THINGS LATE IN LIFE, YOU KNOW.

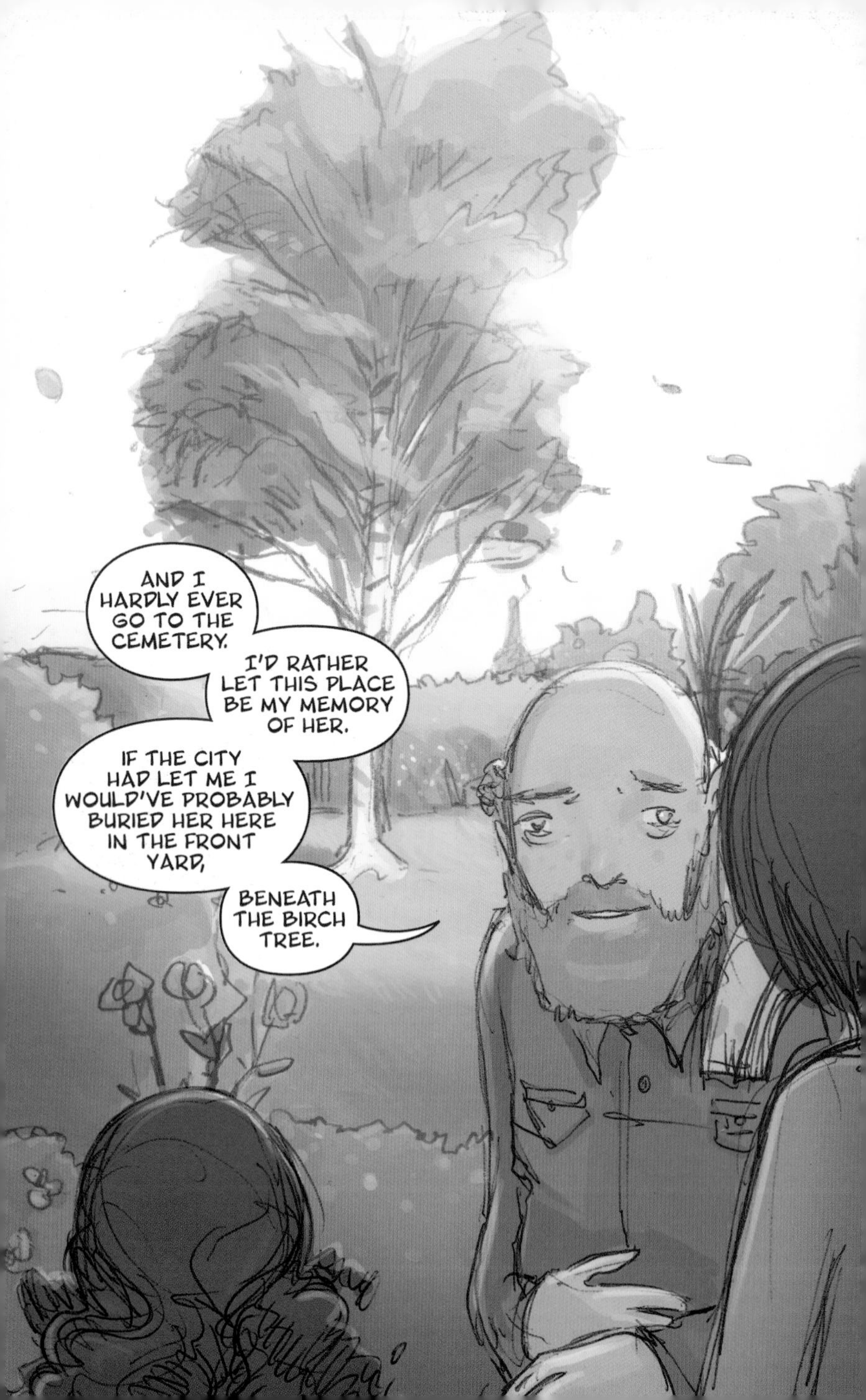
AND I HARDLY EVER GO TO THE CEMETERY.
I'D RATHER LET THIS PLACE BE MY MEMORY OF HER.
IF THE CITY HAD LET ME I WOULD'VE PROBABLY BURIED HER HERE IN THE FRONT YARD,
BENEATH THE BIRCH TREE.

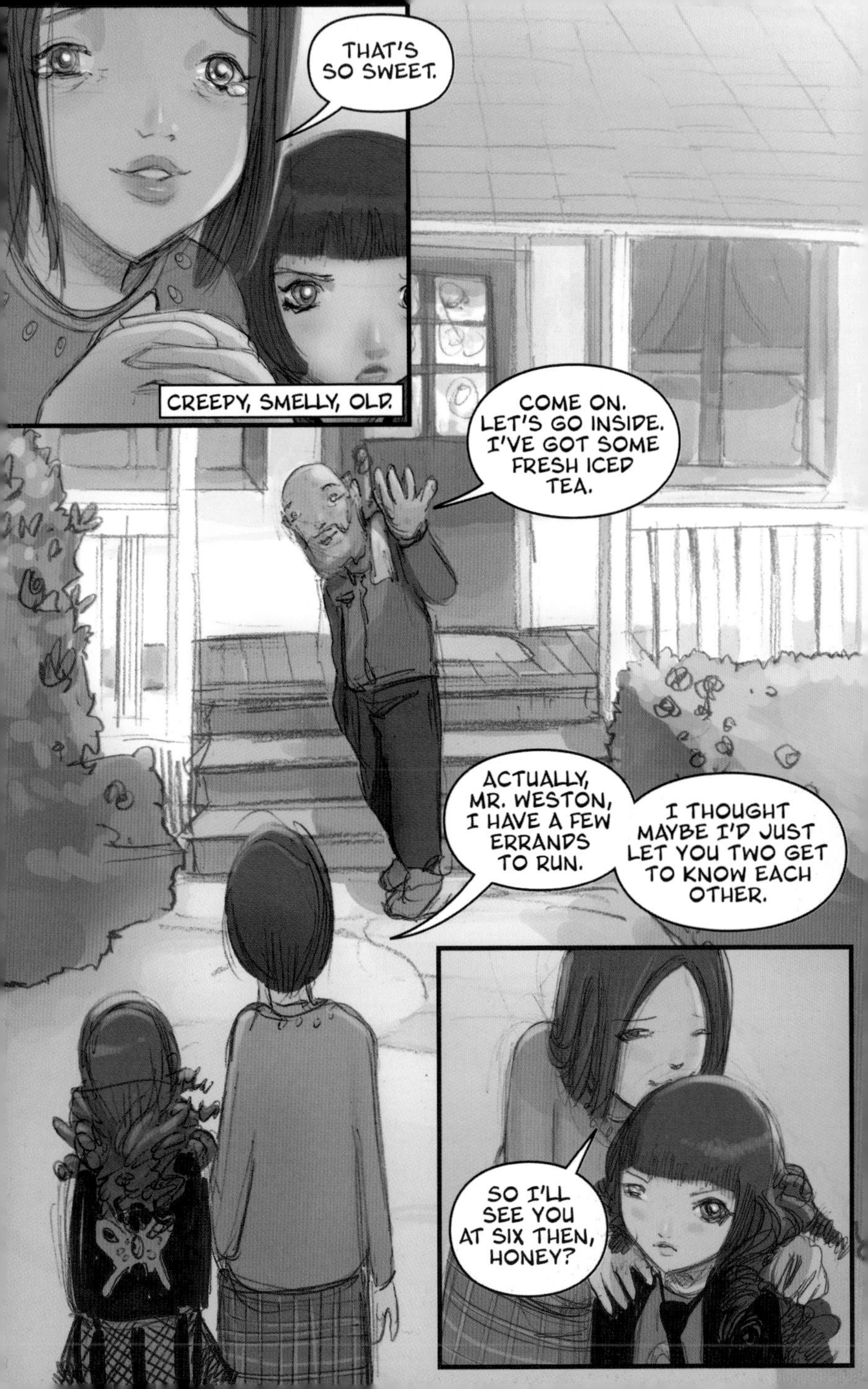
THAT'S SO SWEET.
CREEPY, SMELLY, OLD.
COME ON. LET'S GO INSIDE. I'VE GOT SOME FRESH ICED TEA.
ACTUALLY, MR. WESTON, I HAVE A FEW ERRANDS TO RUN.
I THOUGHT MAYBE I'D JUST LET YOU TWO GET TO KNOW EACH OTHER.
SO I'LL SEE YOU AT SIX THEN, HONEY?

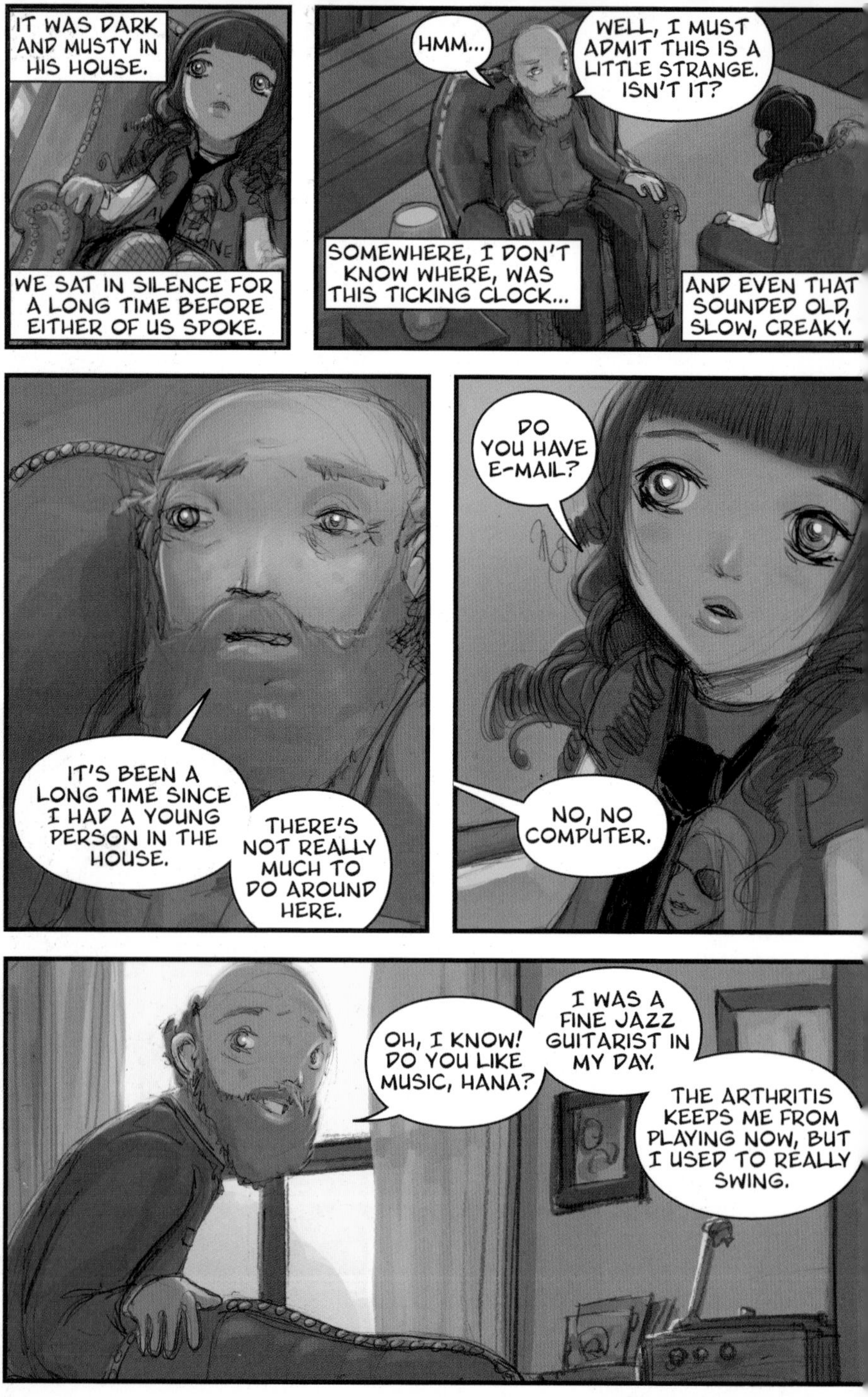
IT WAS DARK AND MUSTY IN HIS HOUSE.
WE SAT IN SILENCE FOR A LONG TIME BEFORE EITHER OF US SPOKE.
HMM...
WELL, I MUST ADMIT THIS IS A LITTLE STRANGE. ISN'T IT?
SOMEWHERE, I DON'T KNOW WHERE, WAS THIS TICKING CLOCK...
AND EVEN THAT SOUNDED OLD, SLOW, CREAKY.
IT'S BEEN A LONG TIME SINCE I HAD A YOUNG PERSON IN THE HOUSE.
THERE'S NOT REALLY MUCH TO DO AROUND HERE.
DO YOU HAVE E-MAIL?
NO, NO COMPUTER.
OH, I KNOW! DO YOU LIKE MUSIC, HANA?
I WAS A FINE JAZZ GUITARIST IN MY DAY.
THE ARTHRITIS KEEPS ME FROM PLAYING NOW, BUT I USED TO REALLY SWING.

YOU KNOW WHAT A RECORD IS?

OH GOD...

OH... OF COURSE YOU DO...

SORRY...

I JUST DIDN'T KNOW WITH ALL THE UHM... M3 PLAYERS TODAY.

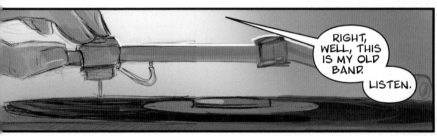

RIGHT, WELL, THIS IS MY OLD BAND.

LISTEN.

YOU LIKE IT?

DON'T SAY WHAT YOU'RE THINKING.

HE'S TRYING TO BE NICE.

IT'S SLOW...

IT'S BORING.

STOP IT, HANA.

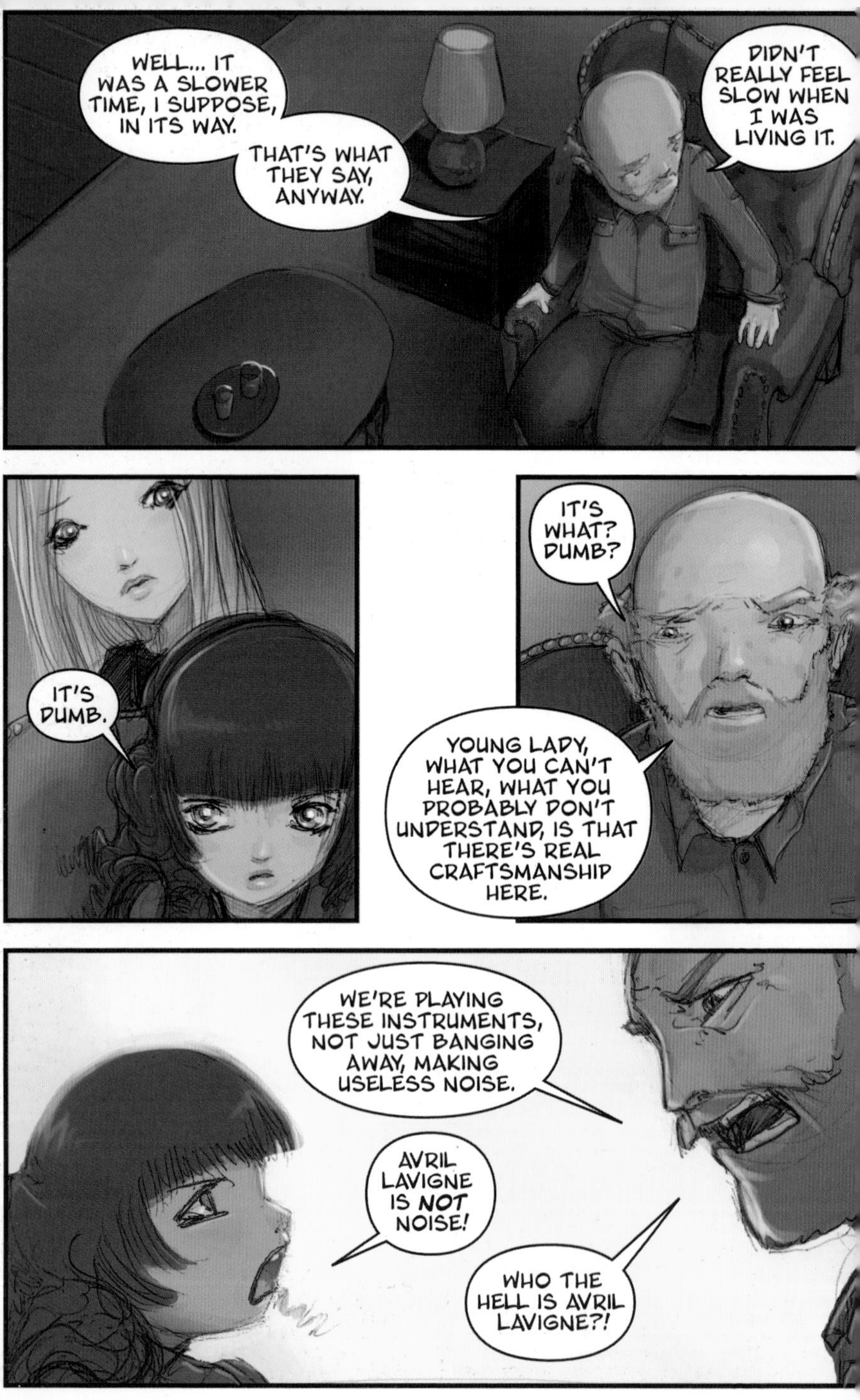
WELL... IT WAS A SLOWER TIME, I SUPPOSE, IN ITS WAY.
THAT'S WHAT THEY SAY, ANYWAY.
DIDN'T REALLY FEEL SLOW WHEN I WAS LIVING IT.
IT'S DUMB.
IT'S WHAT? DUMB?
YOUNG LADY, WHAT YOU CAN'T HEAR, WHAT YOU PROBABLY DON'T UNDERSTAND, IS THAT THERE'S REAL CRAFTSMANSHIP HERE.
WE'RE PLAYING THESE INSTRUMENTS, NOT JUST BANGING AWAY, MAKING USELESS NOISE.
AVRIL LAVIGNE IS **NOT** NOISE!
WHO THE HELL IS AVRIL LAVIGNE?!

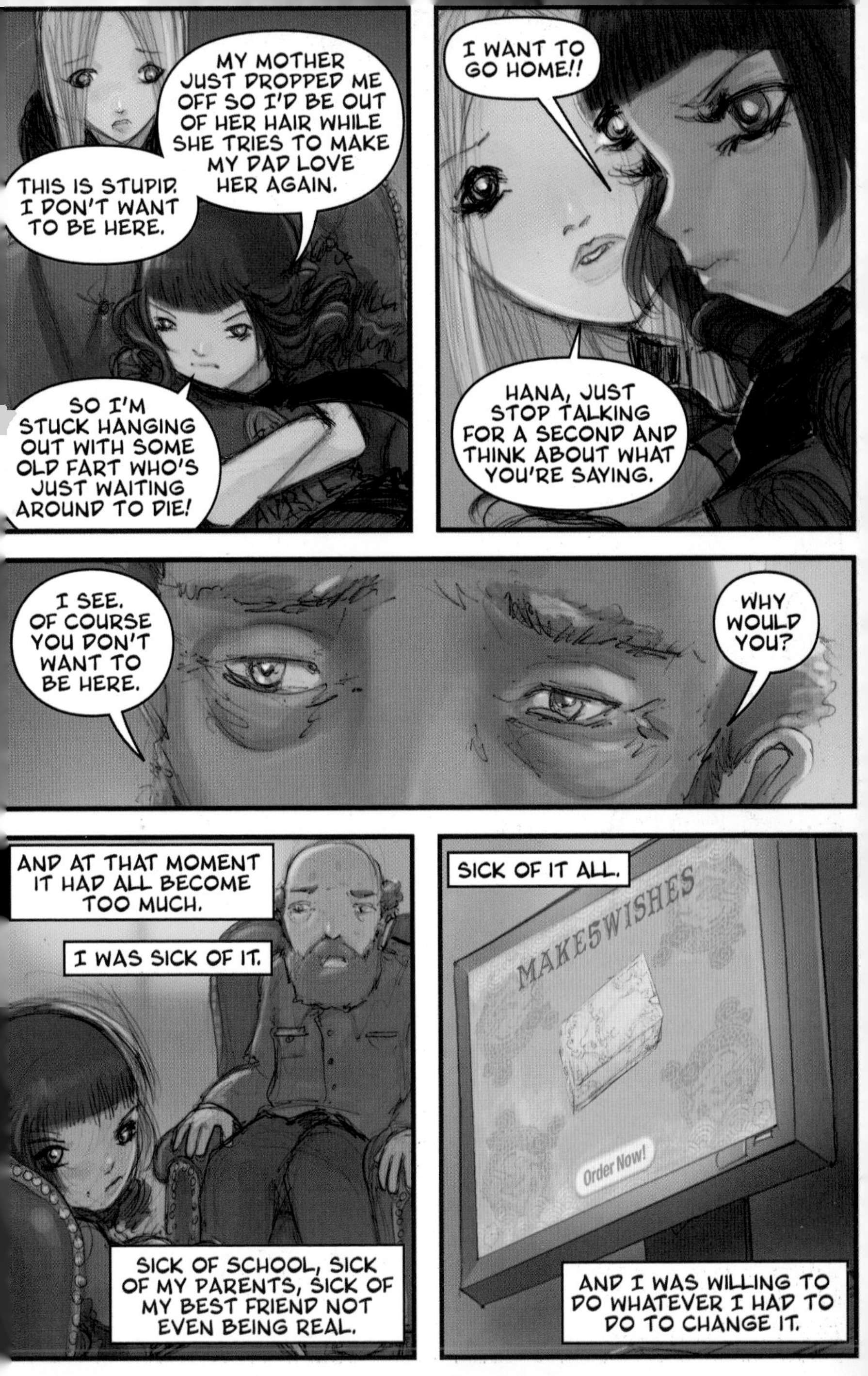
THIS IS STUPID. I DON'T WANT TO BE HERE.
MY MOTHER JUST DROPPED ME OFF SO I'D BE OUT OF HER HAIR WHILE SHE TRIES TO MAKE MY DAD LOVE HER AGAIN.
SO I'M STUCK HANGING OUT WITH SOME OLD FART WHO'S JUST WAITING AROUND TO DIE!
I WANT TO GO HOME!!
HANA, JUST STOP TALKING FOR A SECOND AND THINK ABOUT WHAT YOU'RE SAYING.
I SEE. OF COURSE YOU DON'T WANT TO BE HERE.
WHY WOULD YOU?
AND AT THAT MOMENT IT HAD ALL BECOME TOO MUCH.
I WAS SICK OF IT.
SICK OF SCHOOL, SICK OF MY PARENTS, SICK OF MY BEST FRIEND NOT EVEN BEING REAL.
SICK OF IT ALL.
MAKE5WISHES
Order Now!
AND I WAS WILLING TO DO WHATEVER I HAD TO DO TO CHANGE IT.

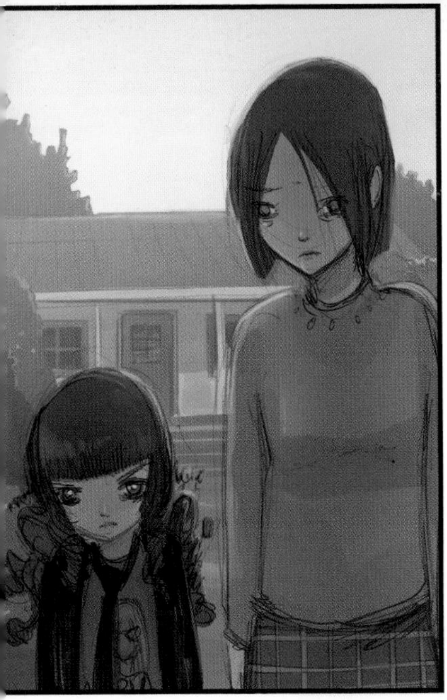

MY FIRST DAY AS A
RENTED GRANDCHILD HAD
BEEN A DISASTER.

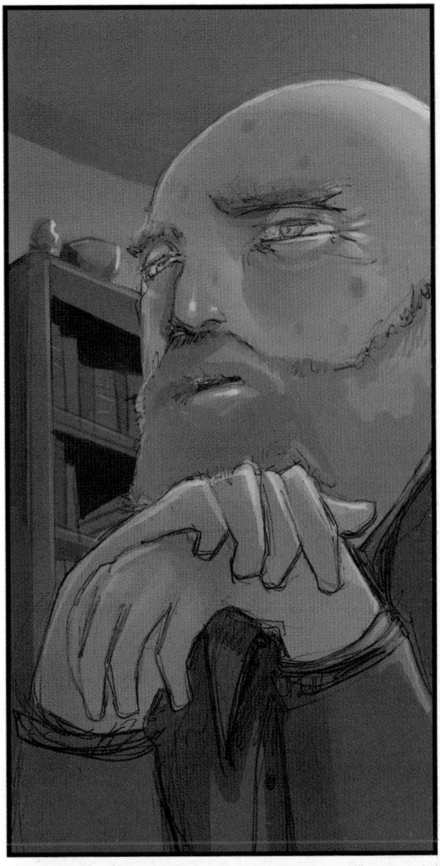

I HADN'T WANTED
TO BE THERE AND
I MADE IT CLEAR.

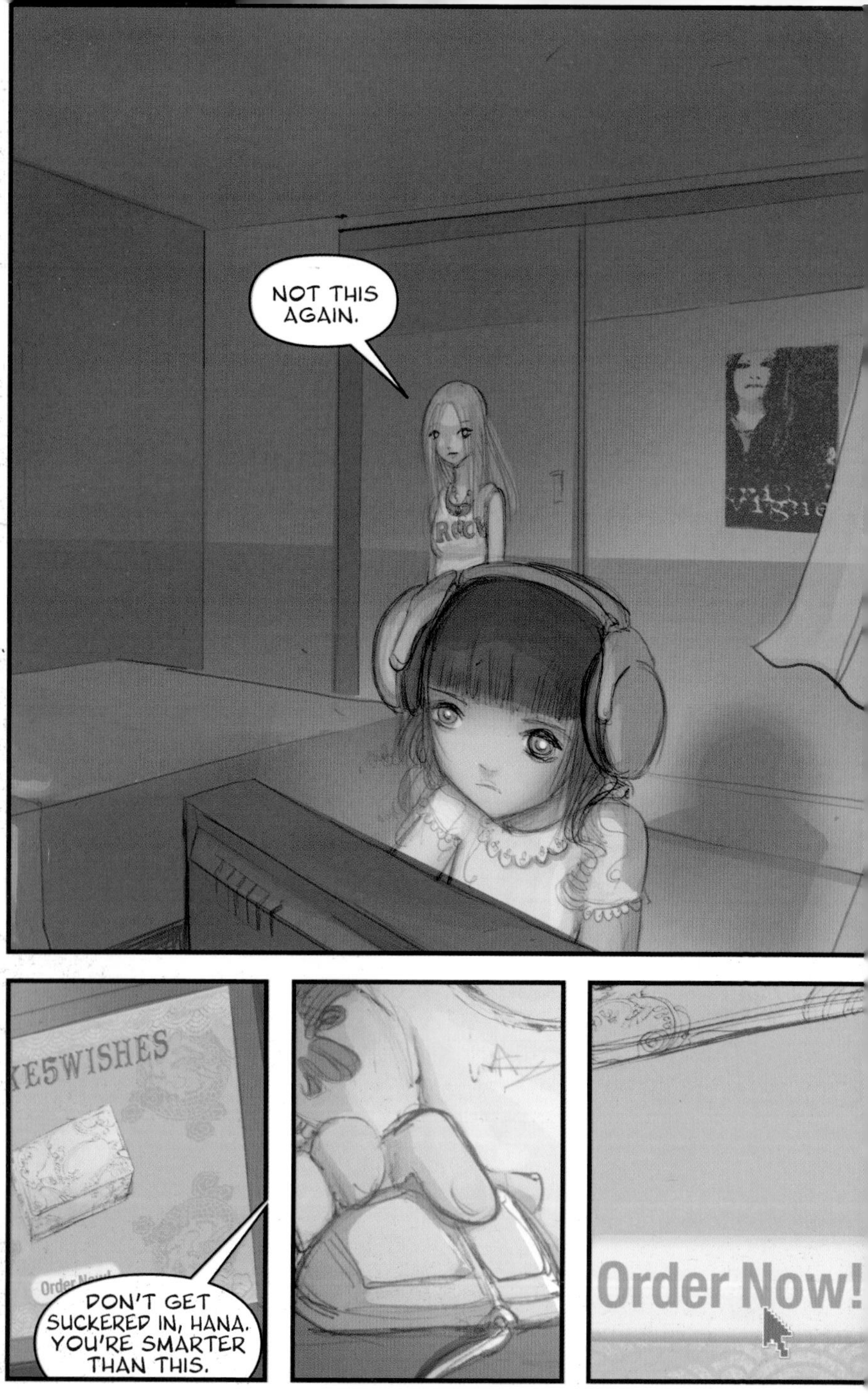
NOT THIS AGAIN.
KE5WISHES
DON'T GET SUCKERED IN, HANA. YOU'RE SMARTER THAN THIS.
Order Now!

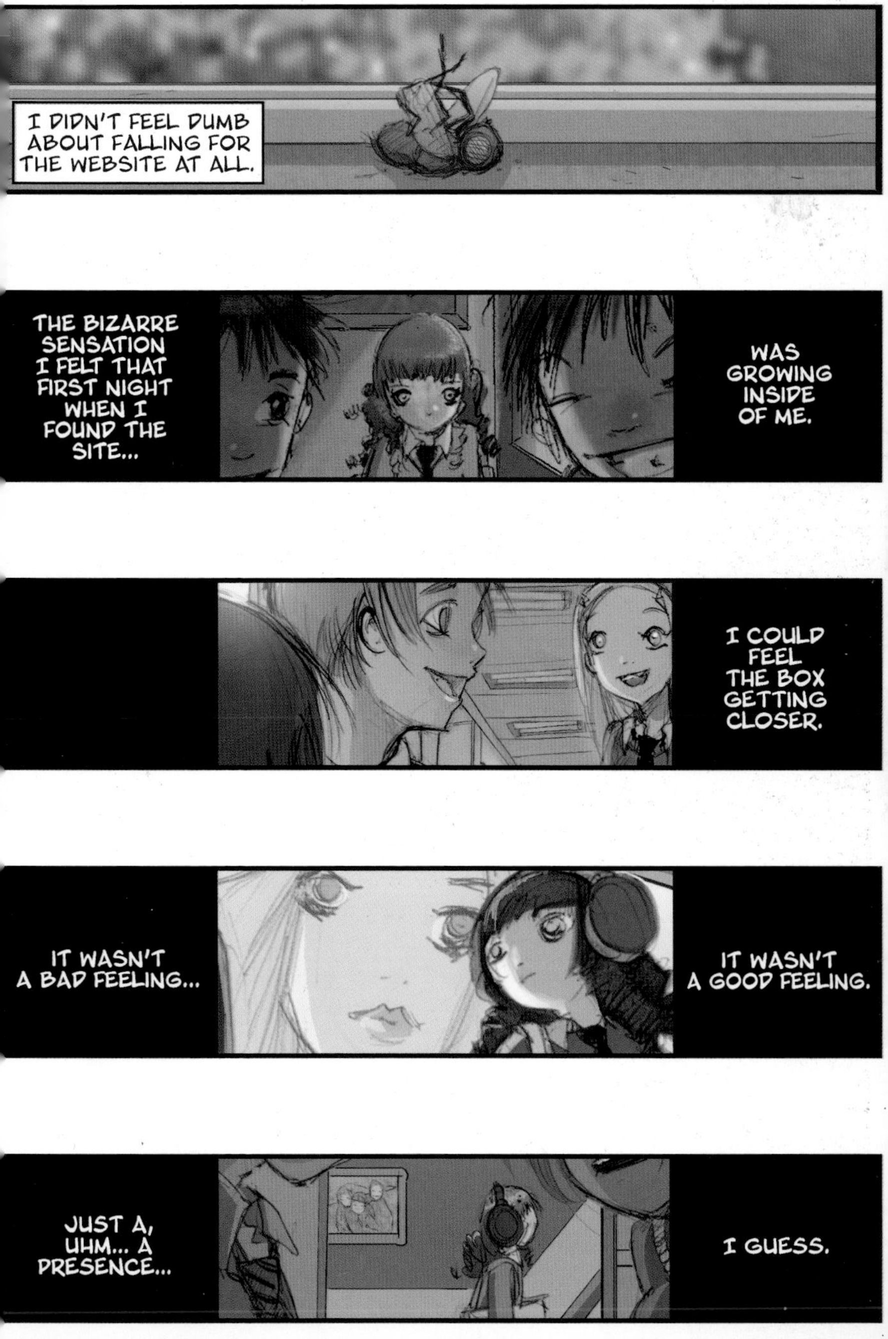
I DIDN'T FEEL DUMB ABOUT FALLING FOR THE WEBSITE AT ALL.
THE BIZARRE SENSATION I FELT THAT FIRST NIGHT WHEN I FOUND THE SITE...
WAS GROWING INSIDE OF ME.
I COULD FEEL THE BOX GETTING CLOSER.
IT WASN'T A BAD FEELING...
IT WASN'T A GOOD FEELING.
JUST A, UHM... A PRESENCE...
I GUESS.

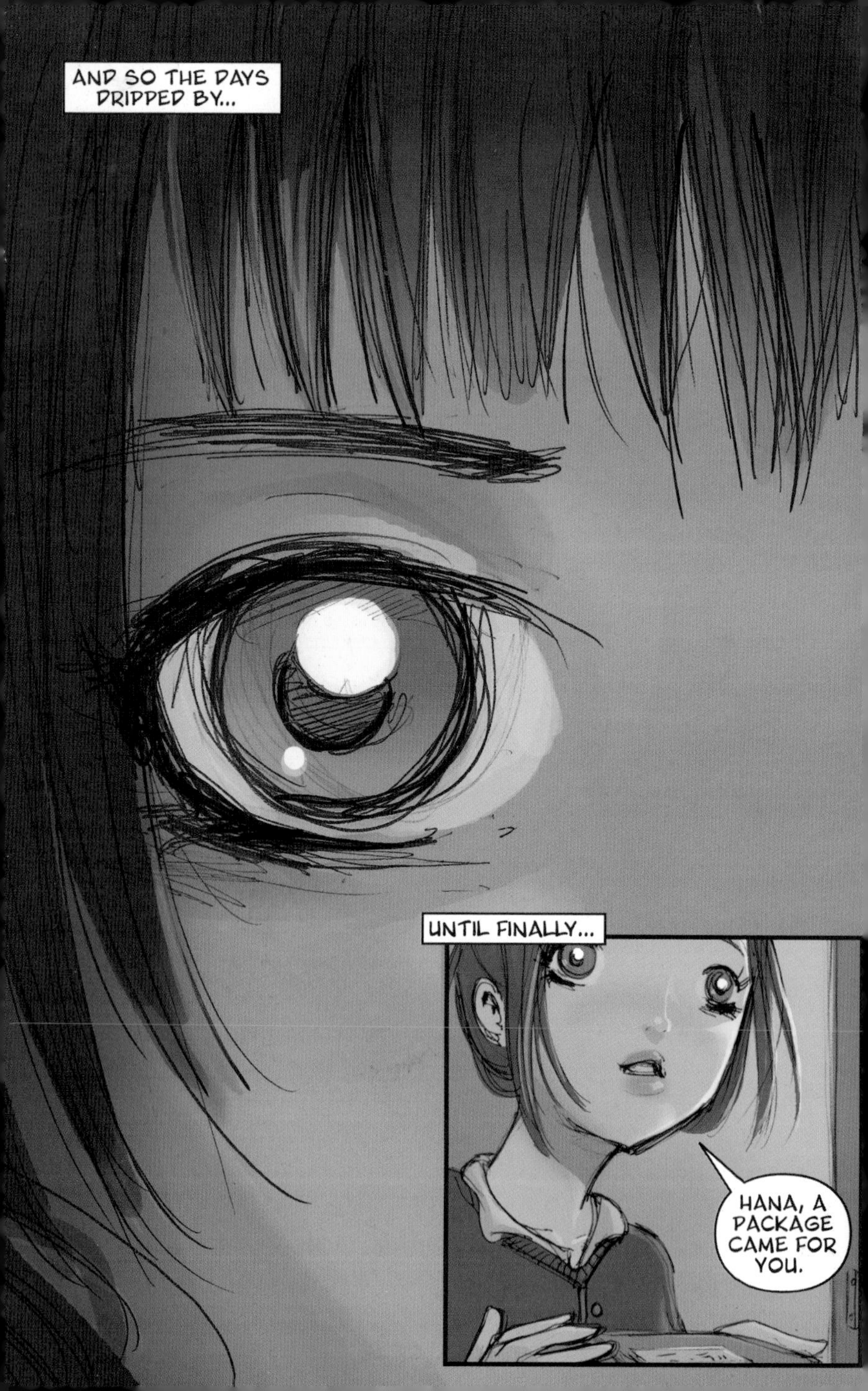
AND SO THE DAYS DRIPPED BY...
UNTIL FINALLY...
HANA, A PACKAGE CAME FOR YOU.

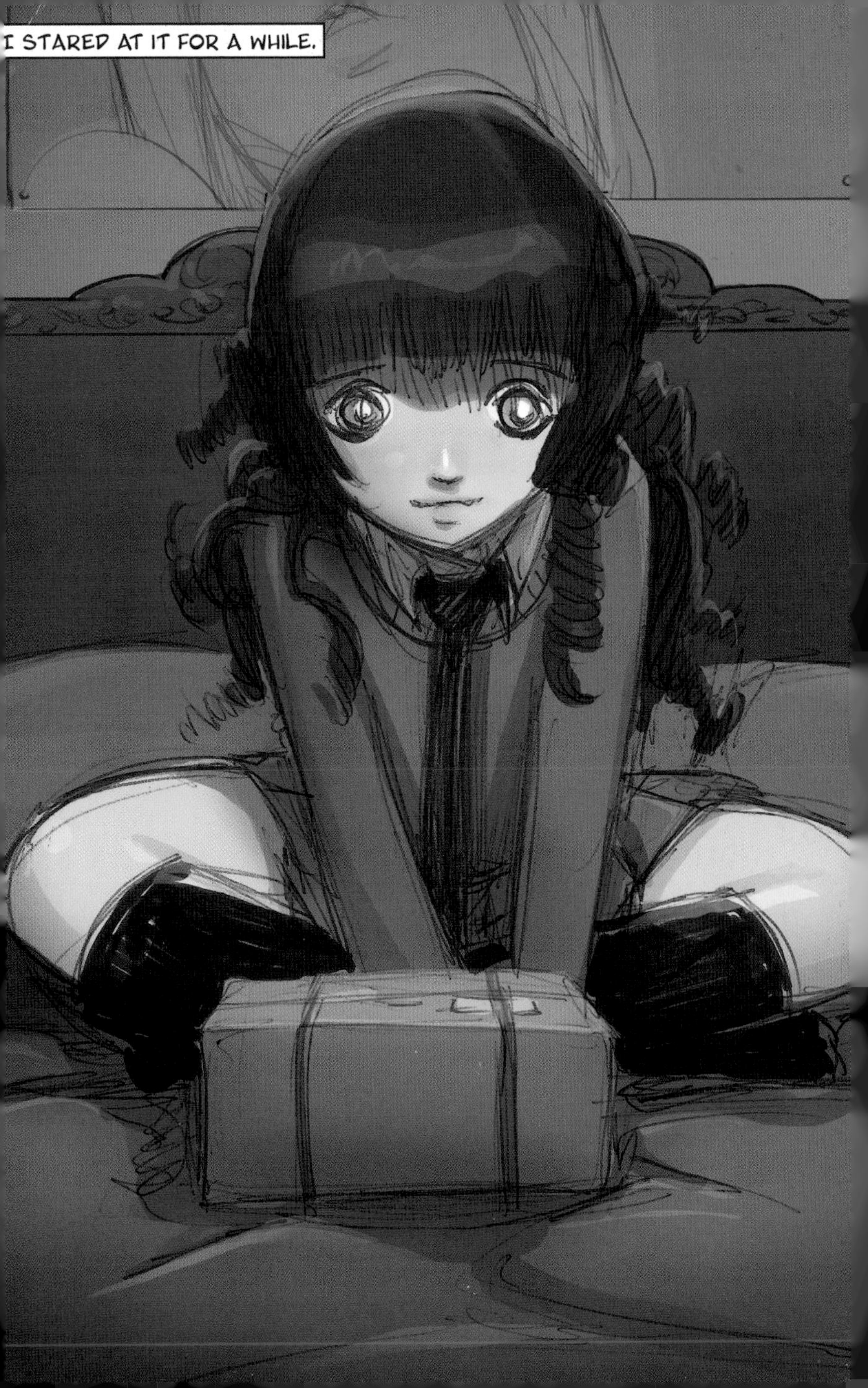
I STARED AT IT FOR A WHILE.

I WAS
PRACTICALLY
BUZZING.

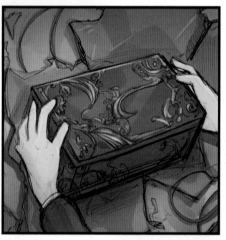

THERE WAS
SOMETHING INSIDE.
A WEIGHT SHIFTING
AROUND.

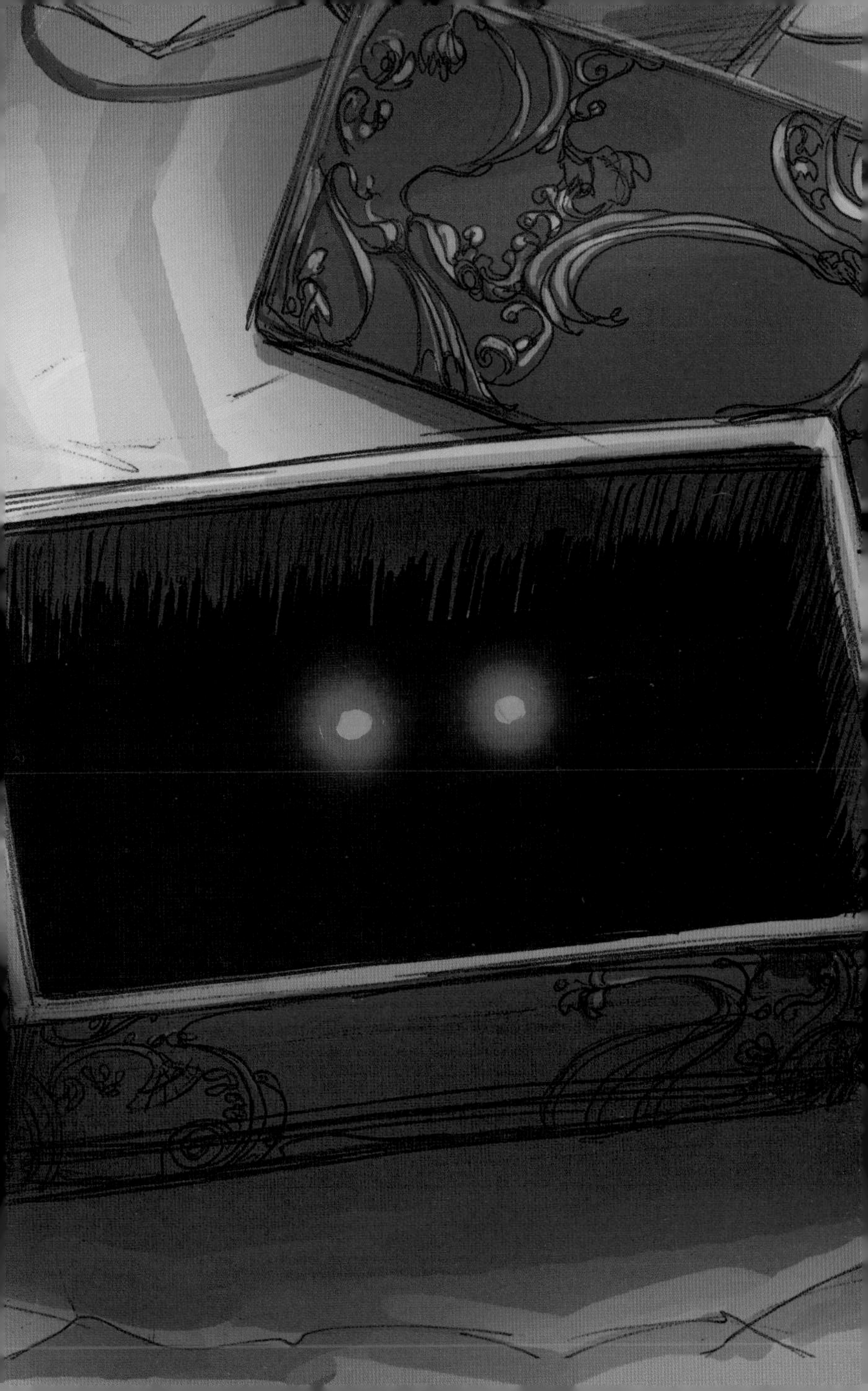

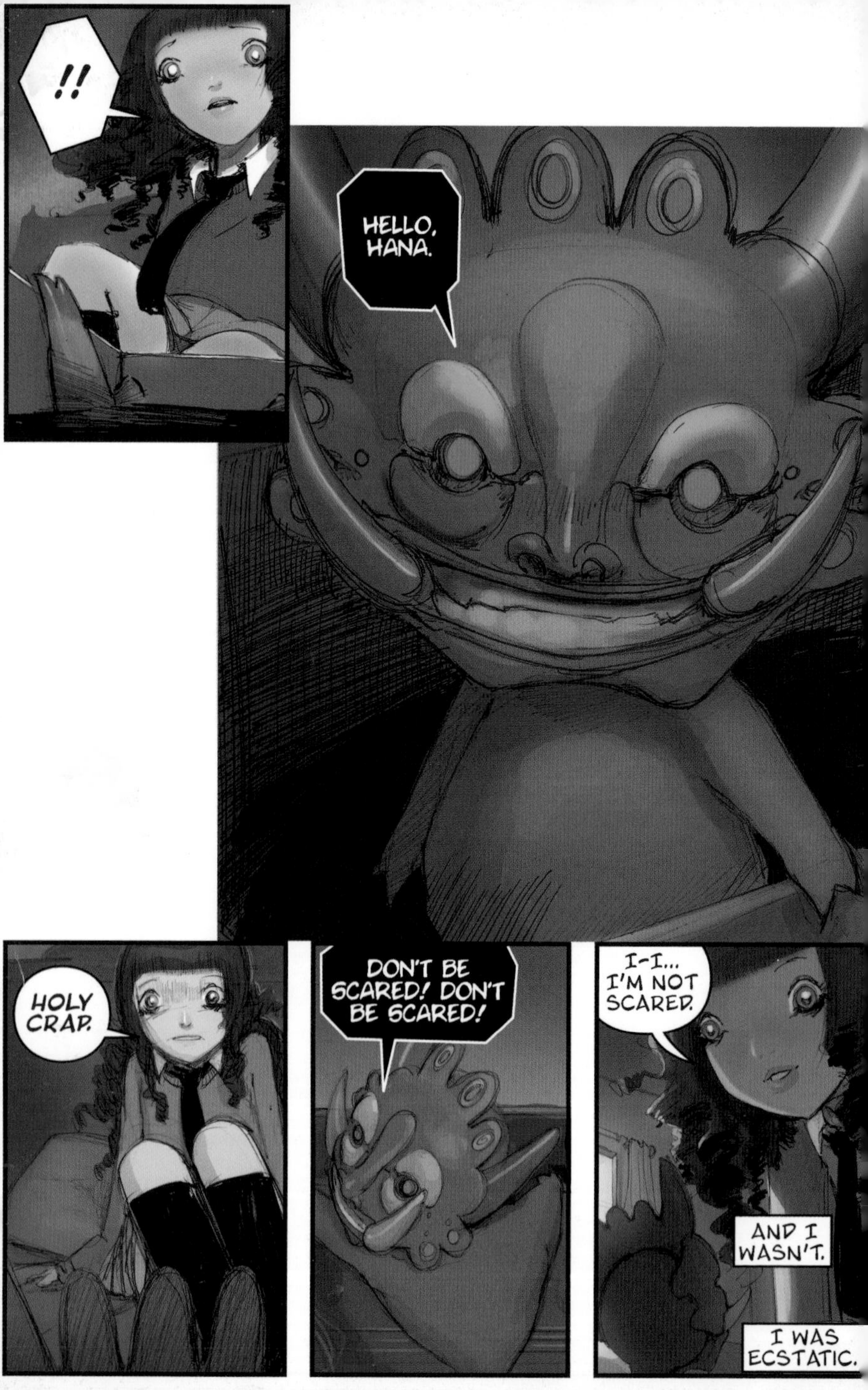
!!
HELLO, HANA.
HOLY CRAP.
DON'T BE SCARED! DON'T BE SCARED!
I-I... I'M NOT SCARED.
AND I WASN'T.
I WAS ECSTATIC.

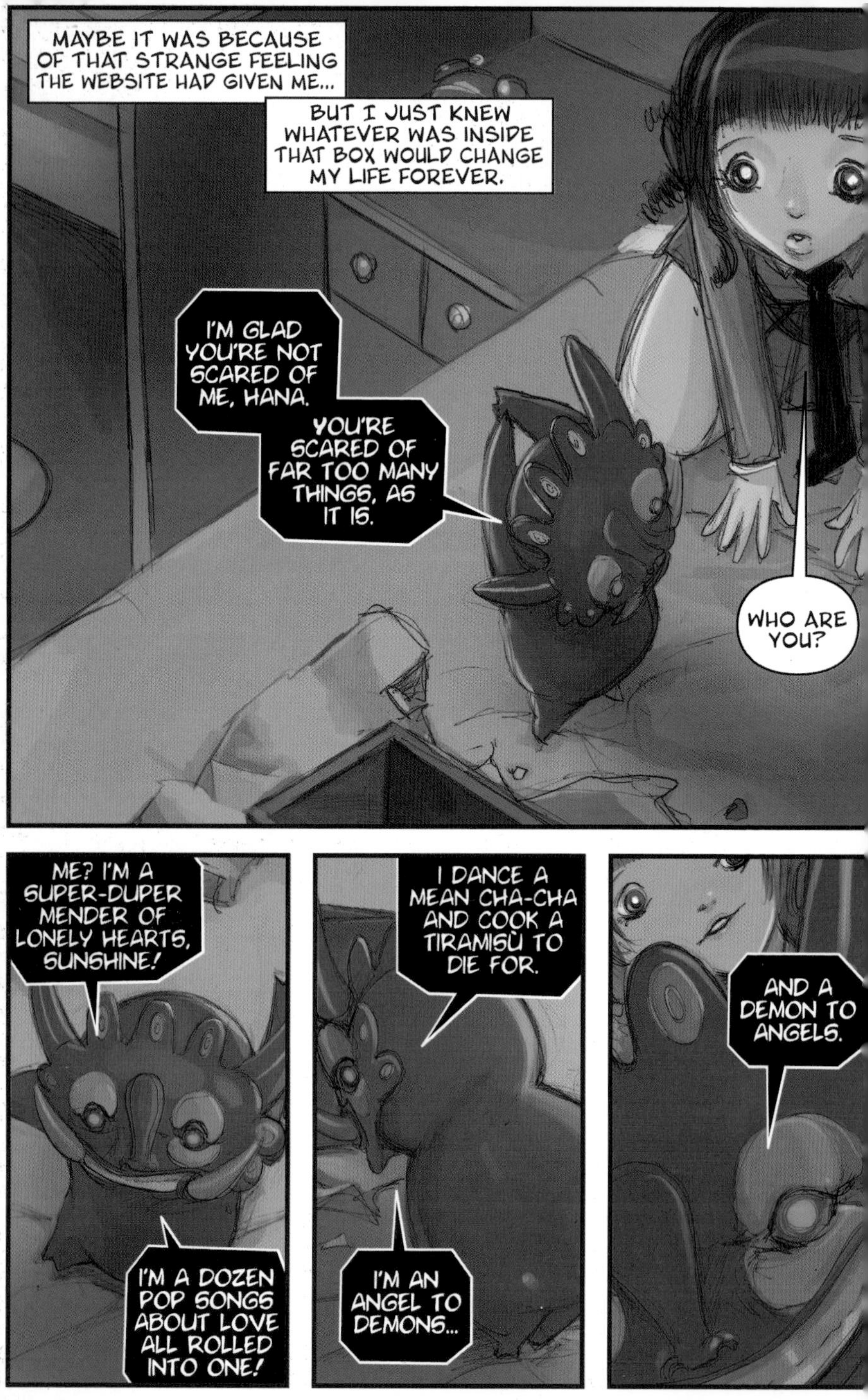
MAYBE IT WAS BECAUSE OF THAT STRANGE FEELING THE WEBSITE HAD GIVEN ME...
BUT I JUST KNEW WHATEVER WAS INSIDE THAT BOX WOULD CHANGE MY LIFE FOREVER.
WHO ARE YOU?
I'M GLAD YOU'RE NOT SCARED OF ME, HANA.
YOU'RE SCARED OF FAR TOO MANY THINGS, AS IT IS.
ME? I'M A SUPER-DUPER MENDER OF LONELY HEARTS, SUNSHINE!
I'M A DOZEN POP SONGS ABOUT LOVE ALL ROLLED INTO ONE!
I DANCE A MEAN CHA-CHA AND COOK A TIRAMISÙ TO DIE FOR.
I'M AN ANGEL TO DEMONS...
AND A DEMON TO ANGELS.

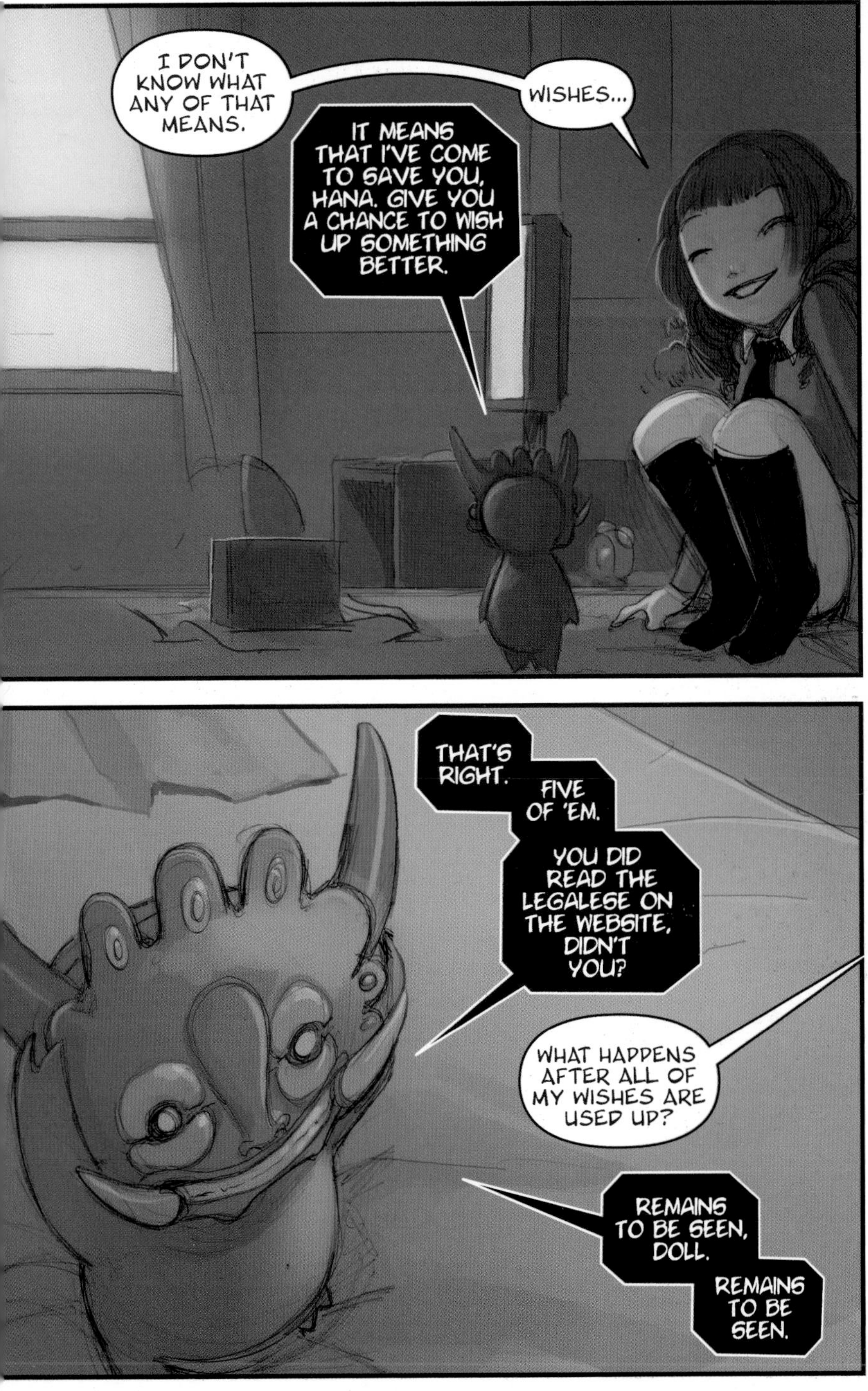
I DON'T KNOW WHAT ANY OF THAT MEANS.
WISHES...
IT MEANS THAT I'VE COME TO SAVE YOU, HANA. GIVE YOU A CHANCE TO WISH UP SOMETHING BETTER.
THAT'S RIGHT.
FIVE OF 'EM.
YOU DID READ THE LEGALESE ON THE WEBSITE, DIDN'T YOU?
WHAT HAPPENS AFTER ALL OF MY WISHES ARE USED UP?
REMAINS TO BE SEEN, DOLL.
REMAINS TO BE SEEN.

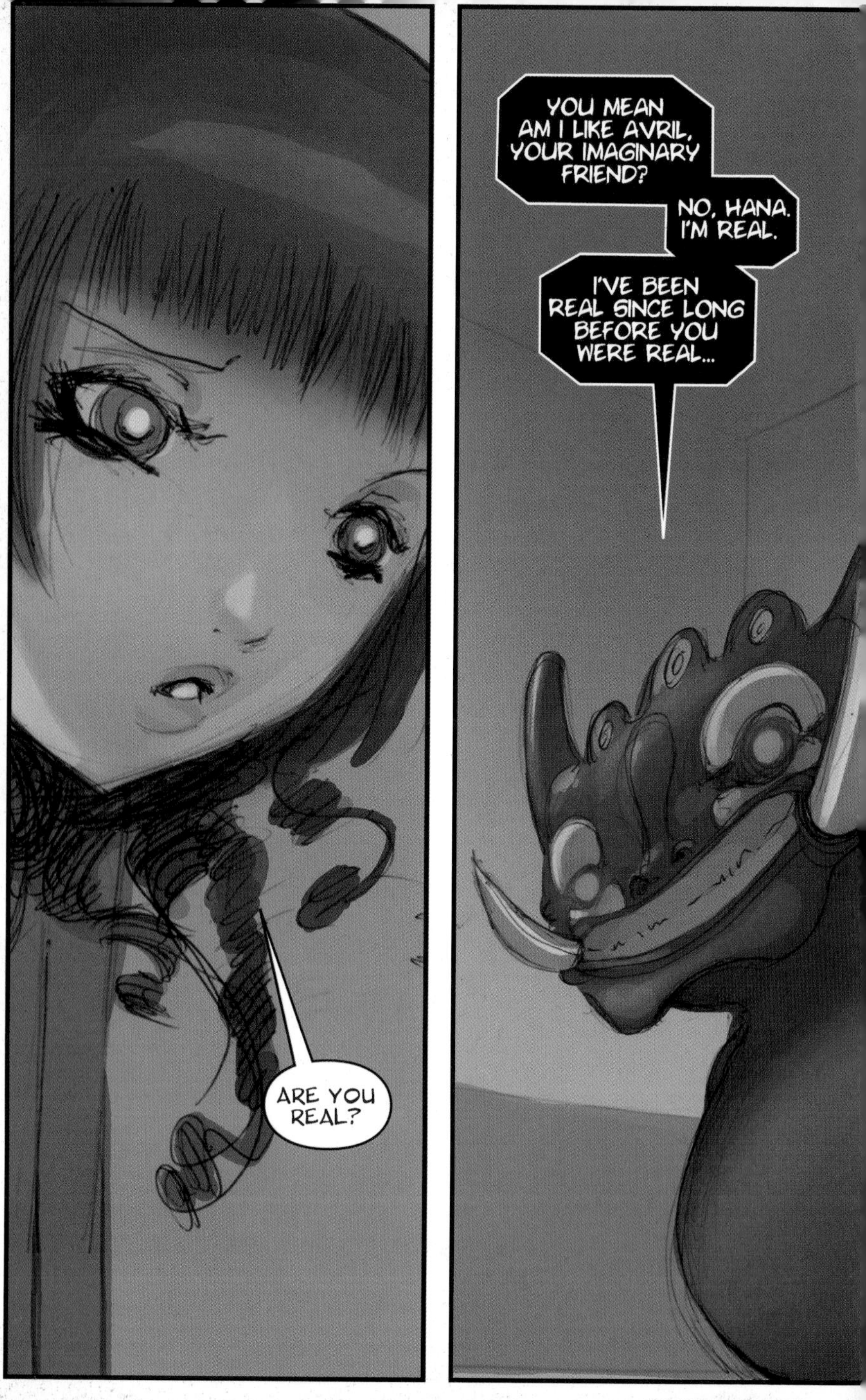
ARE YOU REAL?
YOU MEAN AM I LIKE AVRIL, YOUR IMAGINARY FRIEND?
NO, HANA. I'M REAL.
I'VE BEEN REAL SINCE LONG BEFORE YOU WERE REAL...

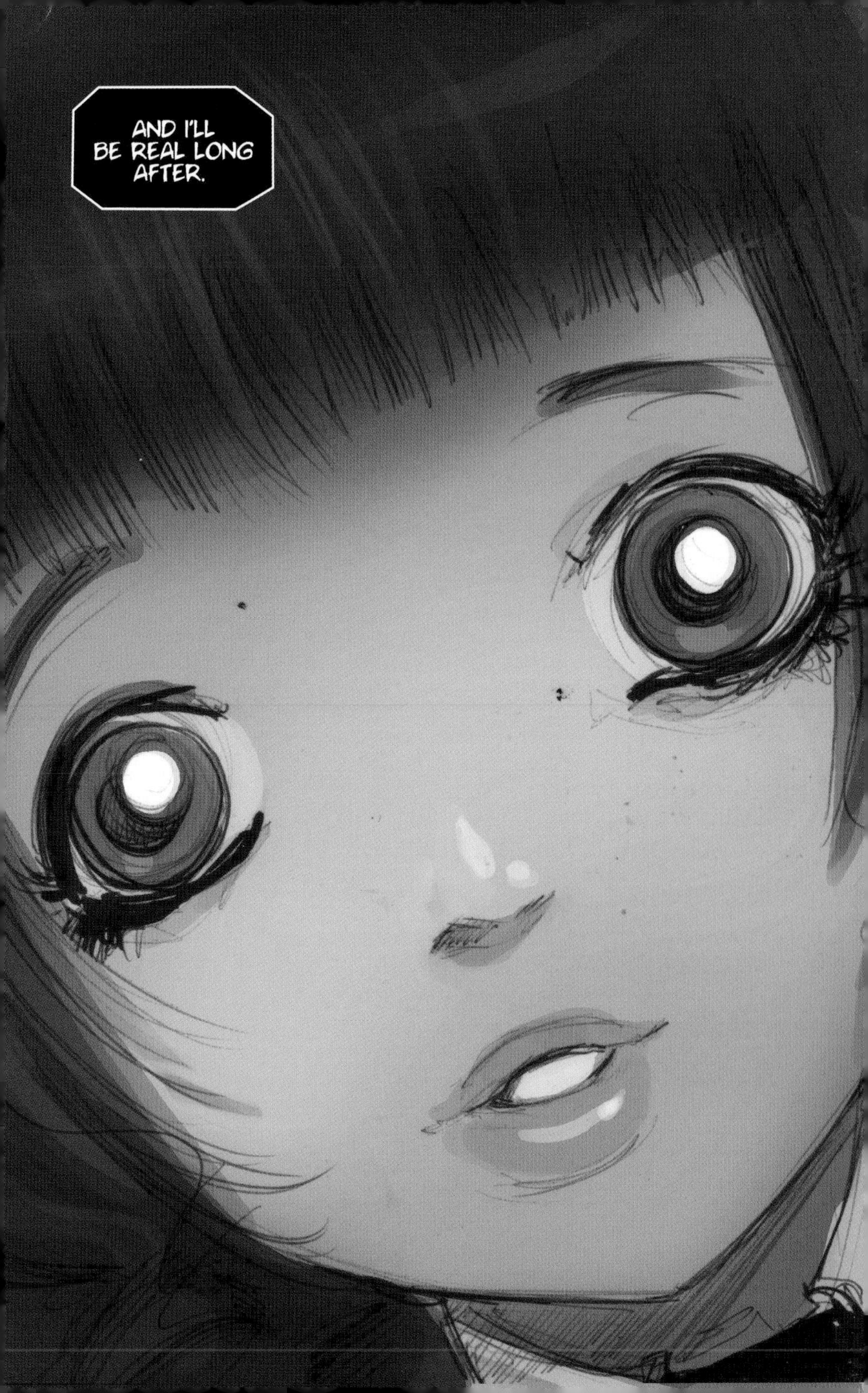
AND I'LL BE REAL LONG AFTER.

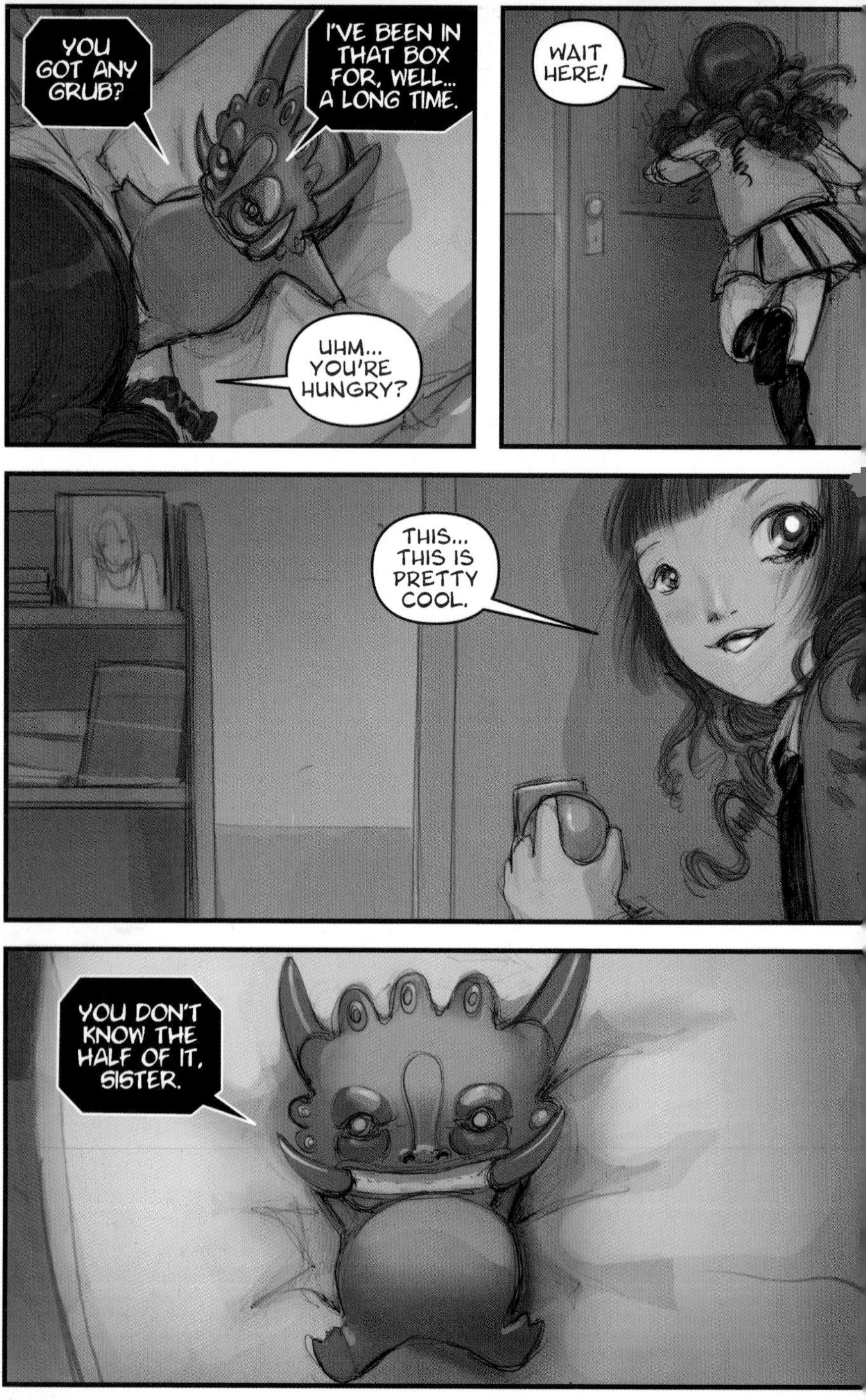
YOU GOT ANY GRUB?
I'VE BEEN IN THAT BOX FOR, WELL... A LONG TIME.
UHM... YOU'RE HUNGRY?
WAIT HERE!
THIS... THIS IS PRETTY COOL.
YOU DON'T KNOW THE HALF OF IT, SISTER.

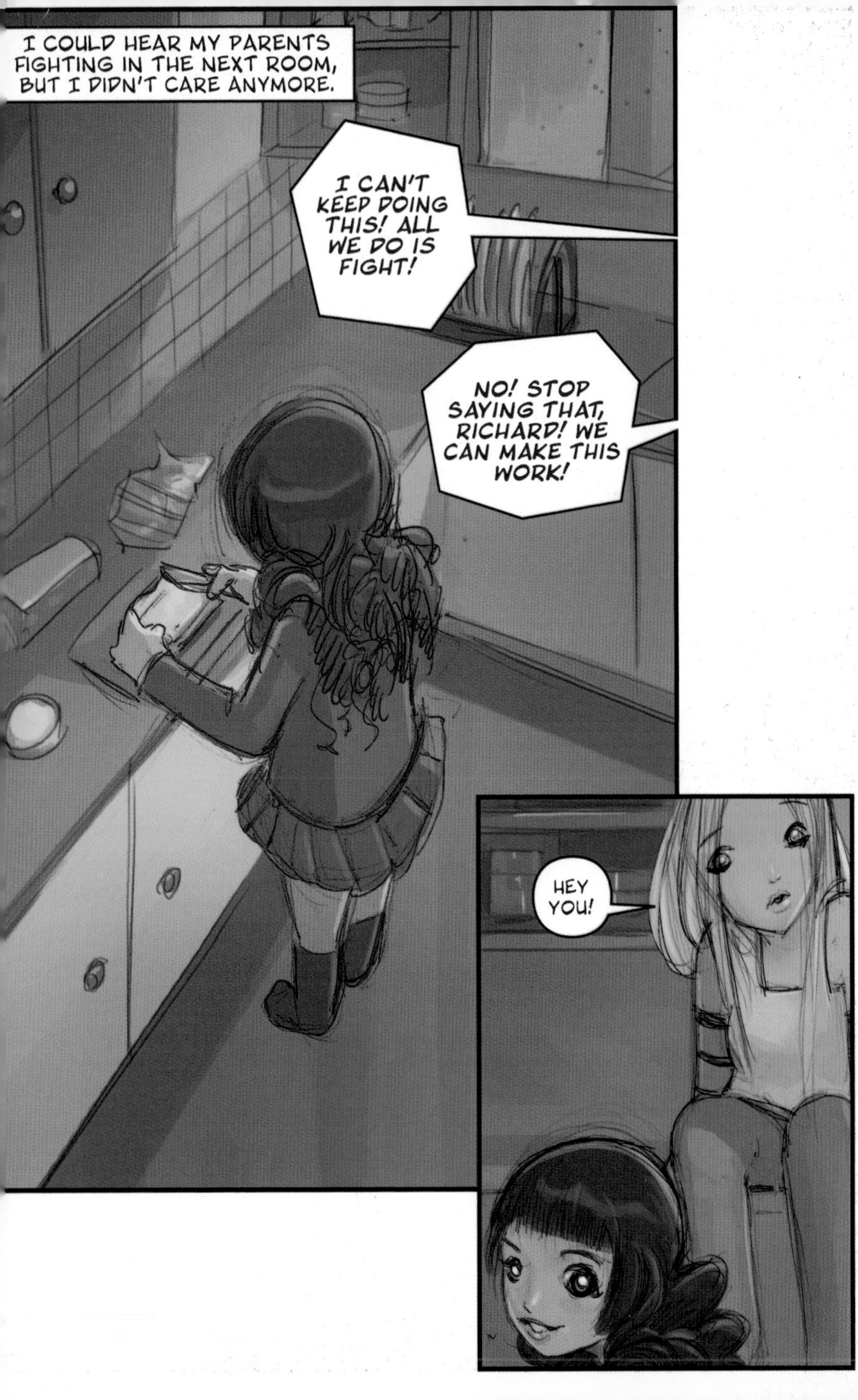
I COULD HEAR MY PARENTS FIGHTING IN THE NEXT ROOM, BUT I DIDN'T CARE ANYMORE.
I CAN'T KEEP DOING THIS! ALL WE DO IS FIGHT!
NO! STOP SAYING THAT, RICHARD! WE CAN MAKE THIS WORK!
HEY YOU!

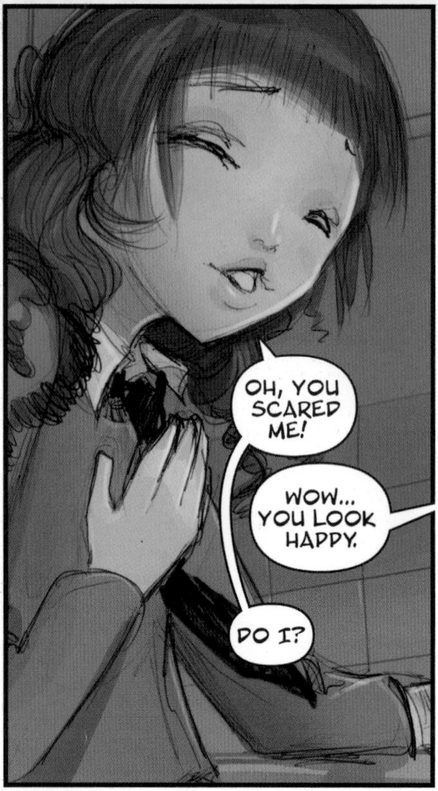
OH, YOU SCARED ME!
WOW... YOU LOOK HAPPY.
DO I?

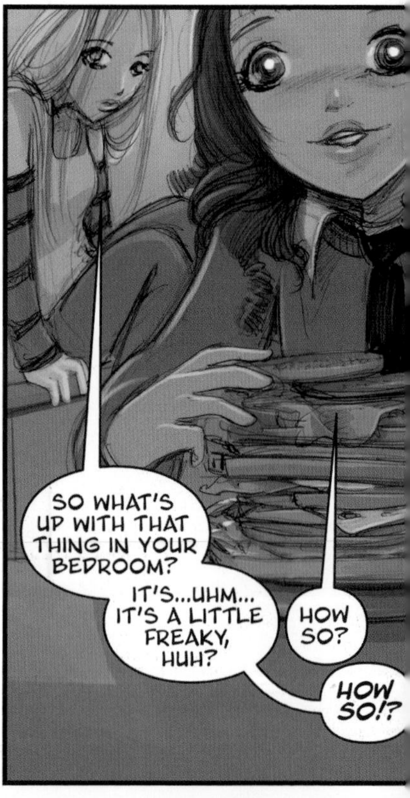
SO WHAT'S UP WITH THAT THING IN YOUR BEDROOM?
IT'S...UHM... IT'S A LITTLE FREAKY, HUH?
HOW SO?
HOW SO!?

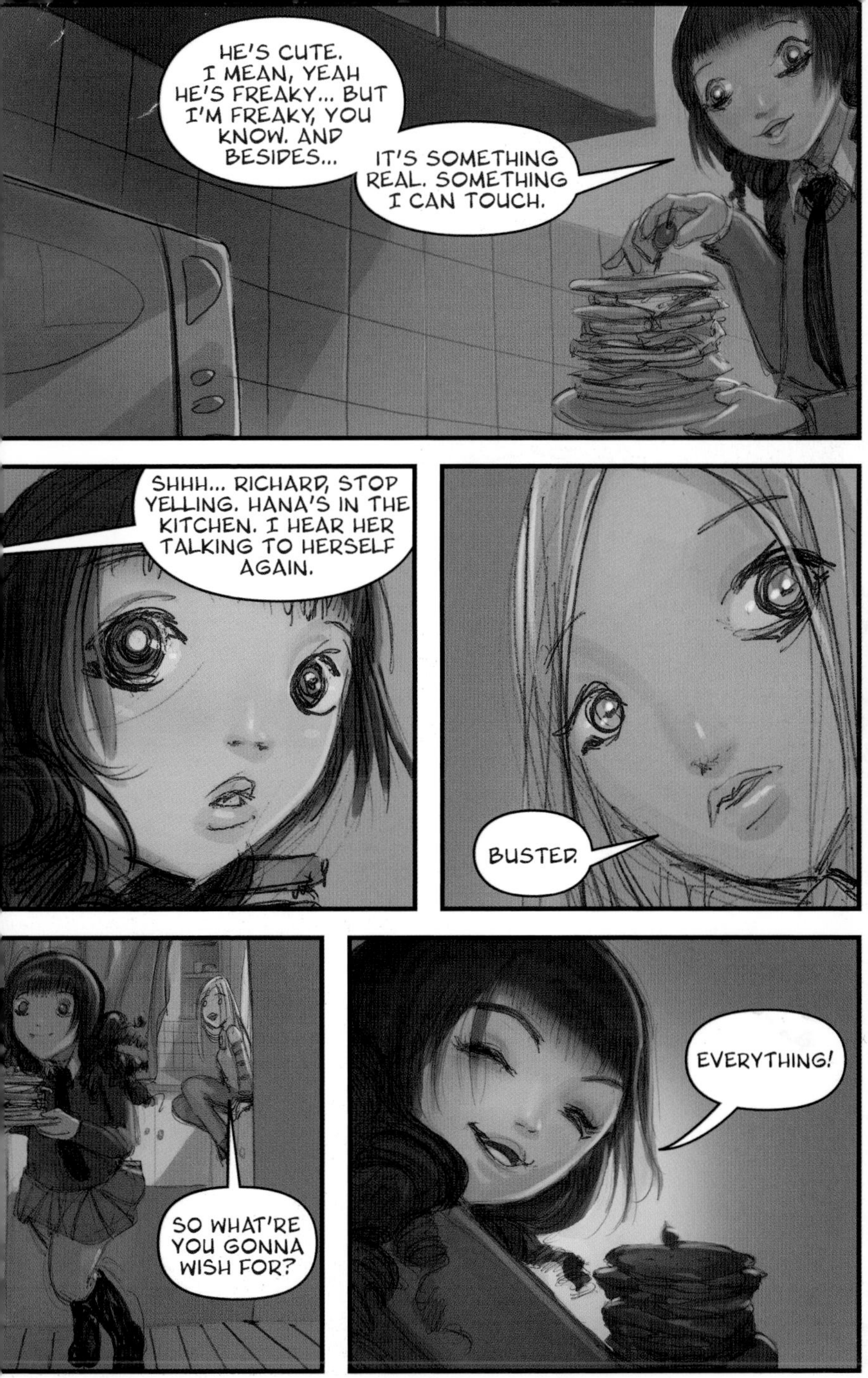
HE'S CUTE. I MEAN, YEAH HE'S FREAKY... BUT I'M FREAKY, YOU KNOW. AND BESIDES...
IT'S SOMETHING REAL. SOMETHING I CAN TOUCH.
SHHH... RICHARD, STOP YELLING. HANA'S IN THE KITCHEN. I HEAR HER TALKING TO HERSELF AGAIN.
BUSTED.
SO WHAT'RE YOU GONNA WISH FOR?
EVERYTHING!

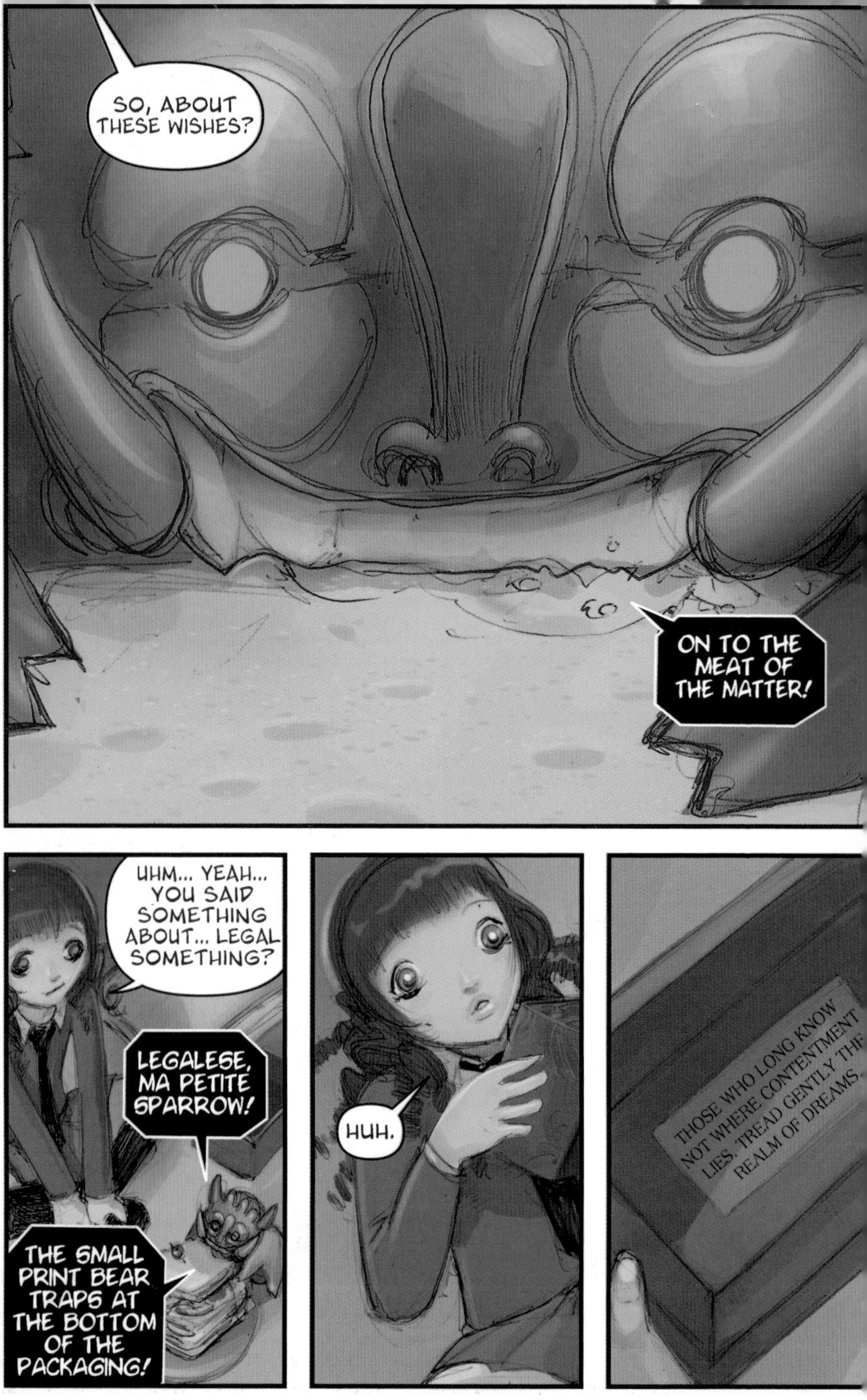
SO, ABOUT THESE WISHES?
ON TO THE MEAT OF THE MATTER!
UHM... YEAH... YOU SAID SOMETHING ABOUT... LEGAL SOMETHING?
LEGALESE, MA PETITE SPARROW!
THE SMALL PRINT BEAR TRAPS AT THE BOTTOM OF THE PACKAGING!
HUH.
THOSE WHO LONG KNOW NOT WHERE CONTENTMENT LIES. TREAD GENTLY THE REALM OF DREAMS.

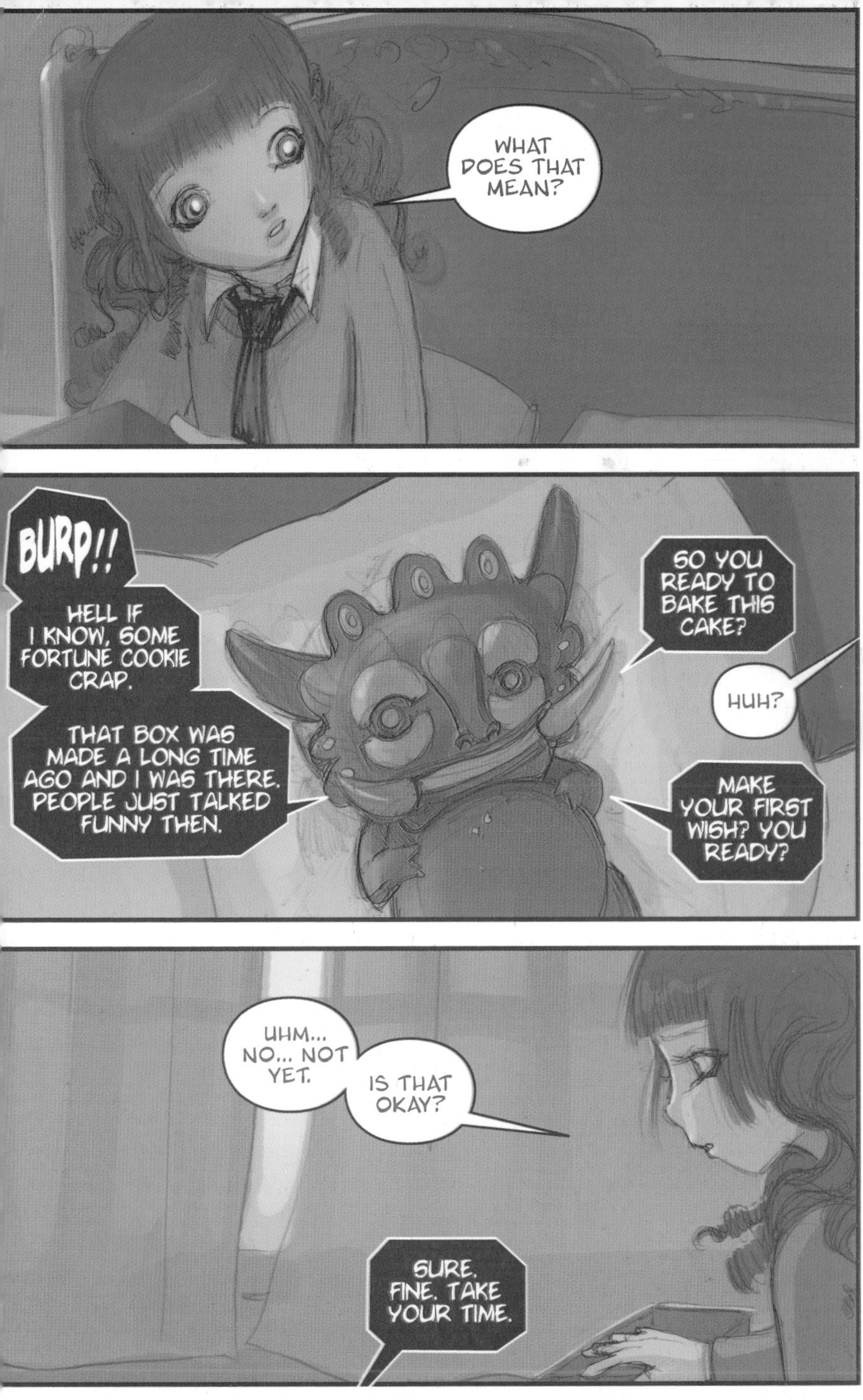
WHAT DOES THAT MEAN?
BURP!!
HELL IF I KNOW, SOME FORTUNE COOKIE CRAP.
THAT BOX WAS MADE A LONG TIME AGO AND I WAS THERE. PEOPLE JUST TALKED FUNNY THEN.
SO YOU READY TO BAKE THIS CAKE?
HUH?
MAKE YOUR FIRST WISH? YOU READY?
UHM... NO... NOT YET.
IS THAT OKAY?
SURE. FINE. TAKE YOUR TIME.

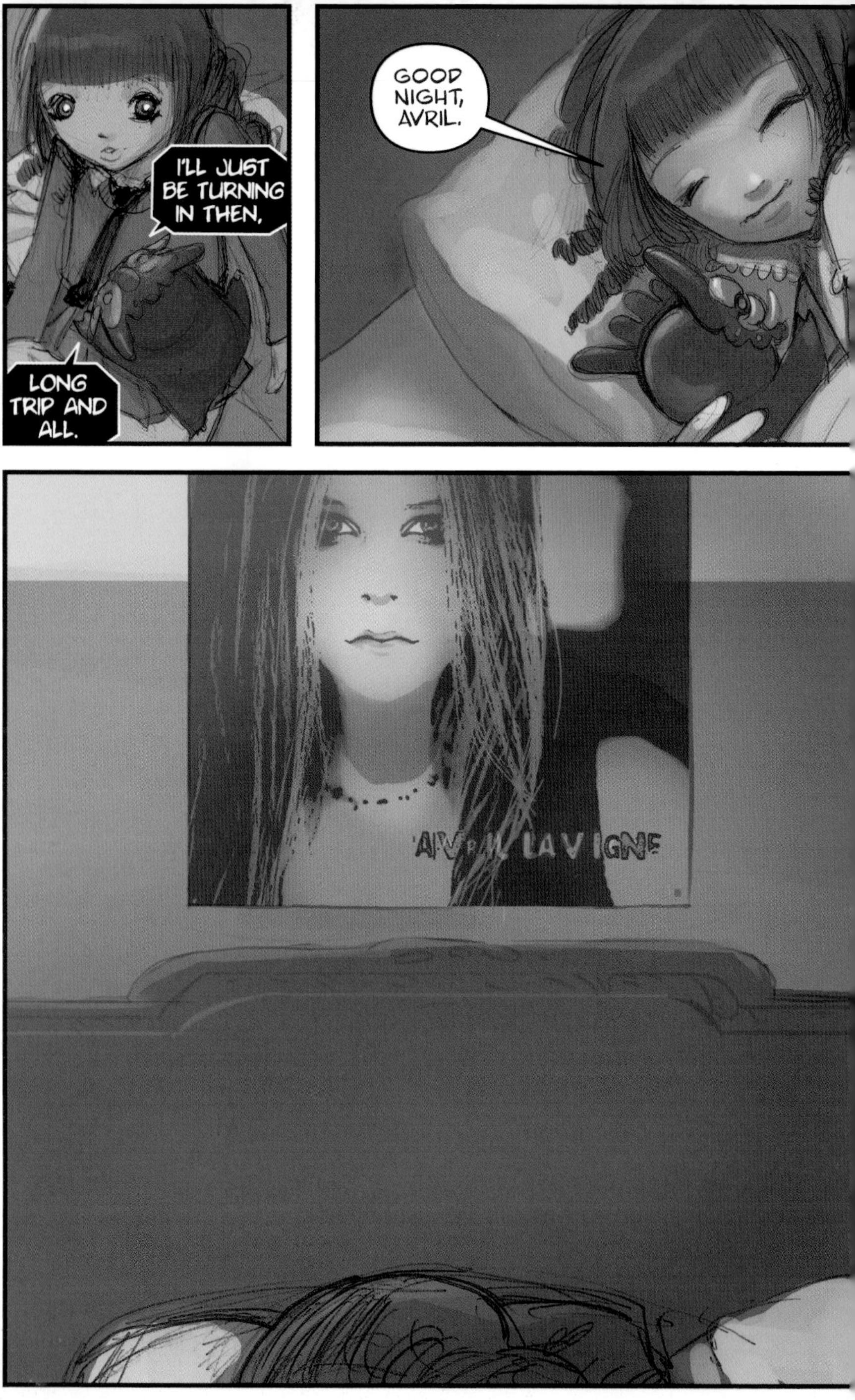
I'LL JUST BE TURNING IN THEN,
LONG TRIP AND ALL.
GOOD NIGHT, AVRIL.
AVRIL LAVIGNE

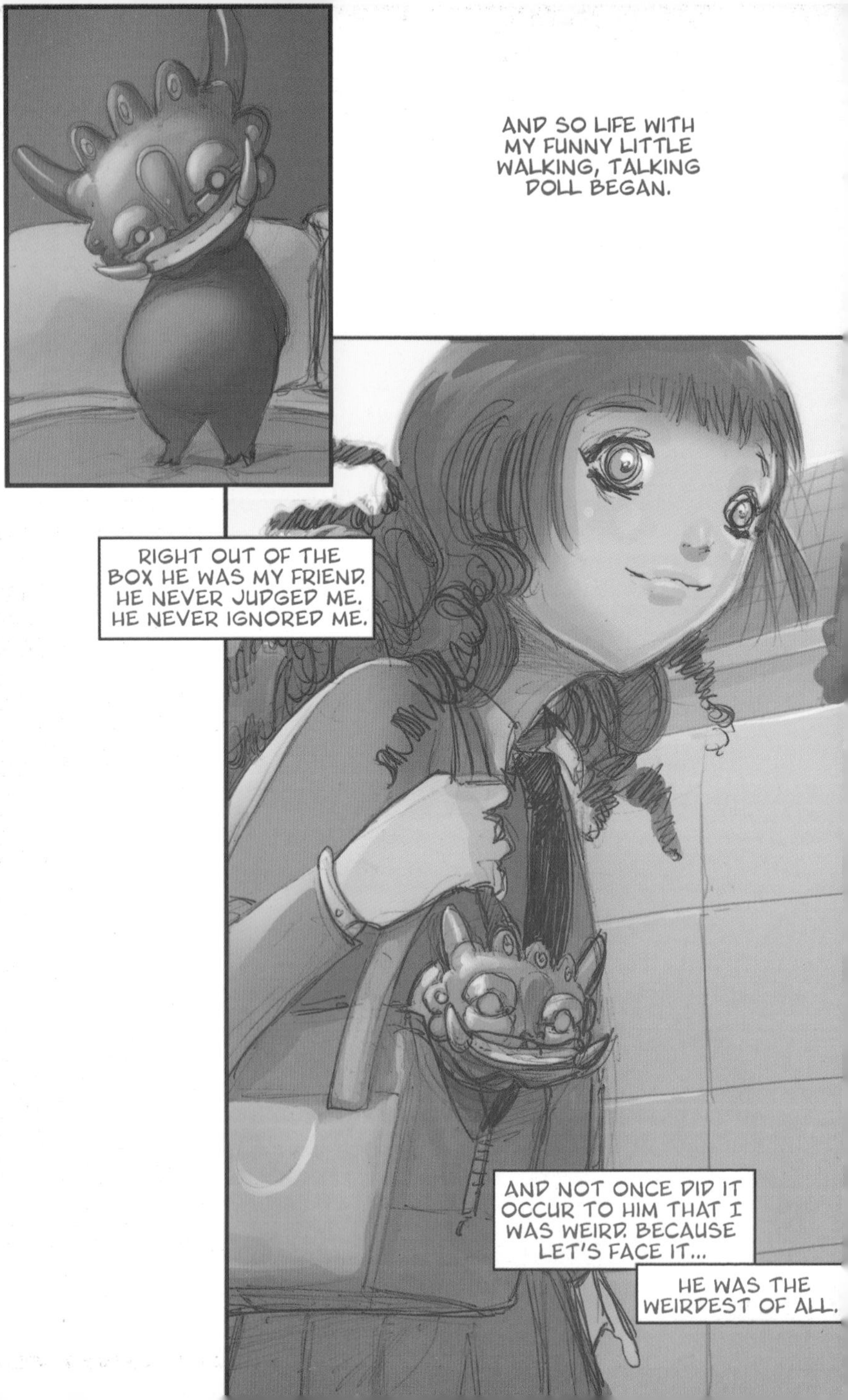
AND SO LIFE WITH MY FUNNY LITTLE WALKING, TALKING DOLL BEGAN.
RIGHT OUT OF THE BOX HE WAS MY FRIEND. HE NEVER JUDGED ME. HE NEVER IGNORED ME.
AND NOT ONCE DID IT OCCUR TO HIM THAT I WAS WEIRD. BECAUSE LET'S FACE IT...
HE WAS THE WEIRDEST OF ALL.

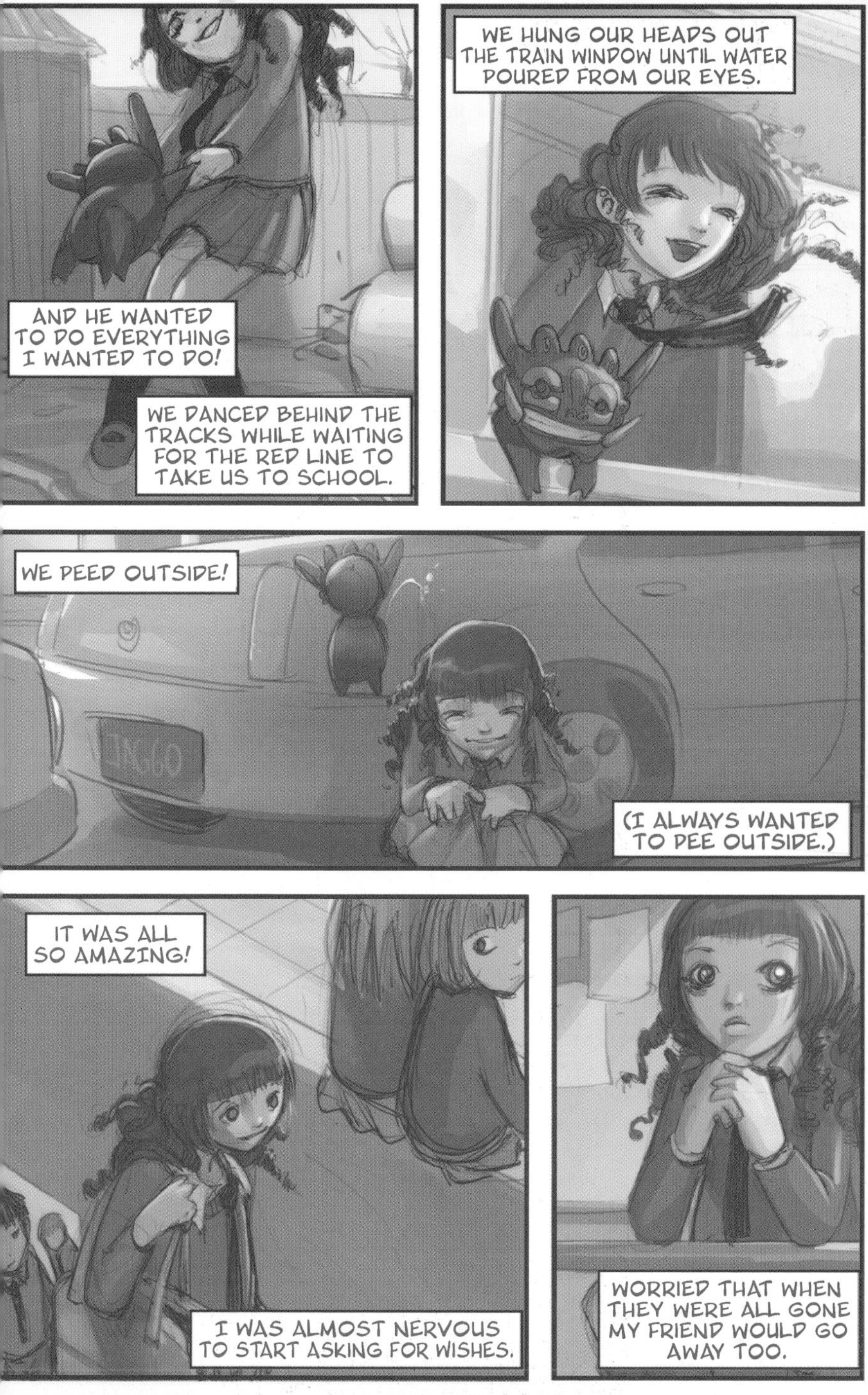
AND HE WANTED TO DO EVERYTHING I WANTED TO DO!
WE DANCED BEHIND THE TRACKS WHILE WAITING FOR THE RED LINE TO TAKE US TO SCHOOL.
WE HUNG OUR HEADS OUT THE TRAIN WINDOW UNTIL WATER POURED FROM OUR EYES.
WE PEED OUTSIDE!
(I ALWAYS WANTED TO PEE OUTSIDE.)
IT WAS ALL SO AMAZING!
I WAS ALMOST NERVOUS TO START ASKING FOR WISHES.
WORRIED THAT WHEN THEY WERE ALL GONE MY FRIEND WOULD GO AWAY TOO.

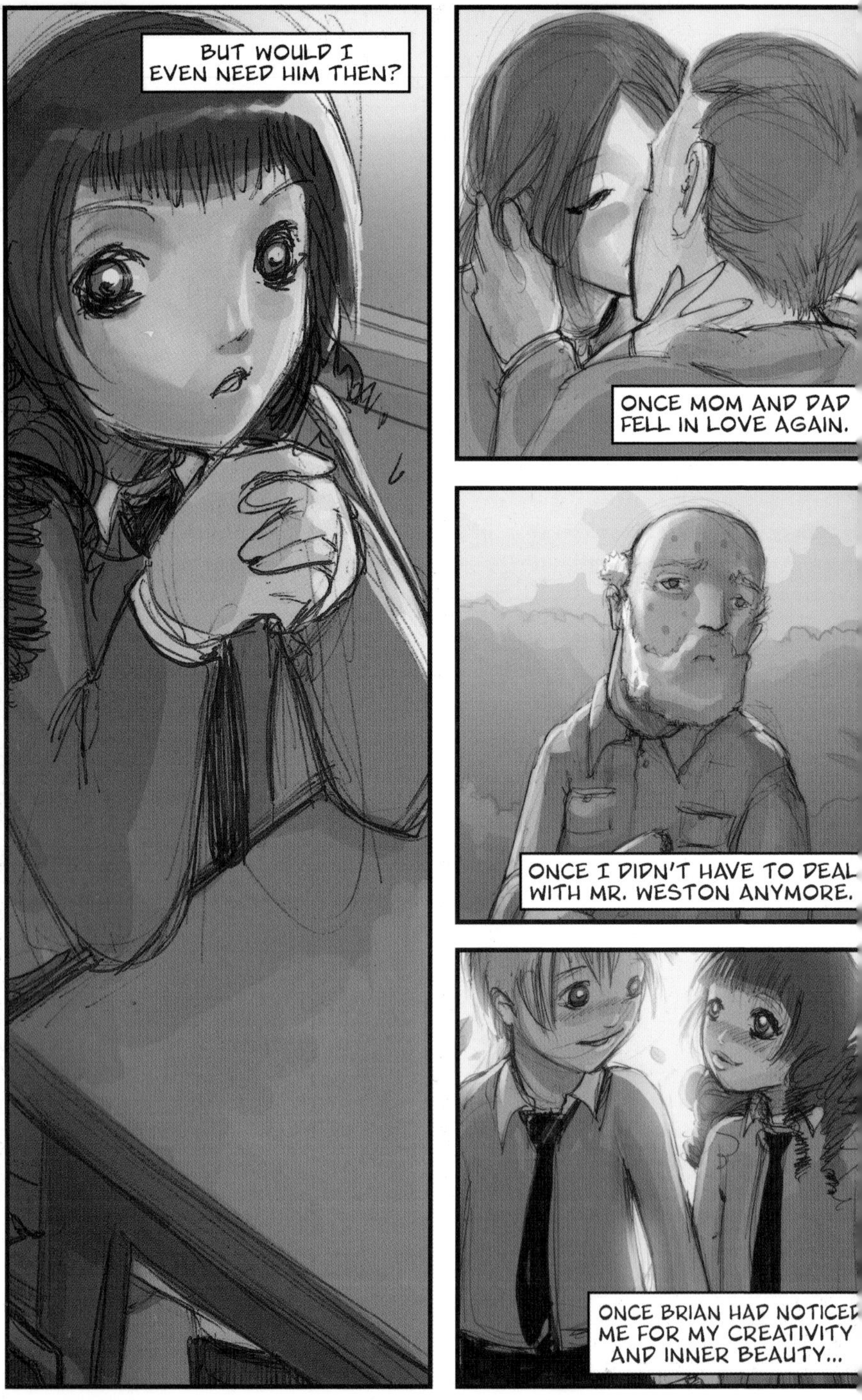
BUT WOULD I EVEN NEED HIM THEN?
ONCE MOM AND DAD FELL IN LOVE AGAIN.
ONCE I DIDN'T HAVE TO DEAL WITH MR. WESTON ANYMORE.
ONCE BRIAN HAD NOTICED ME FOR MY CREATIVITY AND INNER BEAUTY...

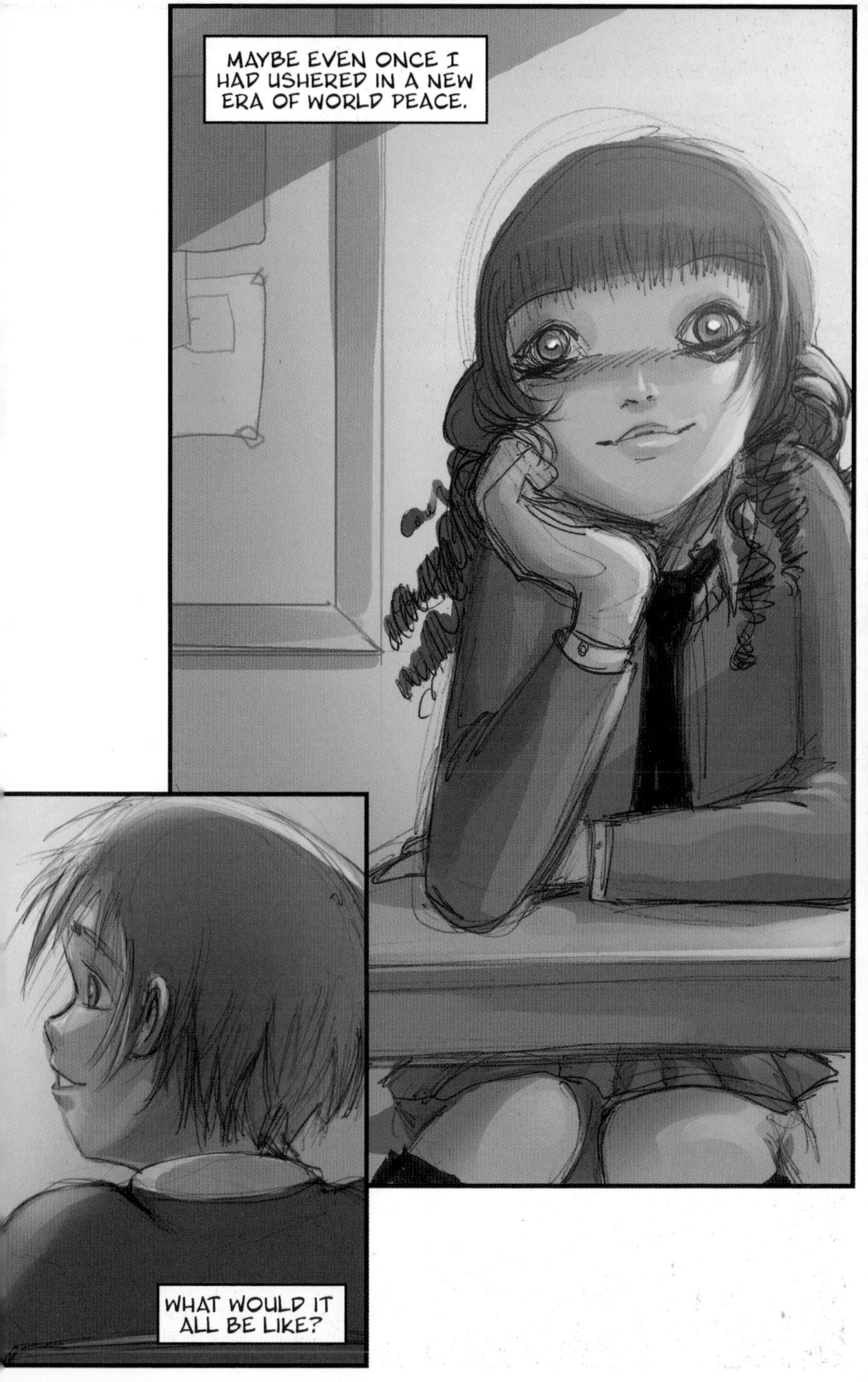
MAYBE EVEN ONCE I HAD USHERED IN A NEW ERA OF WORLD PEACE.
WHAT WOULD IT ALL BE LIKE?

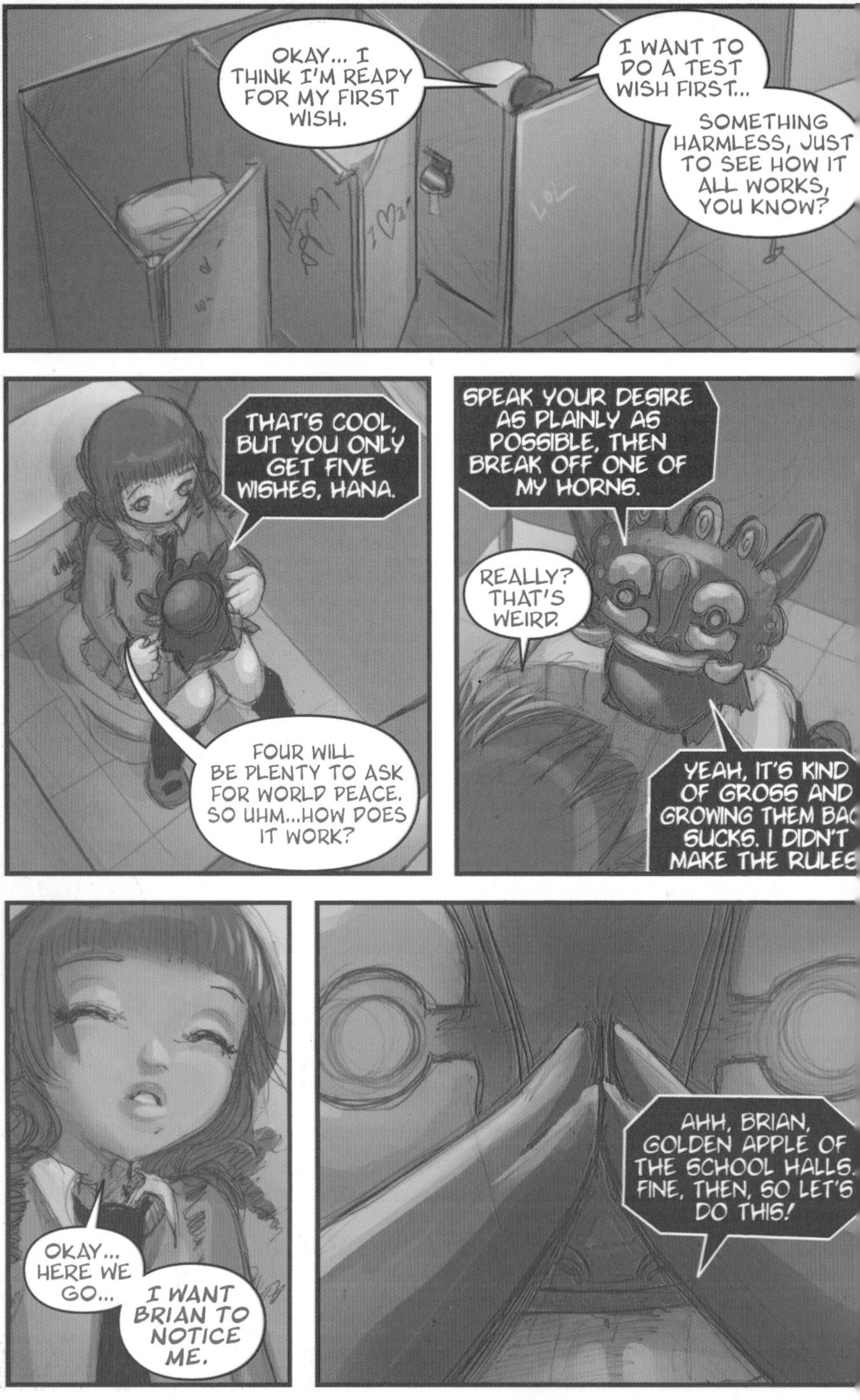
OKAY... I THINK I'M READY FOR MY FIRST WISH.
I WANT TO DO A TEST WISH FIRST...
SOMETHING HARMLESS, JUST TO SEE HOW IT ALL WORKS, YOU KNOW?
THAT'S COOL, BUT YOU ONLY GET FIVE WISHES, HANA.
FOUR WILL BE PLENTY TO ASK FOR WORLD PEACE. SO UHM...HOW DOES IT WORK?
SPEAK YOUR DESIRE AS PLAINLY AS POSSIBLE, THEN BREAK OFF ONE OF MY HORNS.
REALLY? THAT'S WEIRD.
YEAH, IT'S KIND OF GROSS AND GROWING THEM BAC SUCKS. I DIDN'T MAKE THE RULES
OKAY... HERE WE GO...
I WANT BRIAN TO NOTICE ME.
AHH, BRIAN, GOLDEN APPLE OF THE SCHOOL HALLS. FINE, THEN, SO LET'S DO THIS!

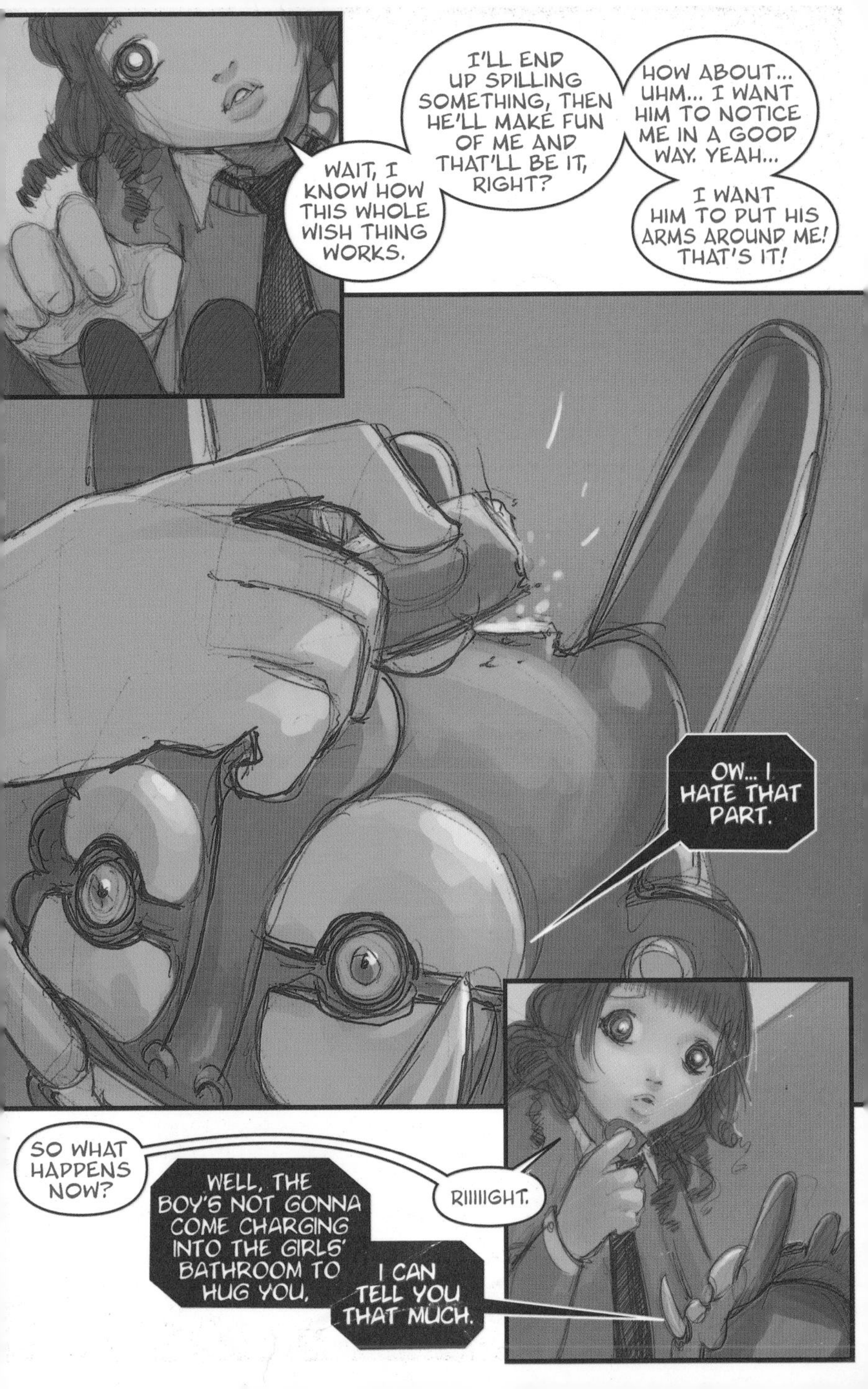
WAIT, I KNOW HOW THIS WHOLE WISH THING WORKS.
I'LL END UP SPILLING SOMETHING, THEN HE'LL MAKE FUN OF ME AND THAT'LL BE IT, RIGHT?
HOW ABOUT... UHM... I WANT HIM TO NOTICE ME IN A GOOD WAY. YEAH...
I WANT HIM TO PUT HIS ARMS AROUND ME! THAT'S IT!
OW... I HATE THAT PART.
SO WHAT HAPPENS NOW?
WELL, THE BOY'S NOT GONNA COME CHARGING INTO THE GIRLS' BATHROOM TO HUG YOU,
I CAN TELL YOU THAT MUCH.
RIIIIGHT.

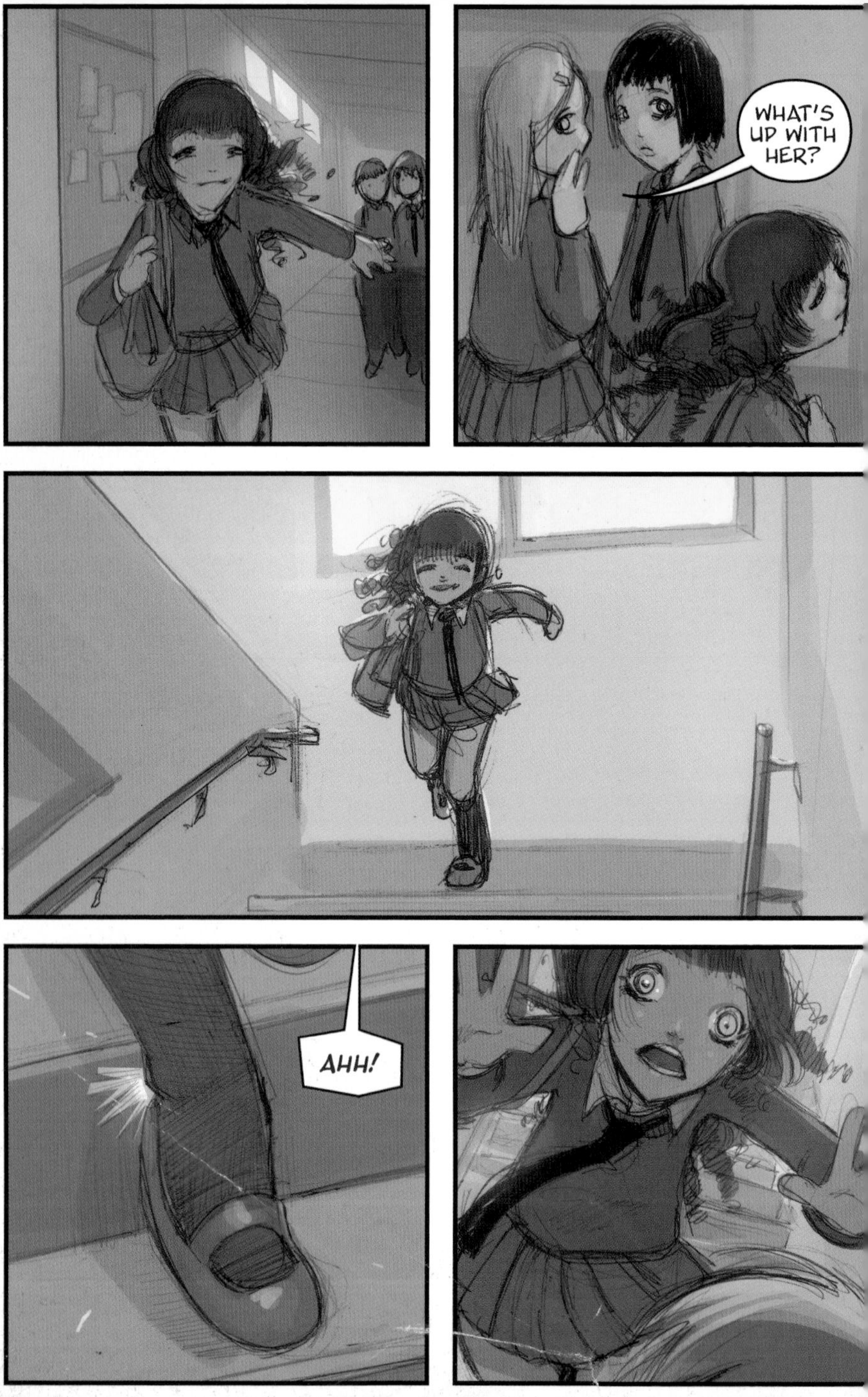
WHAT'S UP WITH HER?
AHH!

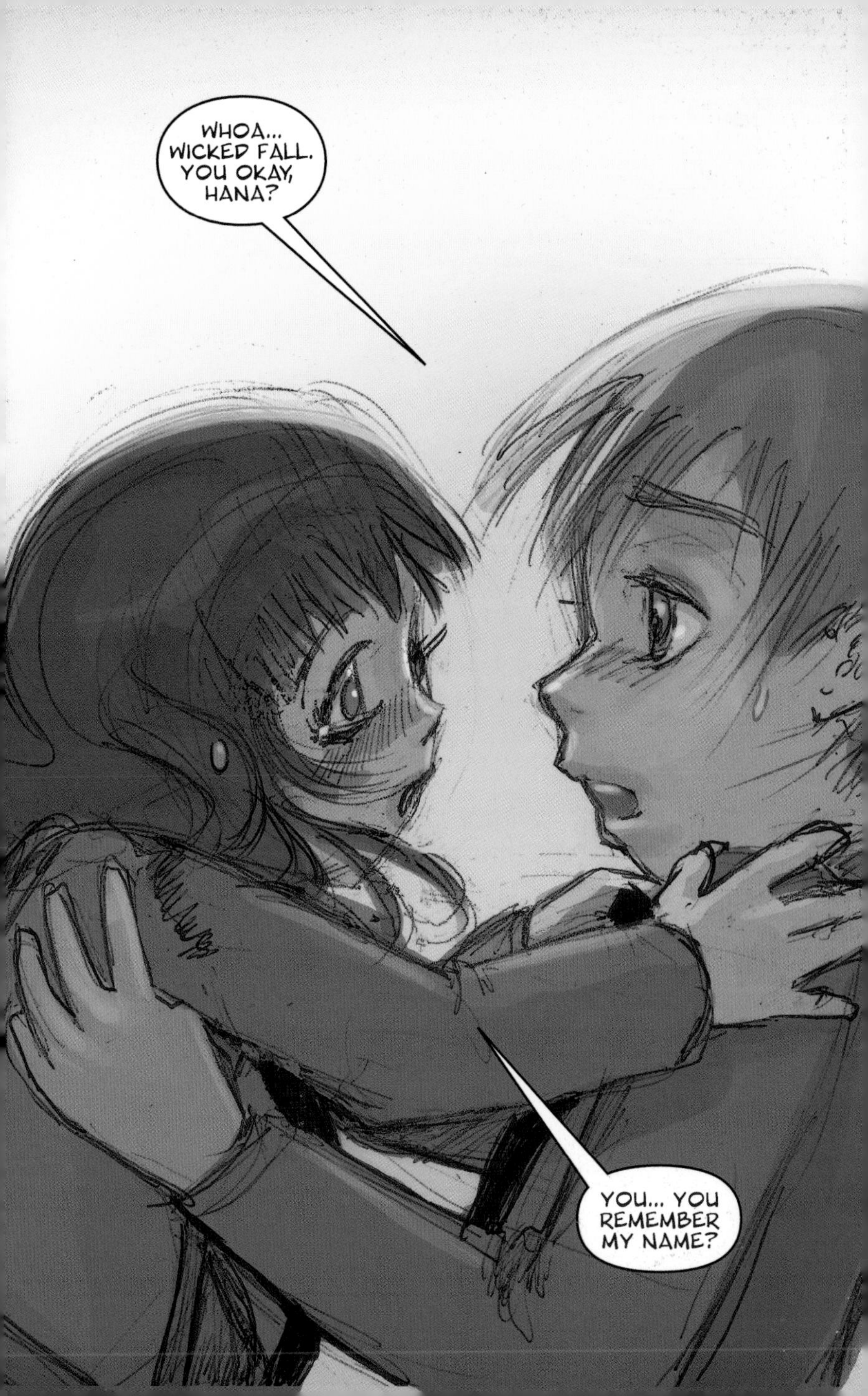
WHOA... WICKED FALL. YOU OKAY, HANA?
YOU... YOU REMEMBER MY NAME?

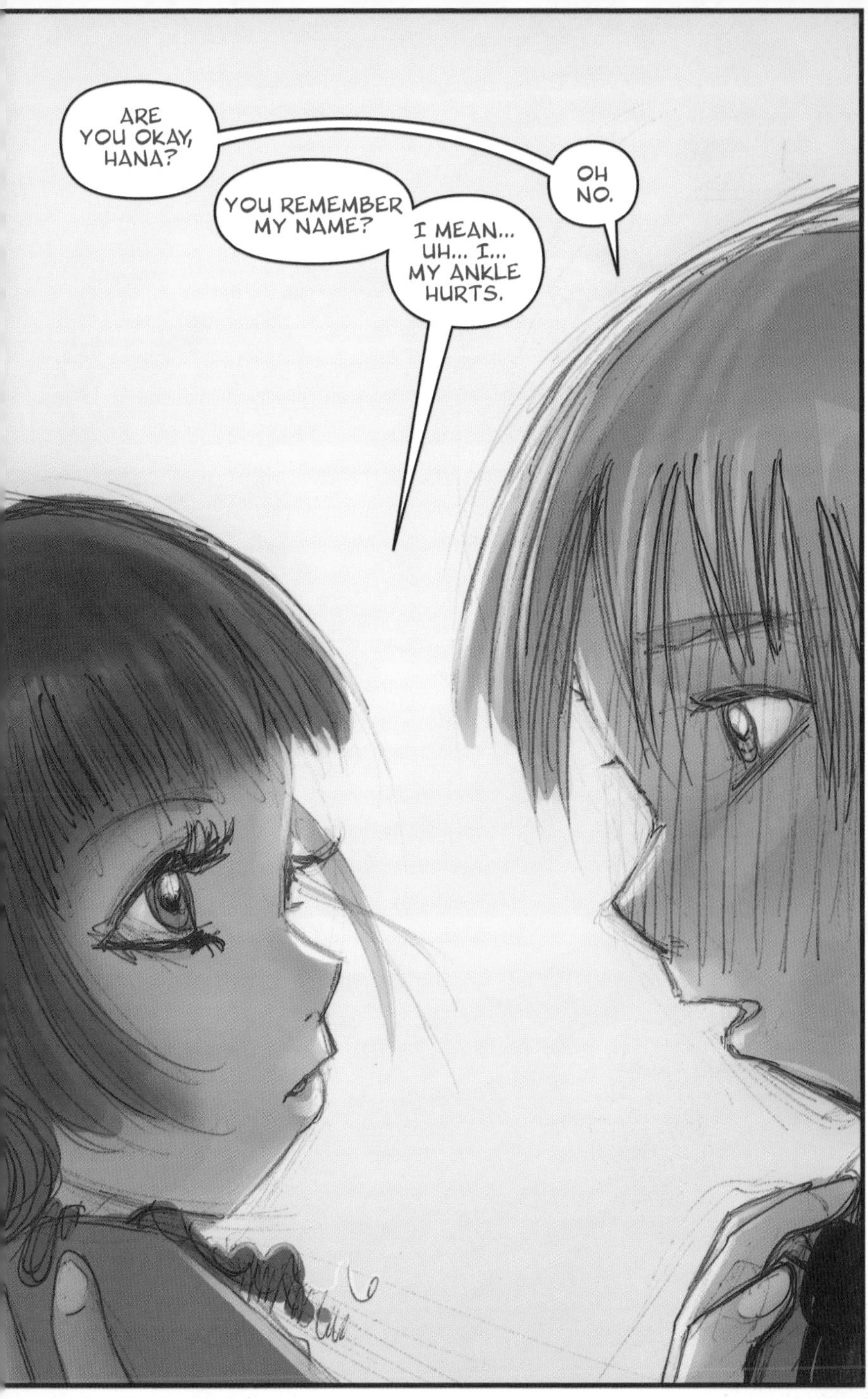
ARE YOU OKAY, HANA?
OH NO.
YOU REMEMBER MY NAME?
I MEAN... UH... I... MY ANKLE HURTS.

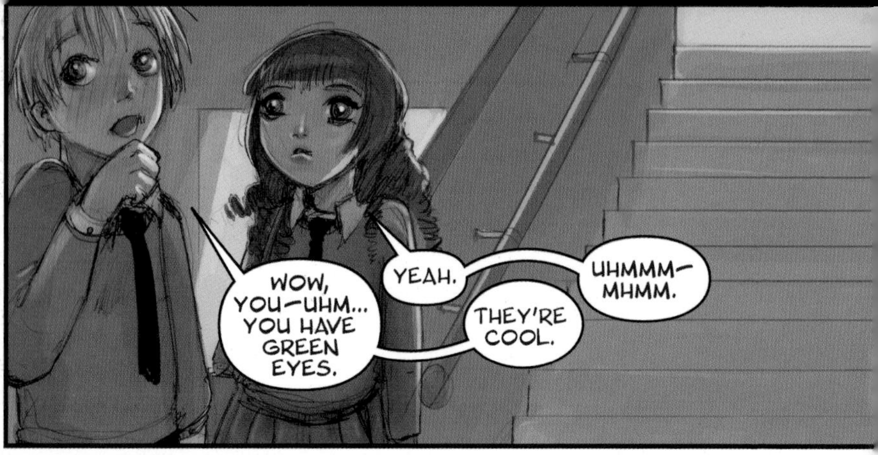
WOW, YOU—UHM... YOU HAVE GREEN EYES.
THEY'RE COOL.
YEAH.
UHMMM-MHMM.

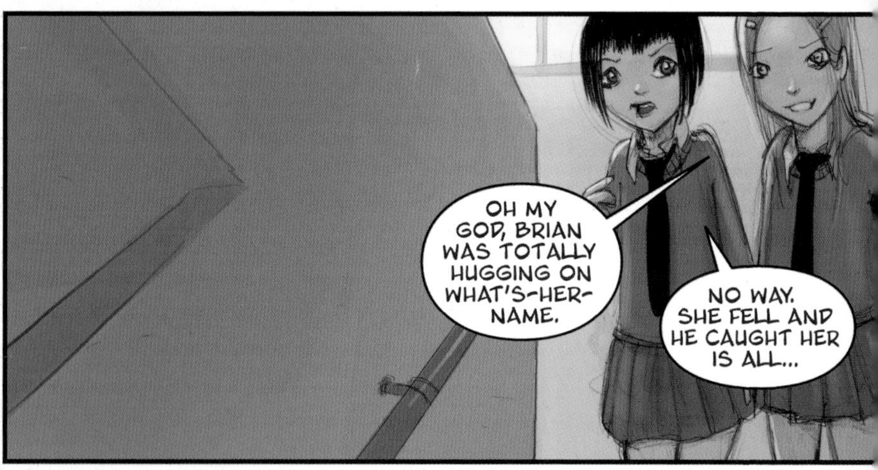
OH MY GOD, BRIAN WAS TOTALLY HUGGING ON WHAT'S-HER-NAME.
NO WAY. SHE FELL AND HE CAUGHT HER IS ALL...

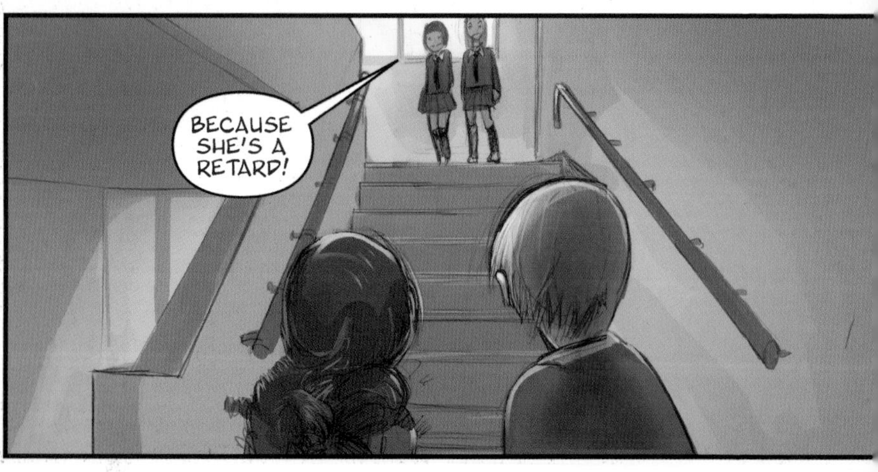
BECAUSE SHE'S A RETARD!

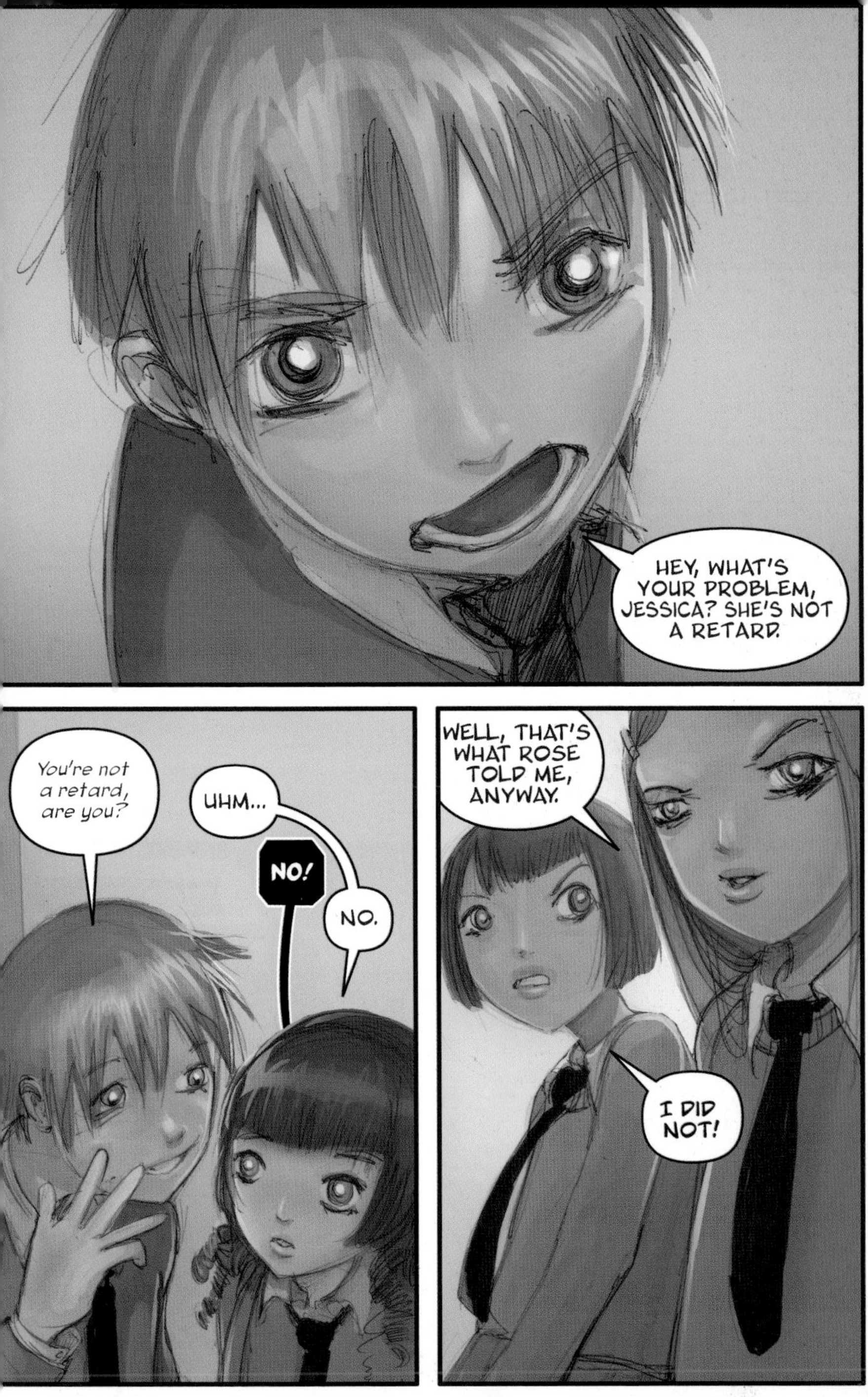
HEY, WHAT'S YOUR PROBLEM, JESSICA? SHE'S NOT A RETARD.
You're not a retard, are you?
UHM...
NO!
NO.
WELL, THAT'S WHAT ROSE TOLD ME, ANYWAY.
I DID NOT!

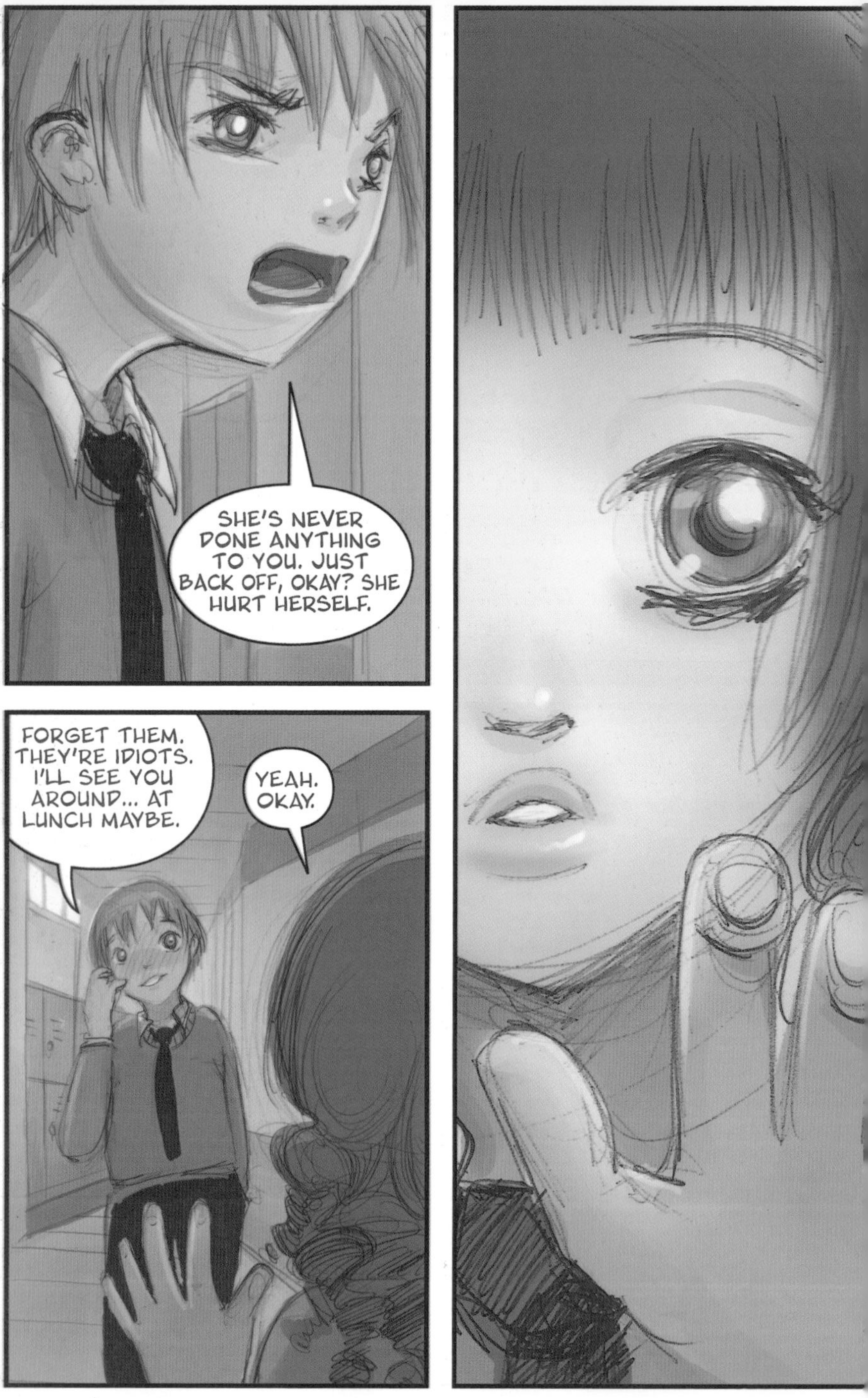
SHE'S NEVER DONE ANYTHING TO YOU. JUST BACK OFF, OKAY? SHE HURT HERSELF.
FORGET THEM. THEY'RE IDIOTS. I'LL SEE YOU AROUND... AT LUNCH MAYBE.
YEAH. OKAY.

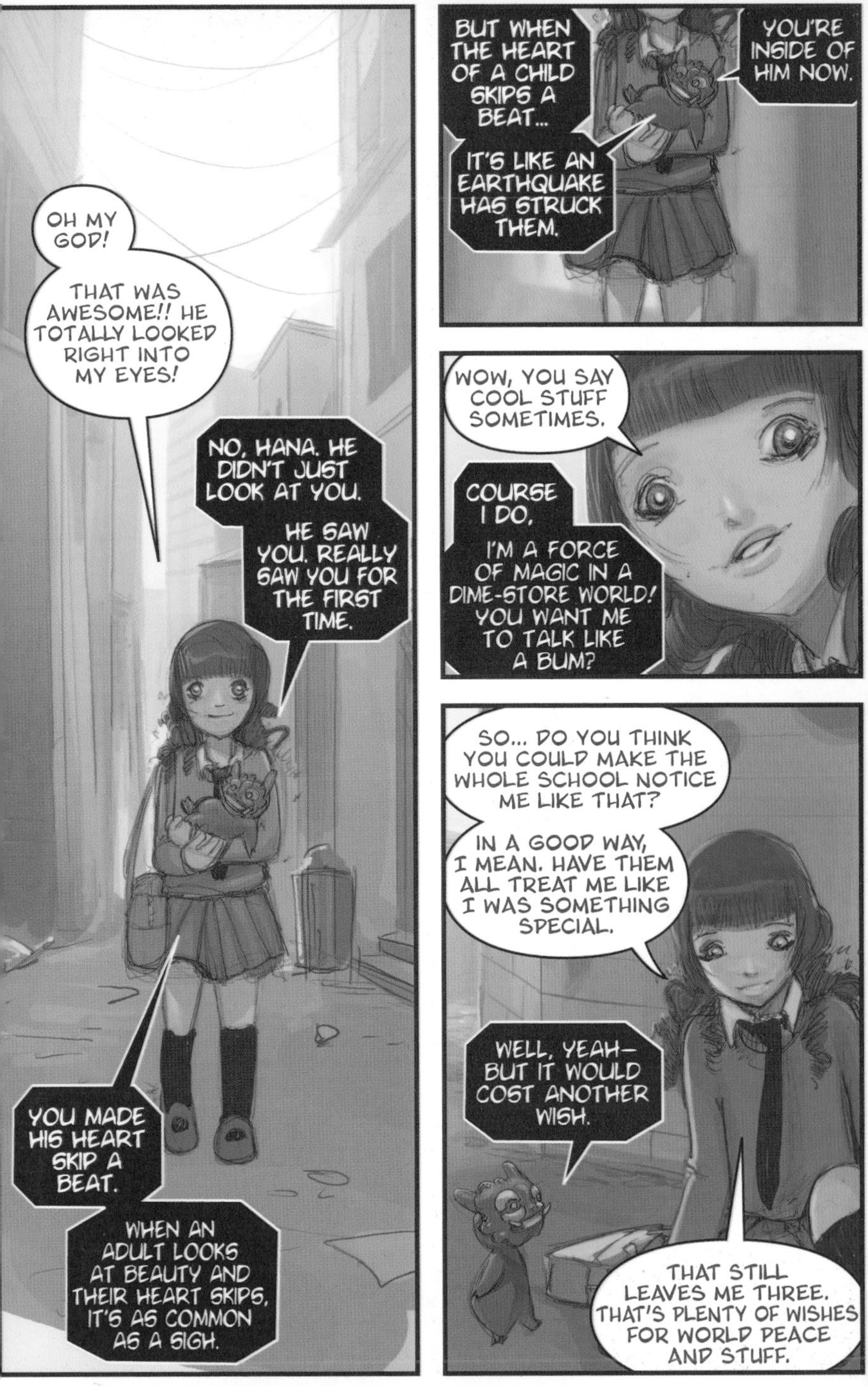
OH MY GOD!
THAT WAS AWESOME!! HE TOTALLY LOOKED RIGHT INTO MY EYES!
NO, HANA. HE DIDN'T JUST LOOK AT YOU.
HE SAW YOU. REALLY SAW YOU FOR THE FIRST TIME.
YOU MADE HIS HEART SKIP A BEAT.
WHEN AN ADULT LOOKS AT BEAUTY AND THEIR HEART SKIPS, IT'S AS COMMON AS A SIGH.
BUT WHEN THE HEART OF A CHILD SKIPS A BEAT...
IT'S LIKE AN EARTHQUAKE HAS STRUCK THEM.
YOU'RE INSIDE OF HIM NOW.
WOW, YOU SAY COOL STUFF SOMETIMES.
COURSE I DO,
I'M A FORCE OF MAGIC IN A DIME-STORE WORLD! YOU WANT ME TO TALK LIKE A BUM?
SO... DO YOU THINK YOU COULD MAKE THE WHOLE SCHOOL NOTICE ME LIKE THAT?
IN A GOOD WAY, I MEAN. HAVE THEM ALL TREAT ME LIKE I WAS SOMETHING SPECIAL.
WELL, YEAH— BUT IT WOULD COST ANOTHER WISH.
THAT STILL LEAVES ME THREE. THAT'S PLENTY OF WISHES FOR WORLD PEACE AND STUFF.

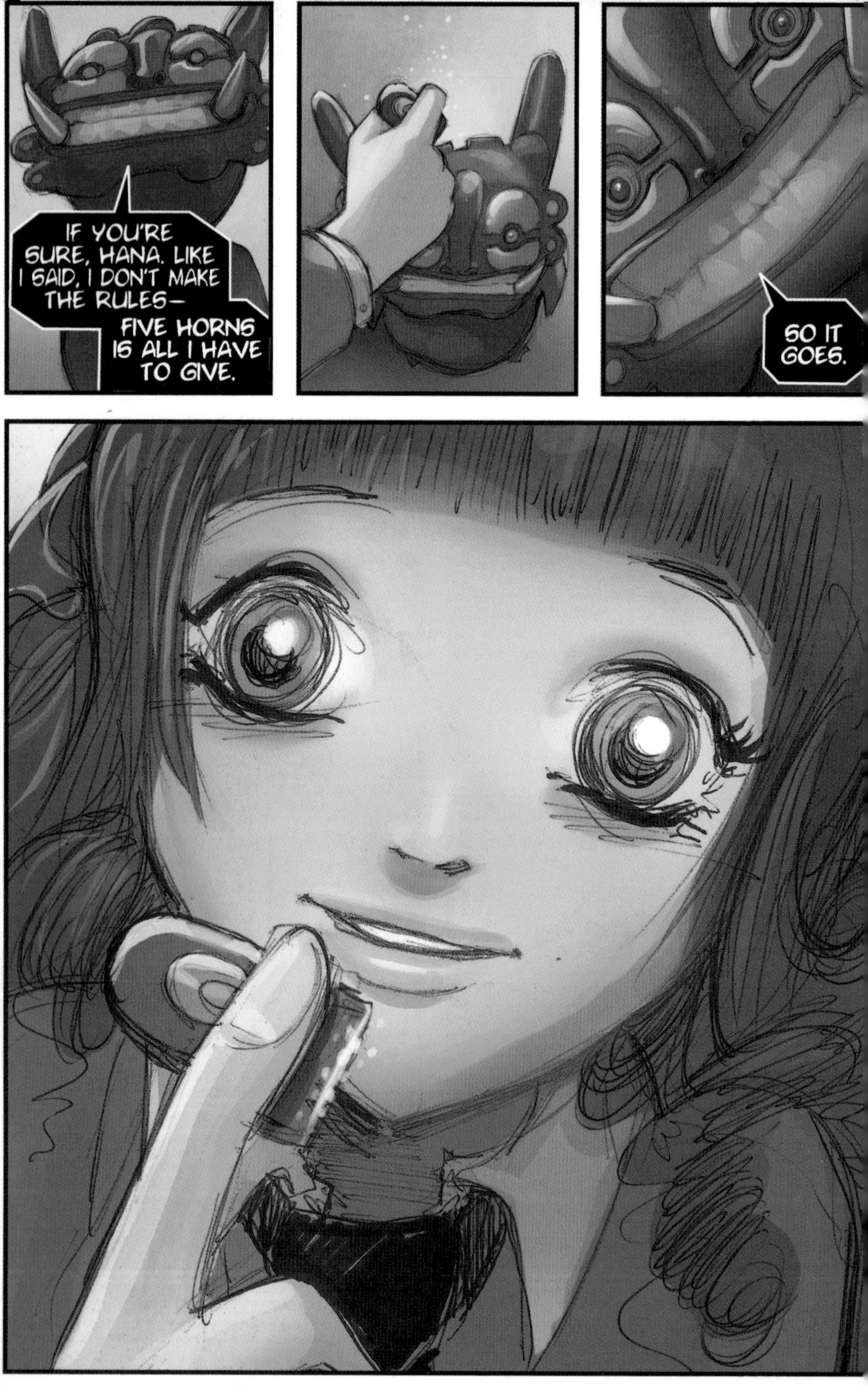
IF YOU'RE SURE, HANA. LIKE I SAID, I DON'T MAKE THE RULES—
FIVE HORNS IS ALL I HAVE TO GIVE.
SO IT GOES.

C'MON, HANA. LET'S ROLL!

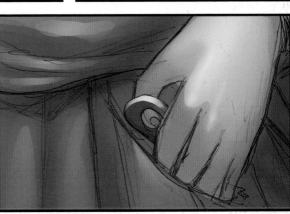

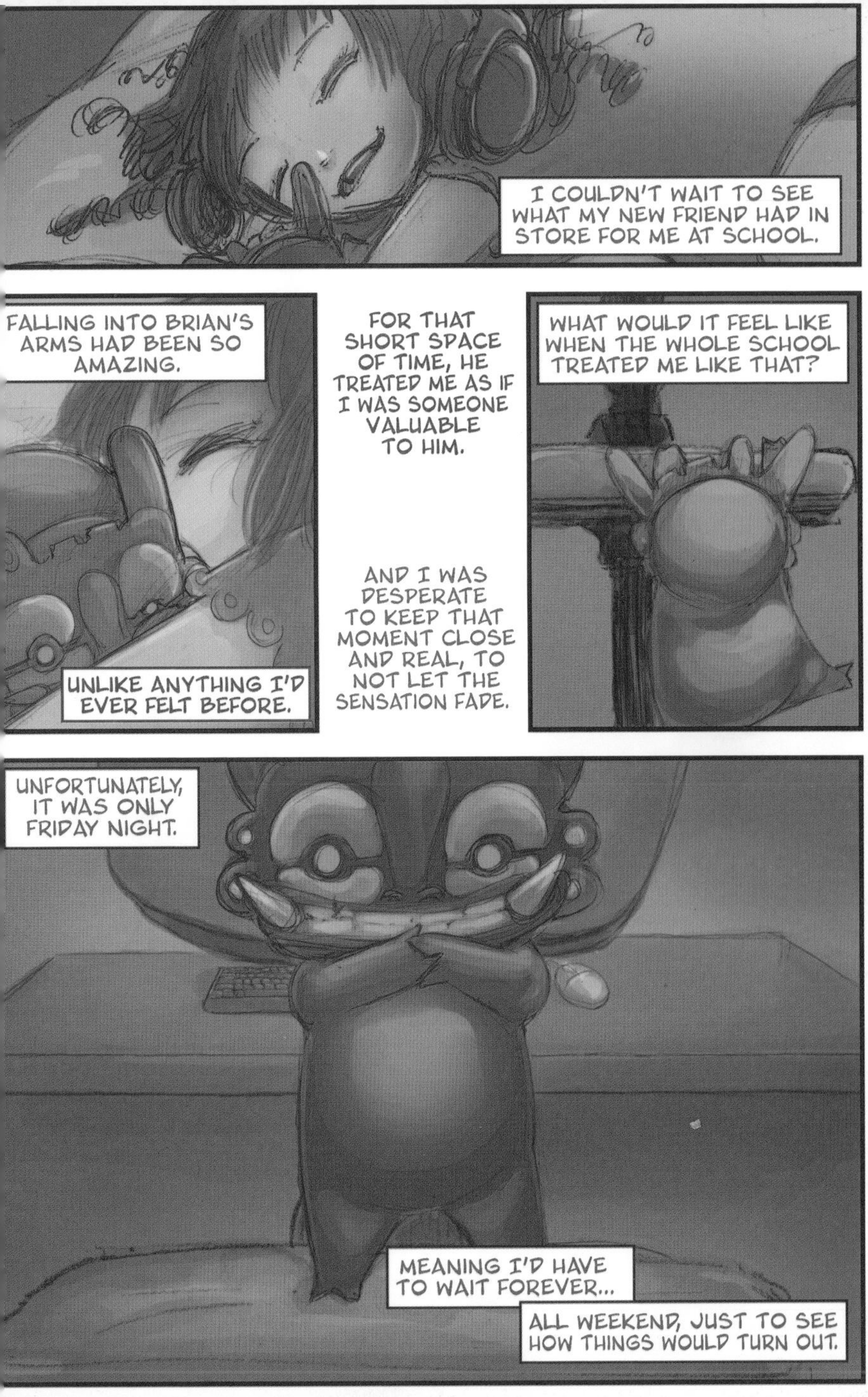
I COULDN'T WAIT TO SEE WHAT MY NEW FRIEND HAD IN STORE FOR ME AT SCHOOL.
FALLING INTO BRIAN'S ARMS HAD BEEN SO AMAZING.
UNLIKE ANYTHING I'D EVER FELT BEFORE.
FOR THAT SHORT SPACE OF TIME, HE TREATED ME AS IF I WAS SOMEONE VALUABLE TO HIM.
AND I WAS DESPERATE TO KEEP THAT MOMENT CLOSE AND REAL, TO NOT LET THE SENSATION FADE.
WHAT WOULD IT FEEL LIKE WHEN THE WHOLE SCHOOL TREATED ME LIKE THAT?
UNFORTUNATELY, IT WAS ONLY FRIDAY NIGHT.
MEANING I'D HAVE TO WAIT FOREVER...
ALL WEEKEND, JUST TO SEE HOW THINGS WOULD TURN OUT.

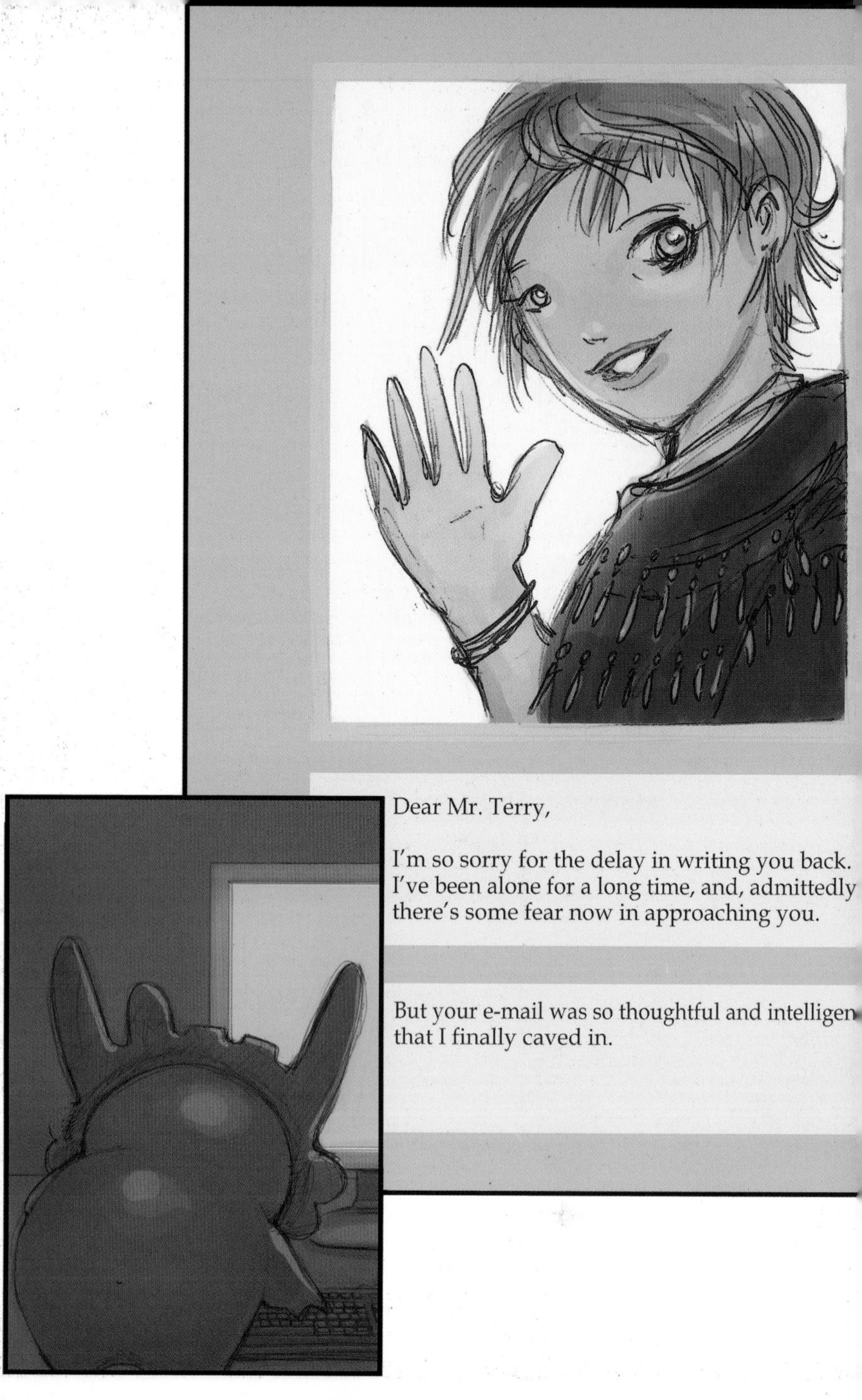
Dear Mr. Terry,
I'm so sorry for the delay in writing you back. I've been alone for a long time, and, admittedly there's some fear now in approaching you.
But your e-mail was so thoughtful and intelligen that I finally caved in.

When I read your thoughts about *Moby-Dick* I suddenly felt *understood* for the first time.

SOMEONE WROTE ME BACK, KOOKS! A WOMAN WROTE ME BACK!

I'm nervous to meet you, but I'm ready.

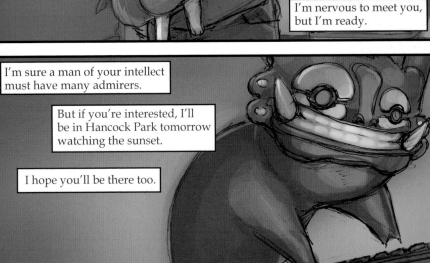

I'm sure a man of your intellect must have many admirers.

But if you're interested, I'll be in Hancock Park tomorrow watching the sunset.

I hope you'll be there too.

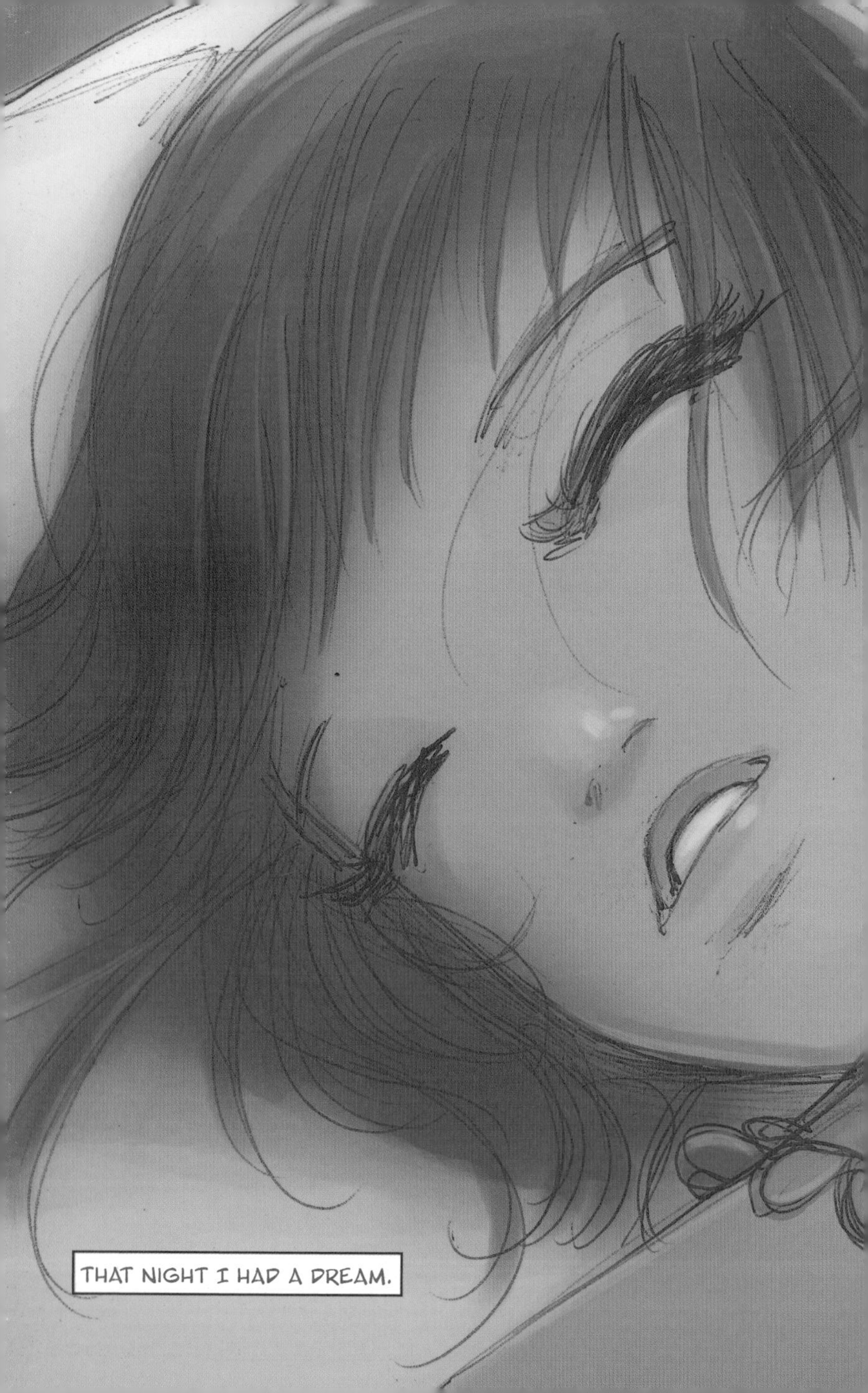
THAT NIGHT I HAD A DREAM.

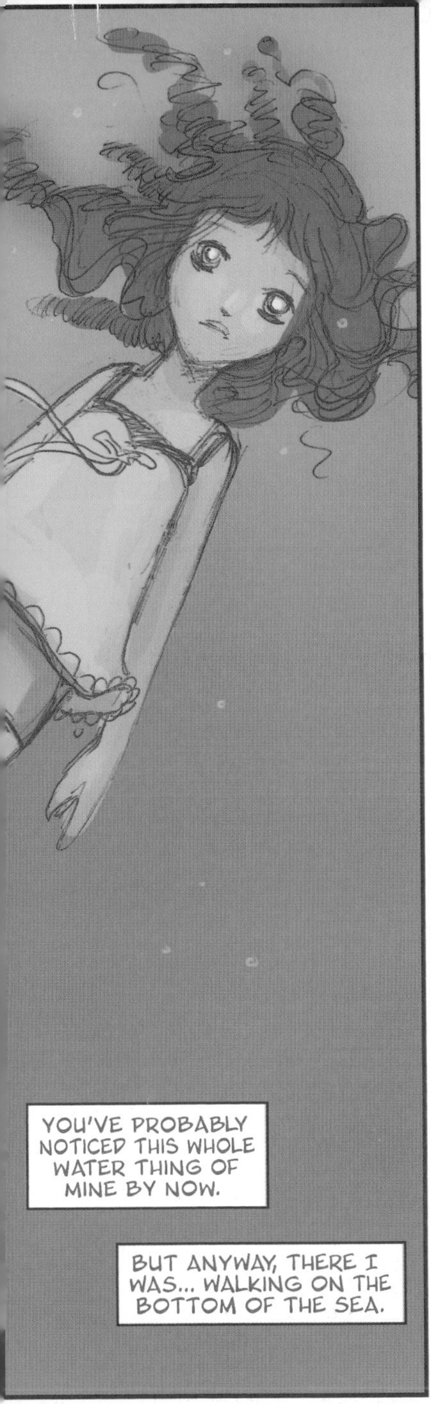
YOU'VE PROBABLY NOTICED THIS WHOLE WATER THING OF MINE BY NOW.
BUT ANYWAY, THERE I WAS... WALKING ON THE BOTTOM OF THE SEA.
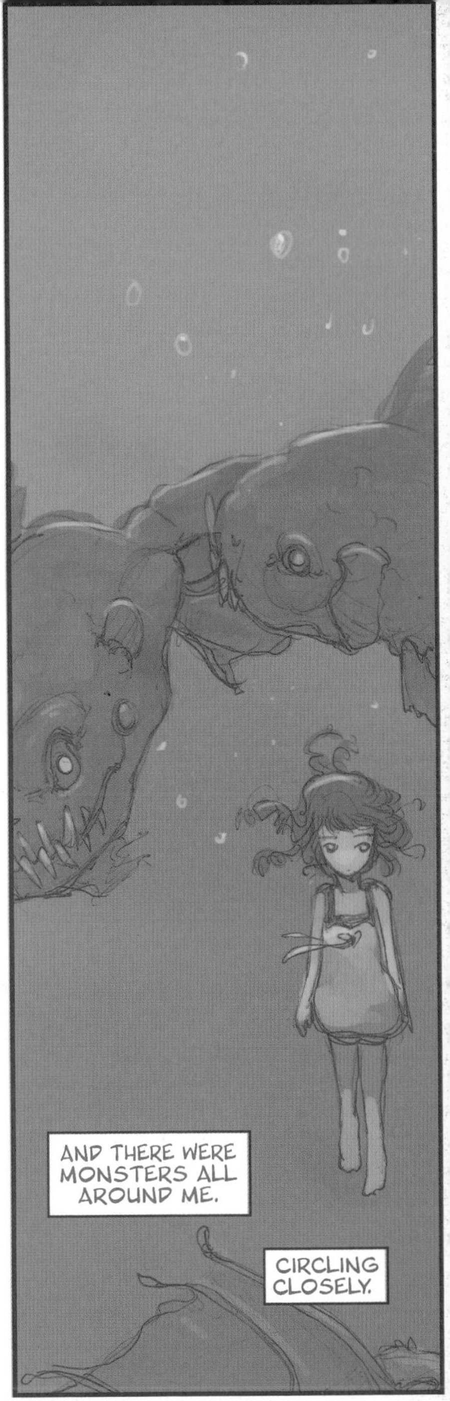
AND THERE WERE MONSTERS ALL AROUND ME.
CIRCLING CLOSELY.

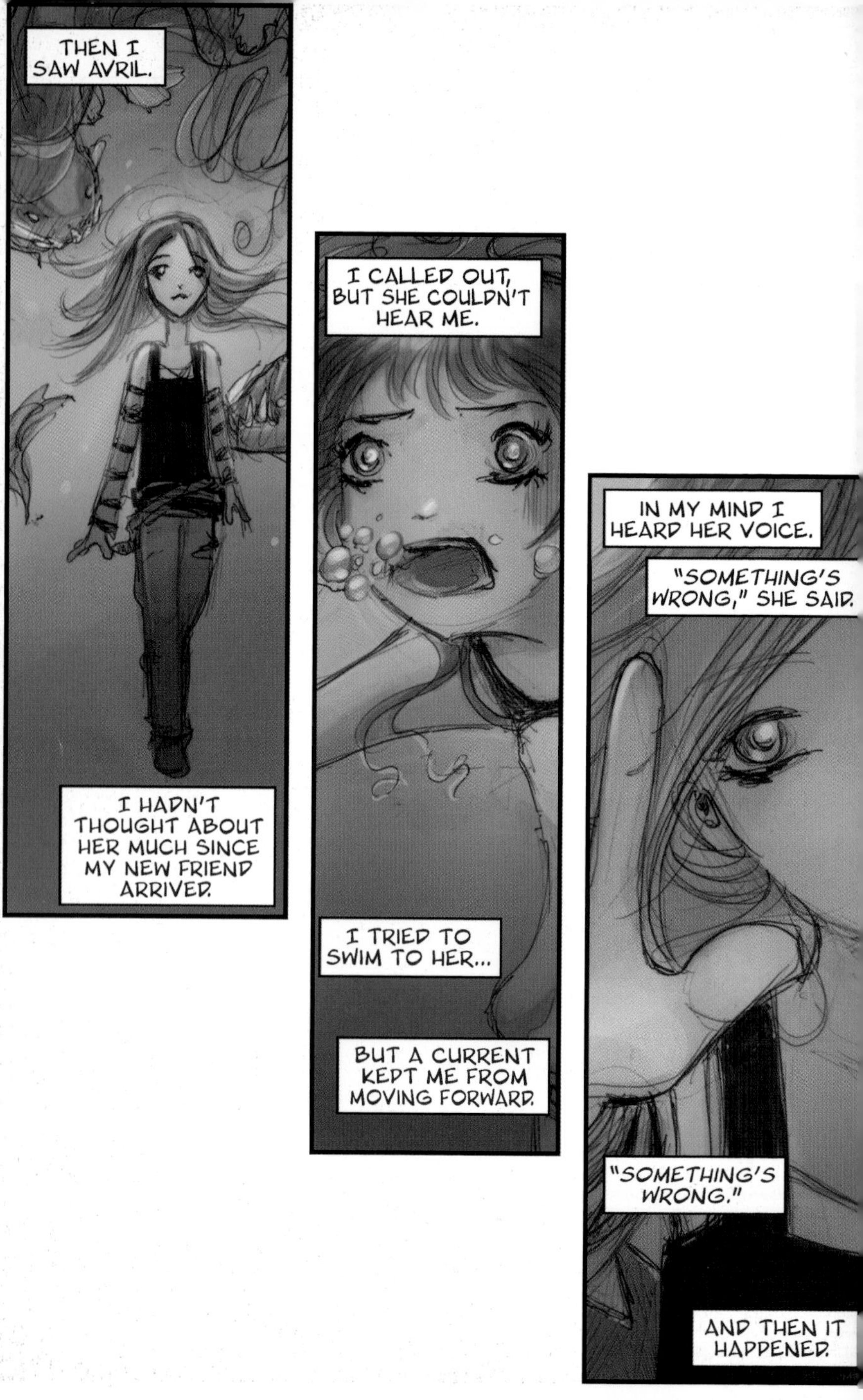
THEN I SAW AVRIL.
I HADN'T THOUGHT ABOUT HER MUCH SINCE MY NEW FRIEND ARRIVED.
I CALLED OUT, BUT SHE COULDN'T HEAR ME.
I TRIED TO SWIM TO HER...
BUT A CURRENT KEPT ME FROM MOVING FORWARD.
IN MY MIND I HEARD HER VOICE.
"SOMETHING'S WRONG," SHE SAID.
"SOMETHING'S WRONG."
AND THEN IT HAPPENED.

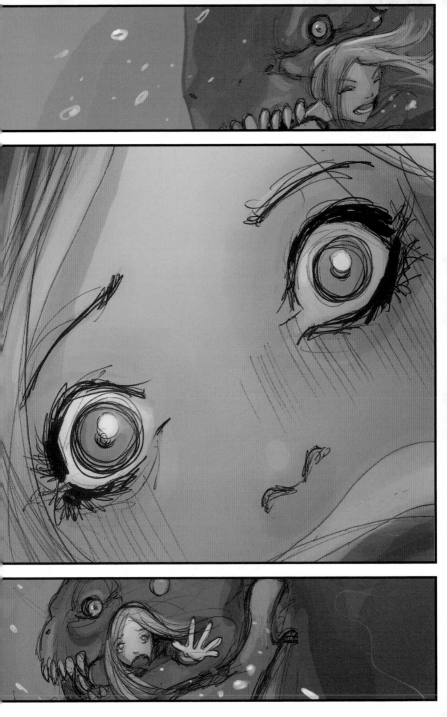

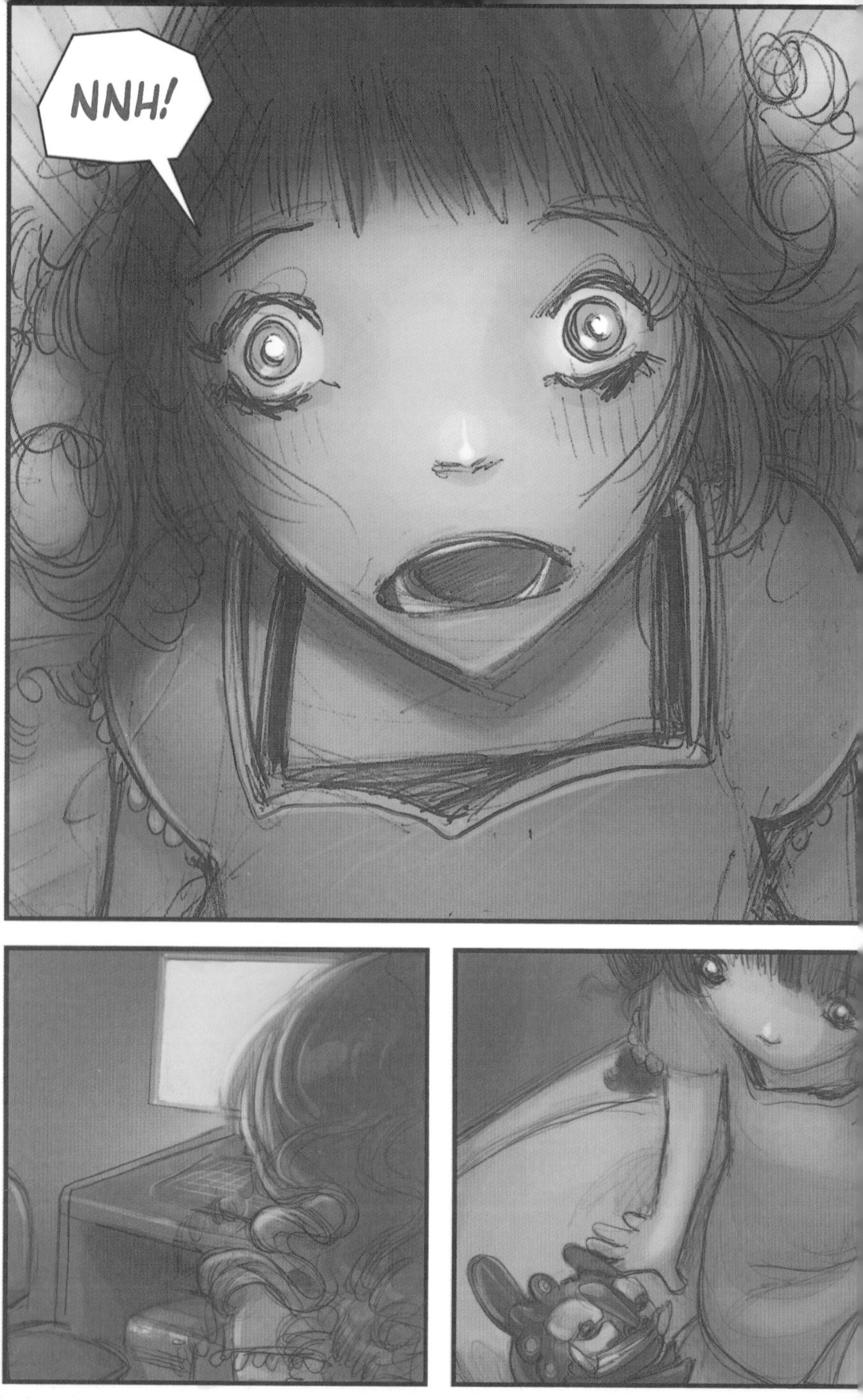
NNH!

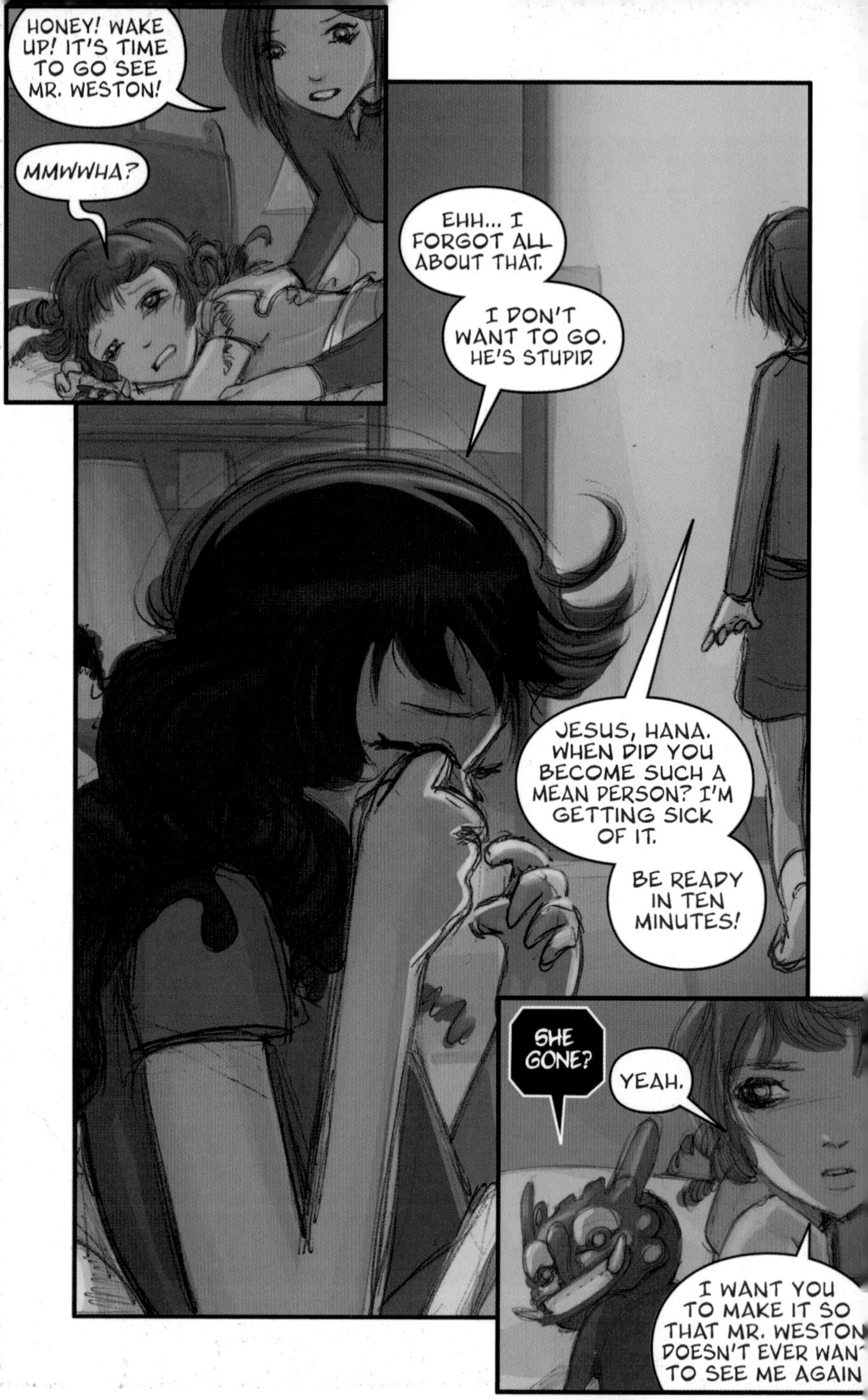
HONEY! WAKE UP! IT'S TIME TO GO SEE MR. WESTON!
MMWWHA?
EHH... I FORGOT ALL ABOUT THAT.
I DON'T WANT TO GO. HE'S STUPID.
JESUS, HANA. WHEN DID YOU BECOME SUCH A MEAN PERSON? I'M GETTING SICK OF IT.
BE READY IN TEN MINUTES!
SHE GONE?
YEAH.
I WANT YOU TO MAKE IT SO THAT MR. WESTON DOESN'T EVER WAN TO SEE ME AGAIN

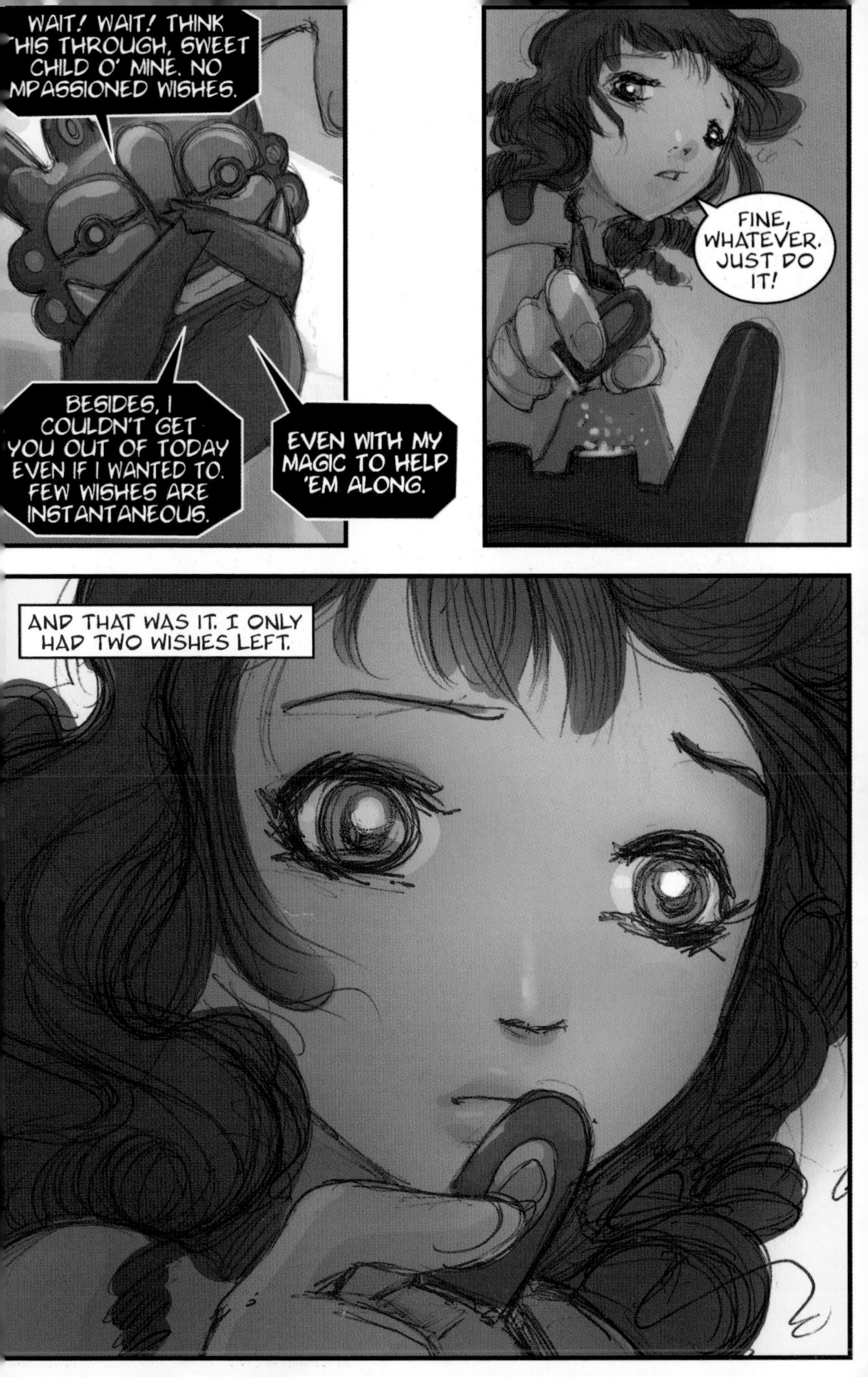
WAIT! WAIT! THINK HIS THROUGH, SWEET CHILD O' MINE. NO MPASSIONED WISHES.
BESIDES, I COULDN'T GET YOU OUT OF TODAY EVEN IF I WANTED TO. FEW WISHES ARE INSTANTANEOUS.
EVEN WITH MY MAGIC TO HELP 'EM ALONG.
FINE, WHATEVER. JUST DO IT!
AND THAT WAS IT. I ONLY HAD TWO WISHES LEFT.

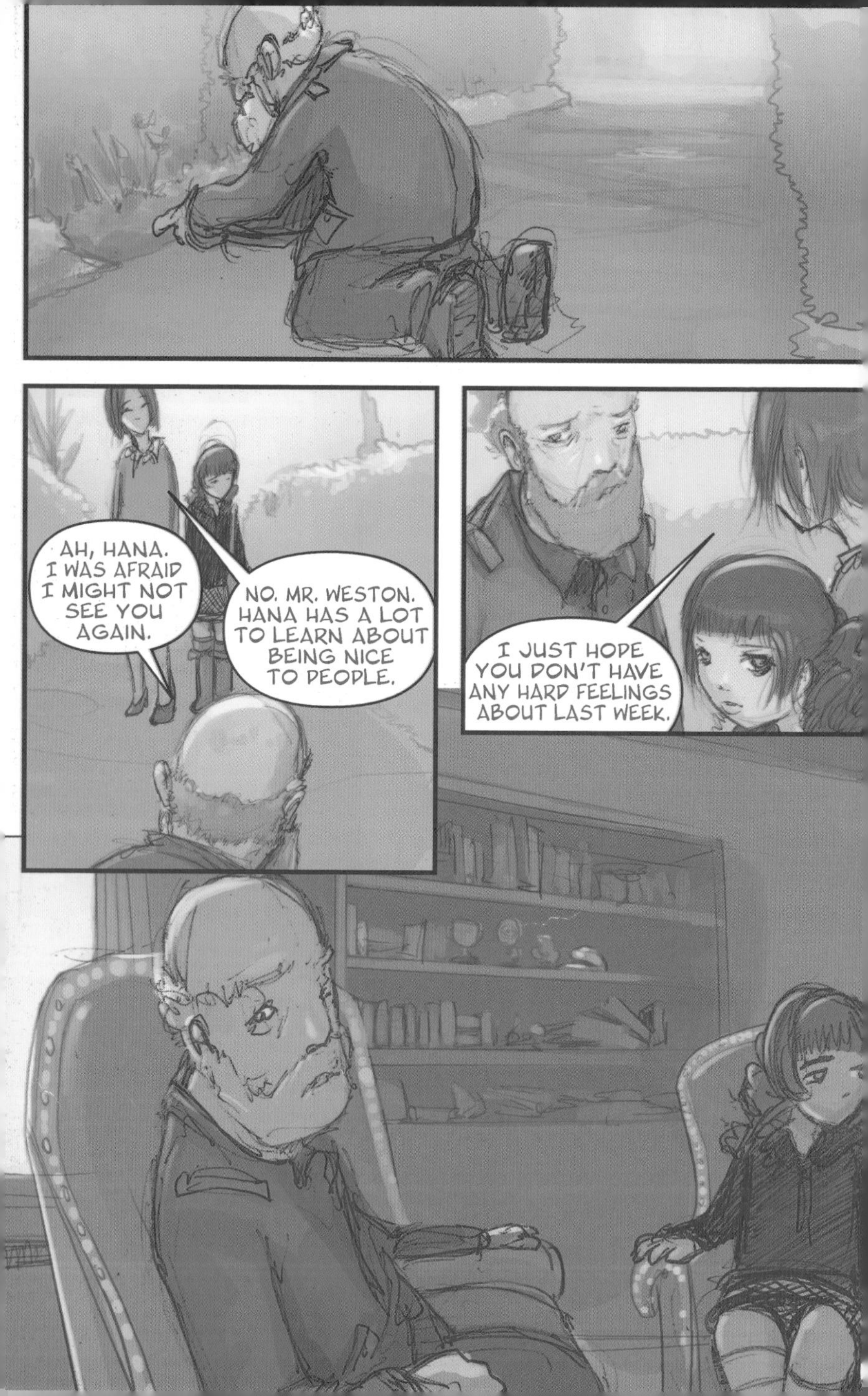
AH, HANA. I WAS AFRAID I MIGHT NOT SEE YOU AGAIN.
NO. MR. WESTON. HANA HAS A LOT TO LEARN ABOUT BEING NICE TO PEOPLE.
I JUST HOPE YOU DON'T HAVE ANY HARD FEELINGS ABOUT LAST WEEK.

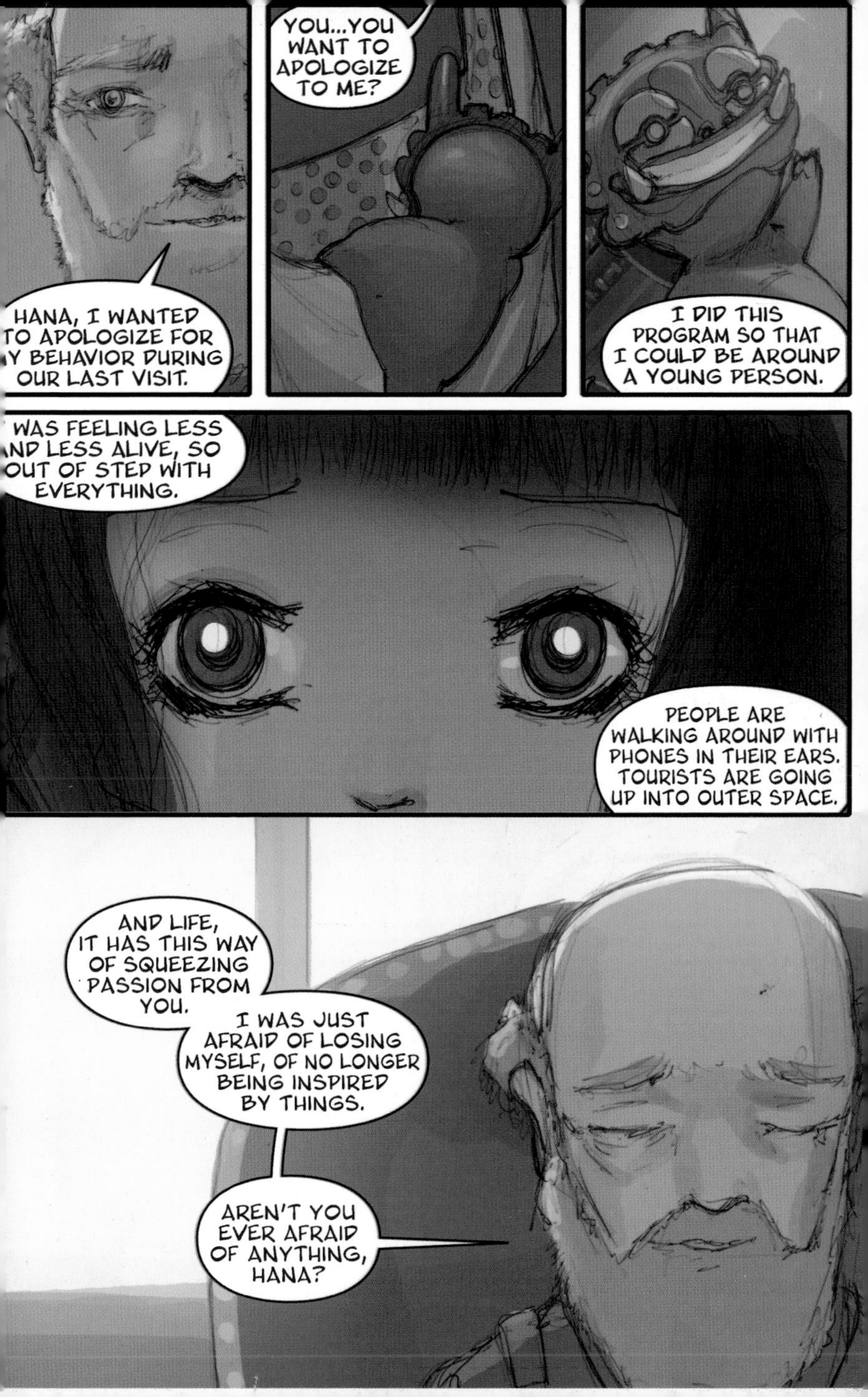
HANA, I WANTED TO APOLOGIZE FOR Y BEHAVIOR DURING OUR LAST VISIT.
YOU...YOU WANT TO APOLOGIZE TO ME?
I DID THIS PROGRAM SO THAT I COULD BE AROUND A YOUNG PERSON.
WAS FEELING LESS ND LESS ALIVE, SO OUT OF STEP WITH EVERYTHING.
PEOPLE ARE WALKING AROUND WITH PHONES IN THEIR EARS. TOURISTS ARE GOING UP INTO OUTER SPACE.
AND LIFE, IT HAS THIS WAY OF SQUEEZING PASSION FROM YOU.
I WAS JUST AFRAID OF LOSING MYSELF, OF NO LONGER BEING INSPIRED BY THINGS.
AREN'T YOU EVER AFRAID OF ANYTHING, HANA?

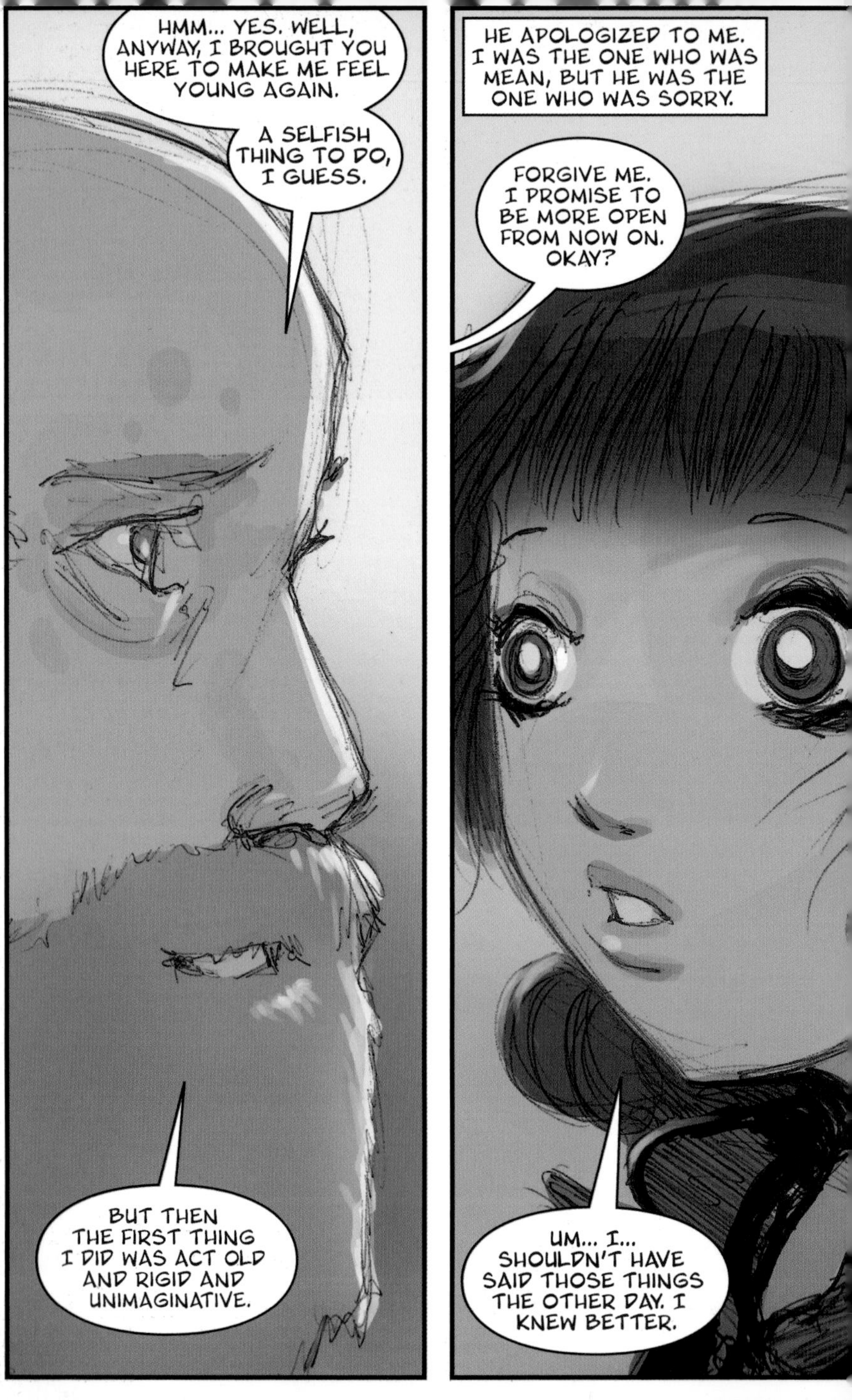
HMM... YES. WELL, ANYWAY, I BROUGHT YOU HERE TO MAKE ME FEEL YOUNG AGAIN.
A SELFISH THING TO DO, I GUESS.
BUT THEN THE FIRST THING I DID WAS ACT OLD AND RIGID AND UNIMAGINATIVE.
HE APOLOGIZED TO ME. I WAS THE ONE WHO WAS MEAN, BUT HE WAS THE ONE WHO WAS SORRY.
FORGIVE ME. I PROMISE TO BE MORE OPEN FROM NOW ON. OKAY?
UM... I... SHOULDN'T HAVE SAID THOSE THINGS THE OTHER DAY. I KNEW BETTER.

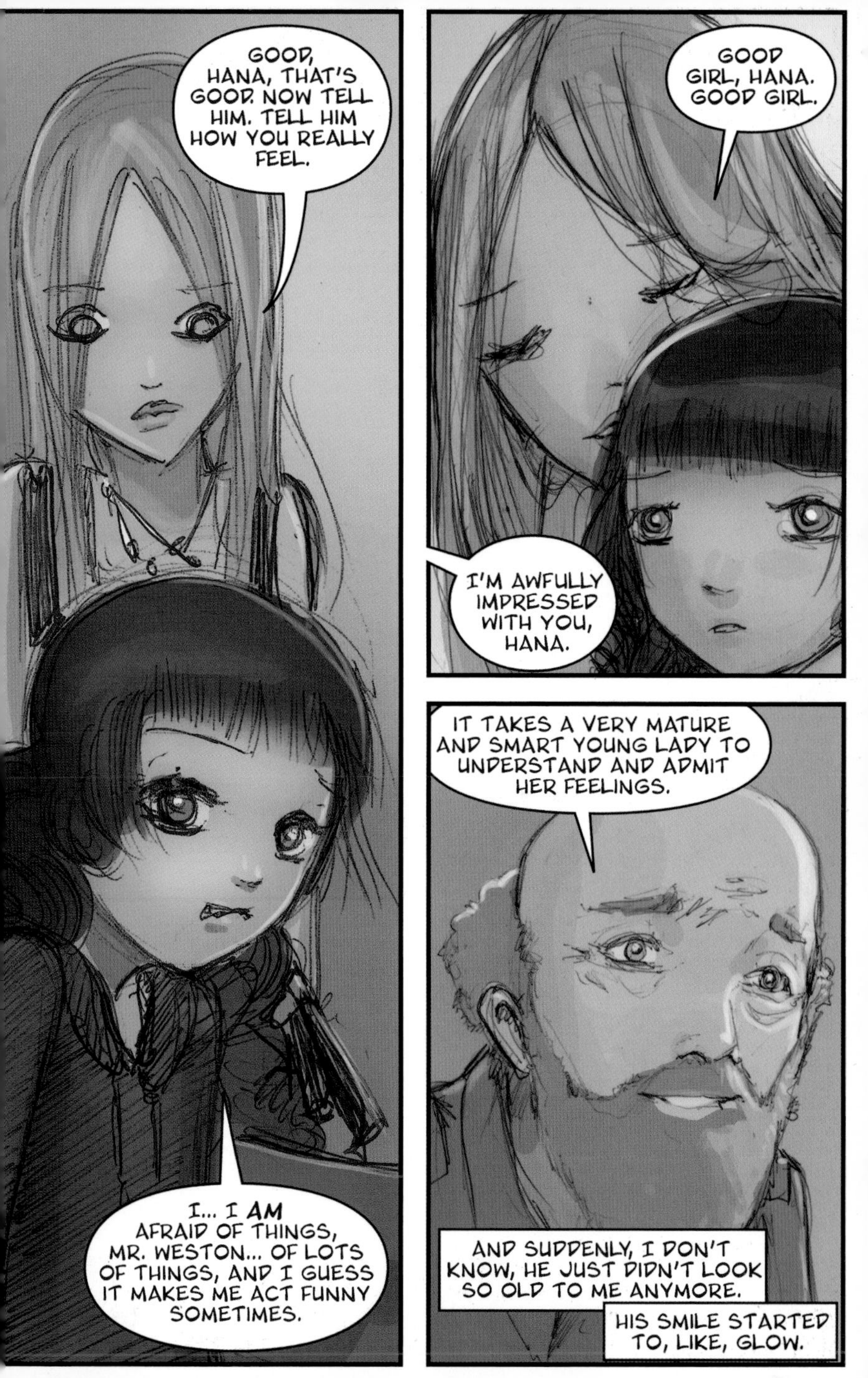
GOOD, HANA, THAT'S GOOD. NOW TELL HIM. TELL HIM HOW YOU REALLY FEEL.
I... I AM AFRAID OF THINGS, MR. WESTON... OF LOTS OF THINGS, AND I GUESS IT MAKES ME ACT FUNNY SOMETIMES.
GOOD GIRL, HANA. GOOD GIRL.
I'M AWFULLY IMPRESSED WITH YOU, HANA.
IT TAKES A VERY MATURE AND SMART YOUNG LADY TO UNDERSTAND AND ADMIT HER FEELINGS.
AND SUDDENLY, I DON'T KNOW, HE JUST DIDN'T LOOK SO OLD TO ME ANYMORE.
HIS SMILE STARTED TO, LIKE, GLOW.

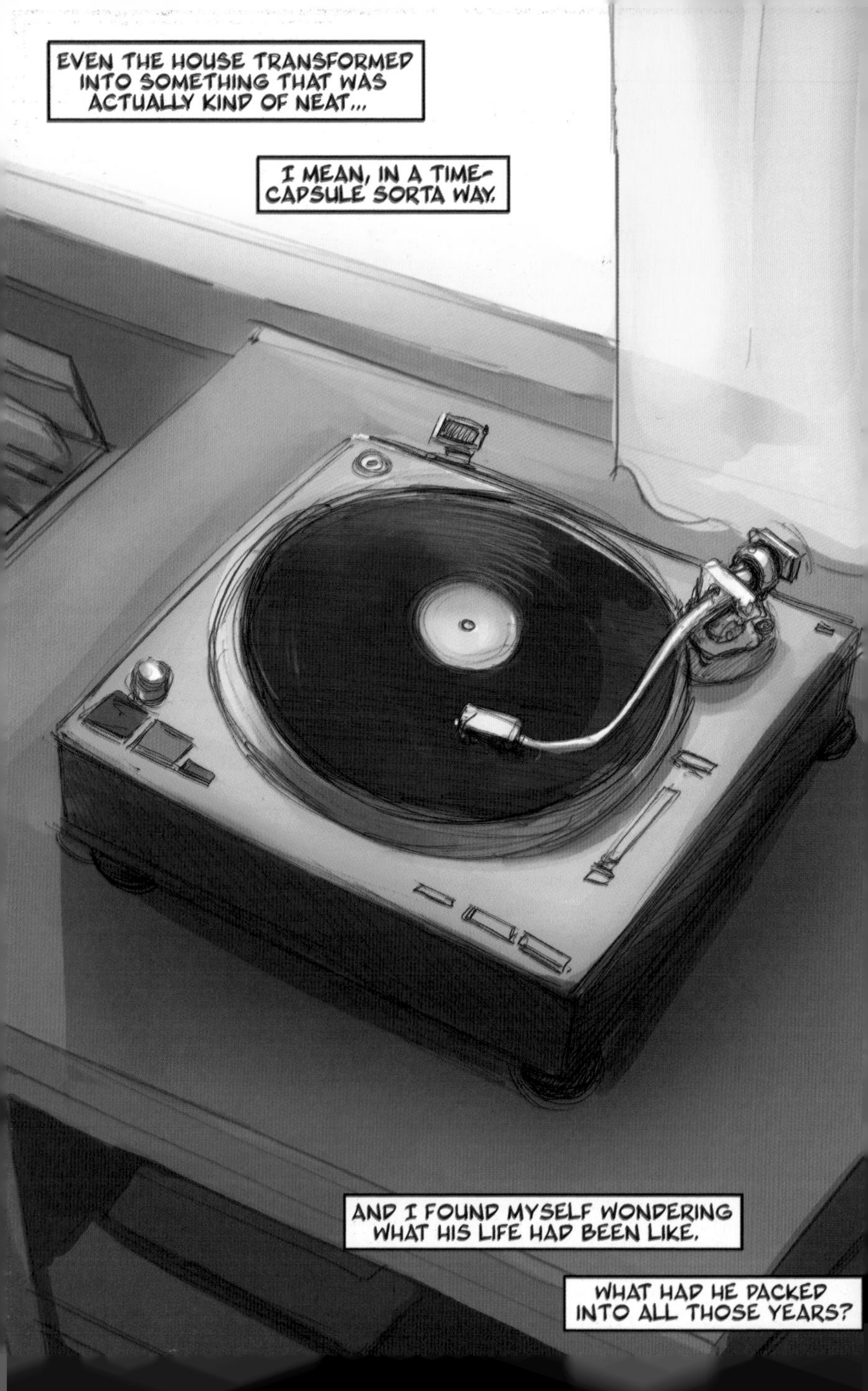
EVEN THE HOUSE TRANSFORMED INTO SOMETHING THAT WAS ACTUALLY KIND OF NEAT...
I MEAN, IN A TIME-CAPSULE SORTA WAY.
AND I FOUND MYSELF WONDERING WHAT HIS LIFE HAD BEEN LIKE.
WHAT HAD HE PACKED INTO ALL THOSE YEARS?

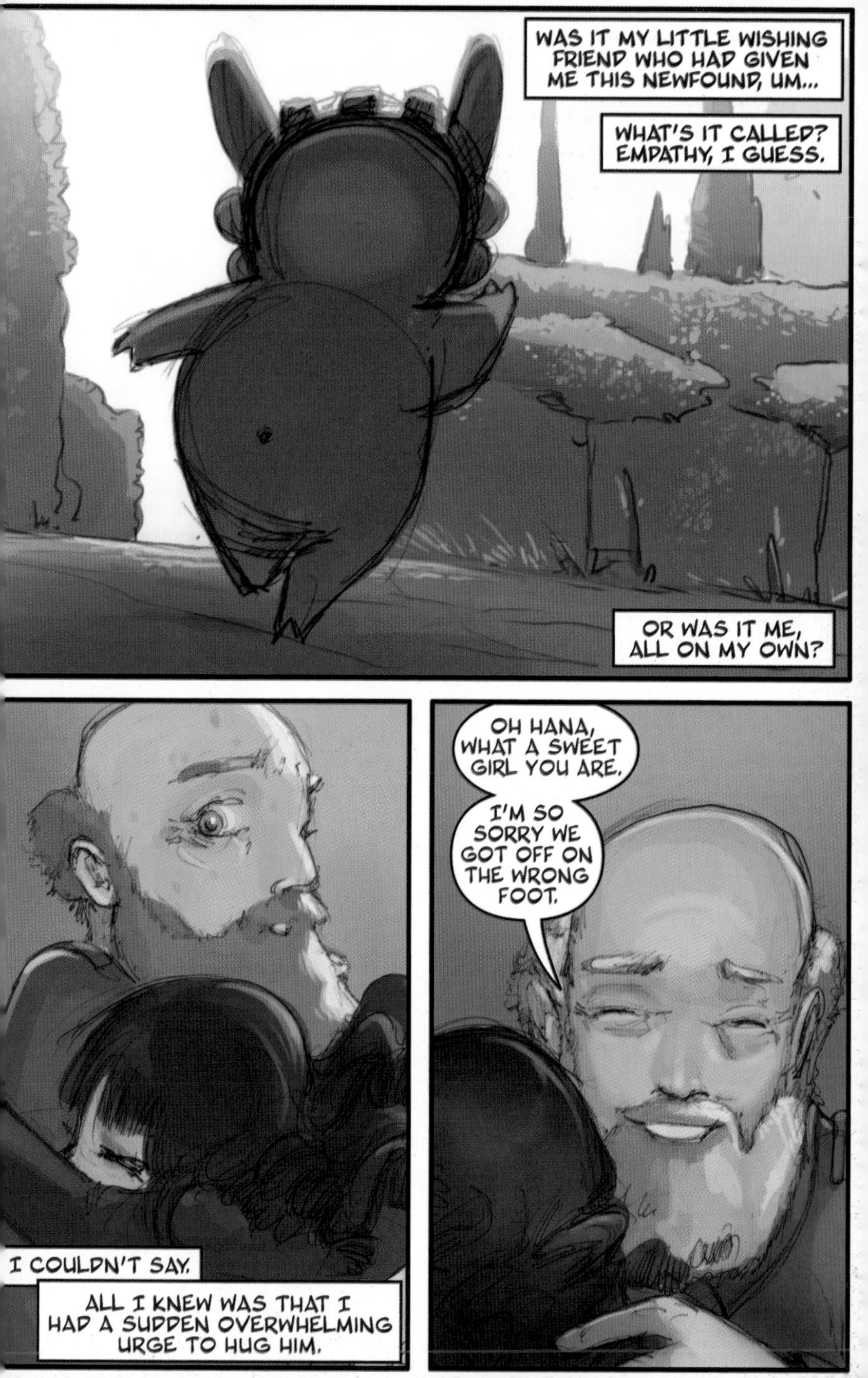
WAS IT MY LITTLE WISHING FRIEND WHO HAD GIVEN ME THIS NEWFOUND, UM...
WHAT'S IT CALLED? EMPATHY, I GUESS.
OR WAS IT ME, ALL ON MY OWN?
I COULDN'T SAY.
ALL I KNEW WAS THAT I HAD A SUDDEN OVERWHELMING URGE TO HUG HIM.
OH HANA, WHAT A SWEET GIRL YOU ARE.
I'M SO SORRY WE GOT OFF ON THE WRONG FOOT.

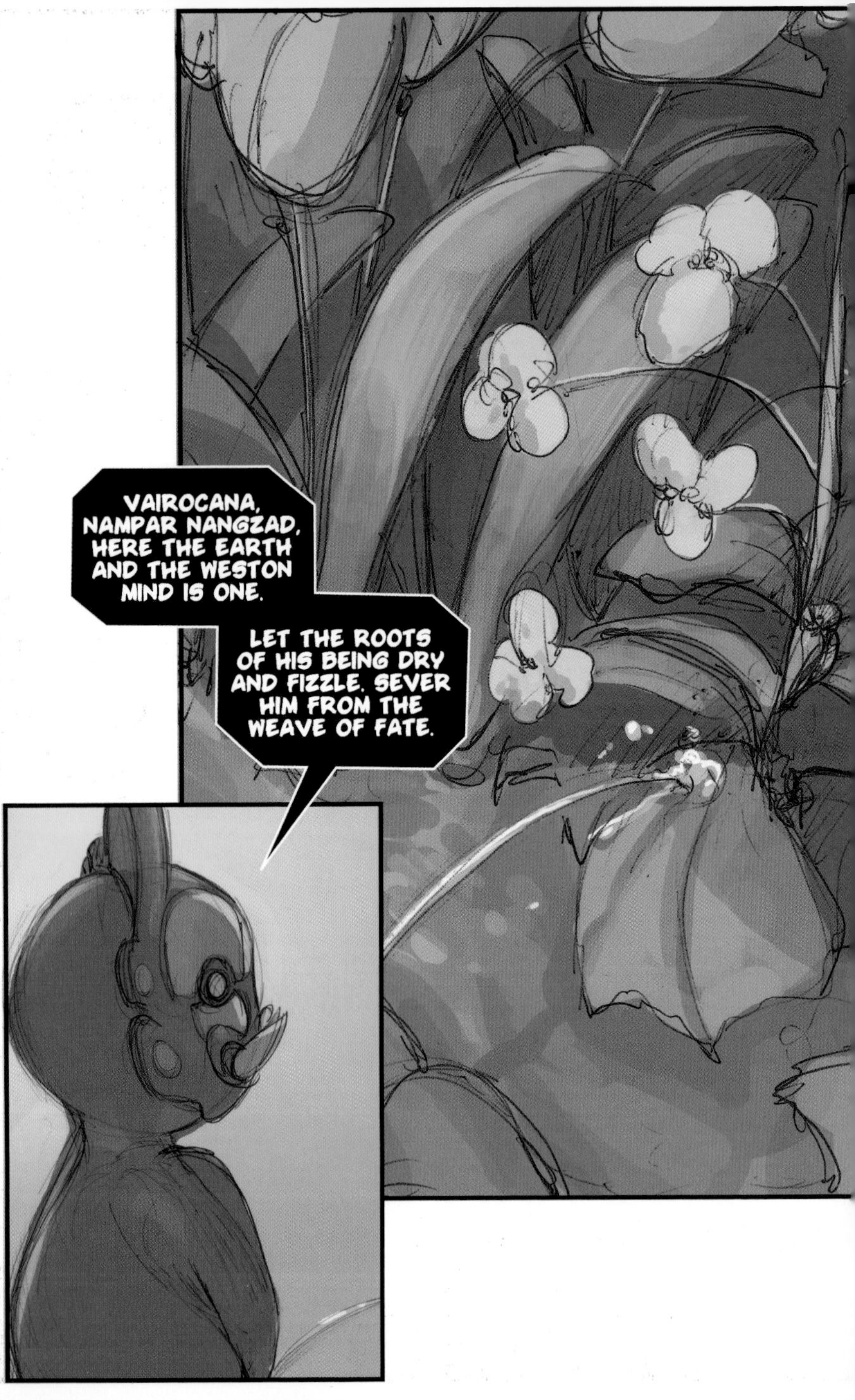
VAIROCANA, NAMPAR NANGZAD, HERE THE EARTH AND THE WESTON MIND IS ONE.
LET THE ROOTS OF HIS BEING DRY AND FIZZLE. SEVER HIM FROM THE WEAVE OF FATE.

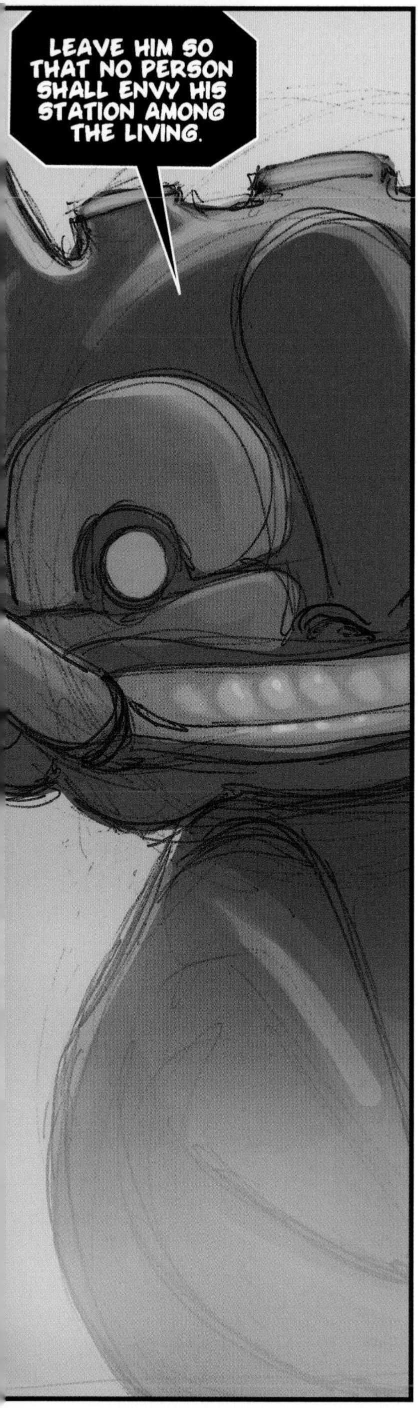
LEAVE HIM SO THAT NO PERSON SHALL ENVY HIS STATION AMONG THE LIVING.

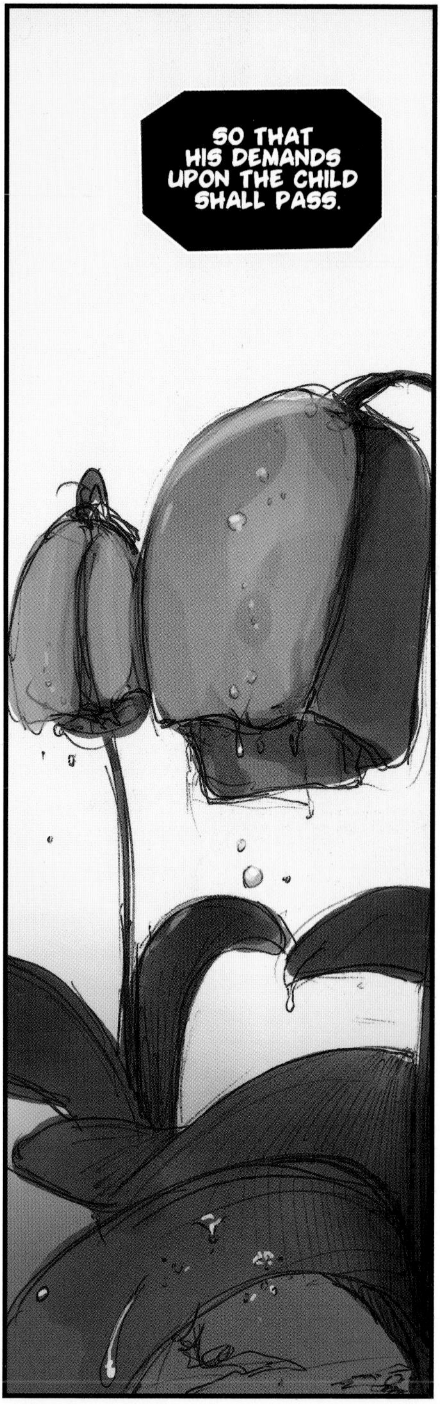
SO THAT HIS DEMANDS UPON THE CHILD SHALL PASS.

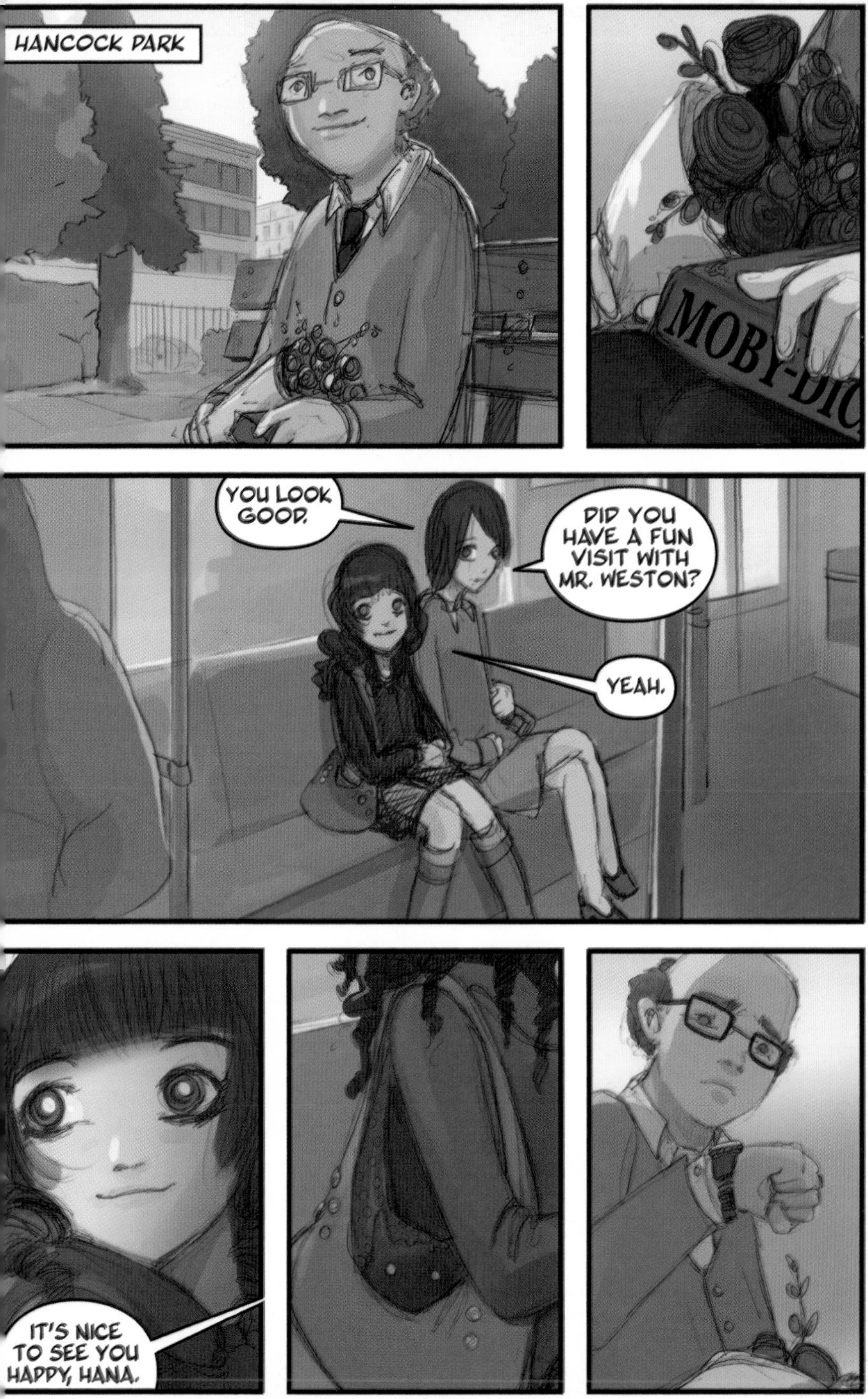
HANCOCK PARK
MOBY-DIC
YOU LOOK GOOD.
DID YOU HAVE A FUN VISIT WITH MR. WESTON?
YEAH.
IT'S NICE TO SEE YOU HAPPY, HANA.

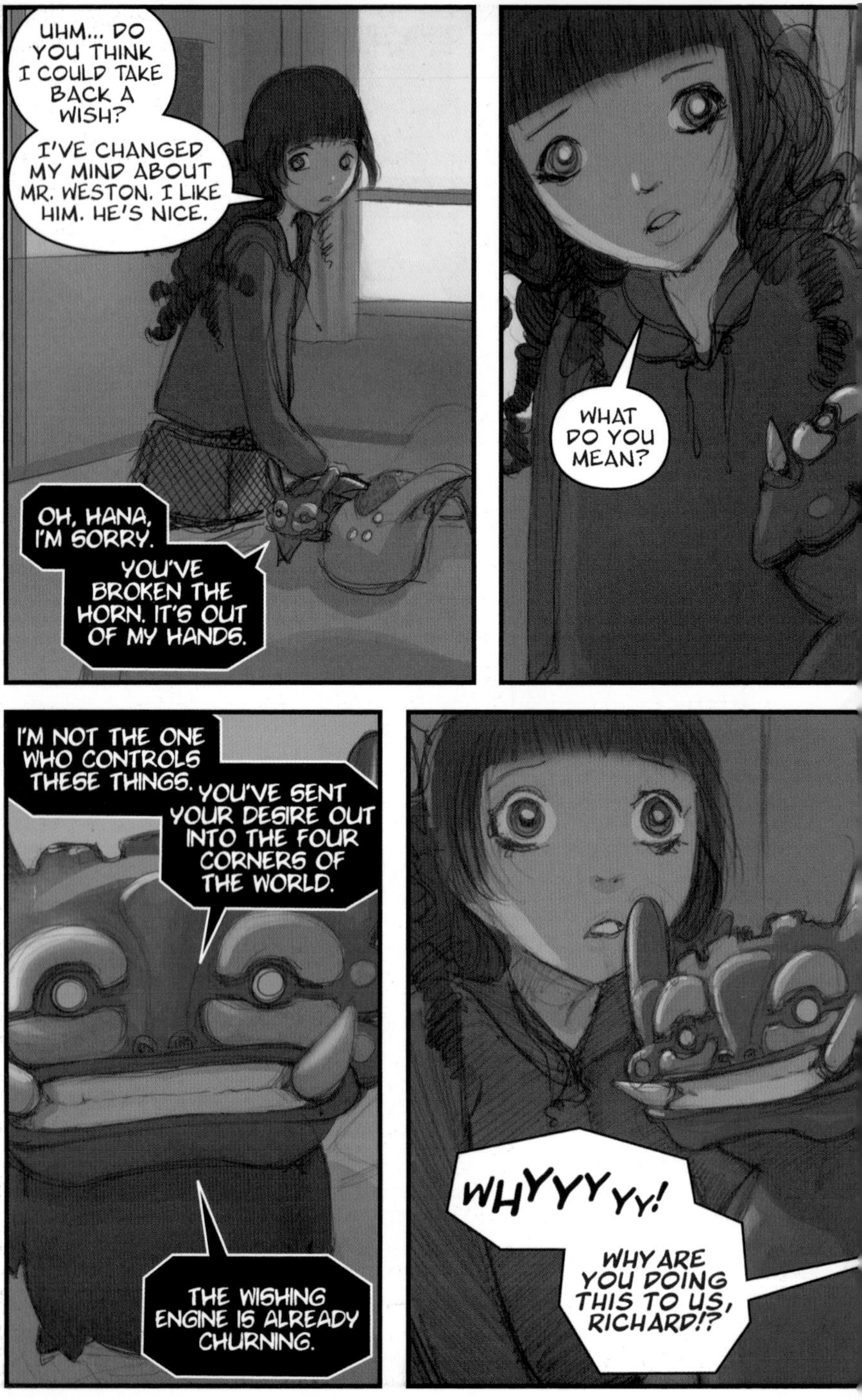
UHM... DO YOU THINK I COULD TAKE BACK A WISH?
I'VE CHANGED MY MIND ABOUT MR. WESTON. I LIKE HIM. HE'S NICE.
OH, HANA, I'M SORRY.
YOU'VE BROKEN THE HORN. IT'S OUT OF MY HANDS.
WHAT DO YOU MEAN?
I'M NOT THE ONE WHO CONTROLS THESE THINGS.
YOU'VE SENT YOUR DESIRE OUT INTO THE FOUR CORNERS OF THE WORLD.
THE WISHING ENGINE IS ALREADY CHURNING.
WHYYYYYY!
WHY ARE YOU DOING THIS TO US, RICHARD!?

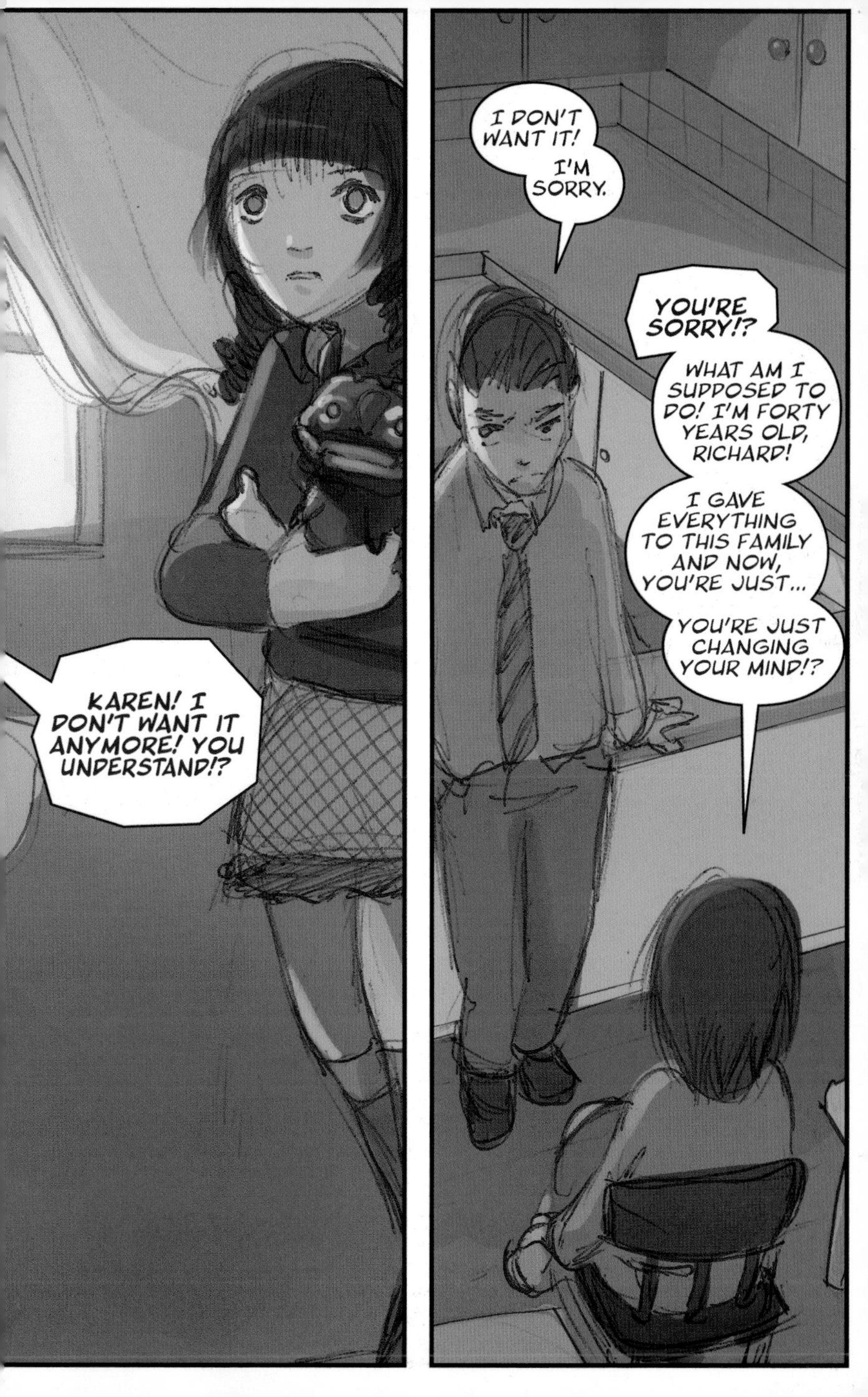
KAREN! I DON'T WANT IT ANYMORE! YOU UNDERSTAND!?
I DON'T WANT IT!
I'M SORRY.
YOU'RE SORRY!?
WHAT AM I SUPPOSED TO DO! I'M FORTY YEARS OLD, RICHARD!
I GAVE EVERYTHING TO THIS FAMILY AND NOW, YOU'RE JUST...
YOU'RE JUST CHANGING YOUR MIND!?

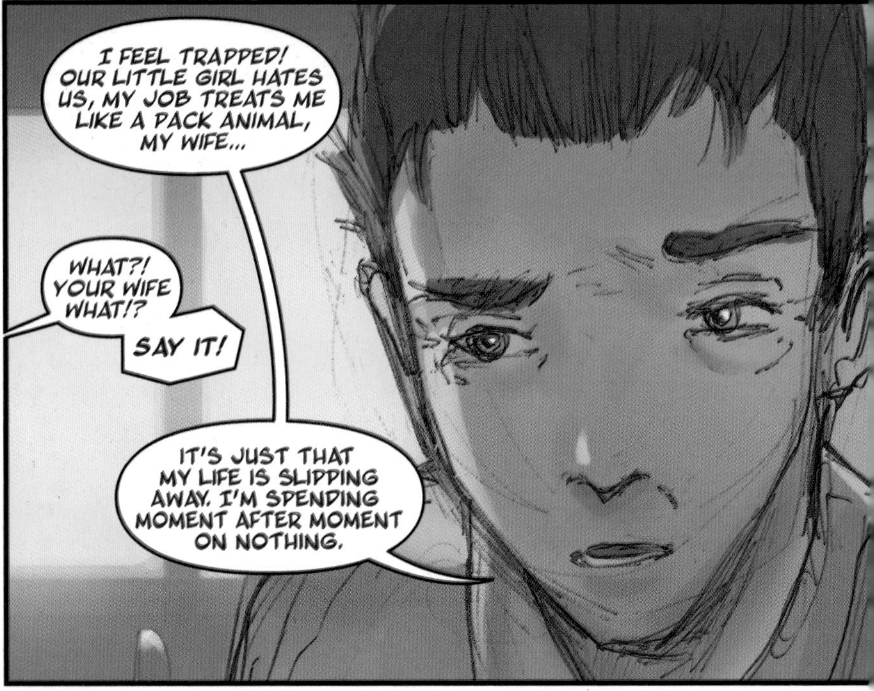
I FEEL TRAPPED! OUR LITTLE GIRL HATES US, MY JOB TREATS ME LIKE A PACK ANIMAL, MY WIFE...
WHAT?! YOUR WIFE WHAT!?
SAY IT!
IT'S JUST THAT MY LIFE IS SLIPPING AWAY. I'M SPENDING MOMENT AFTER MOMENT ON NOTHING.

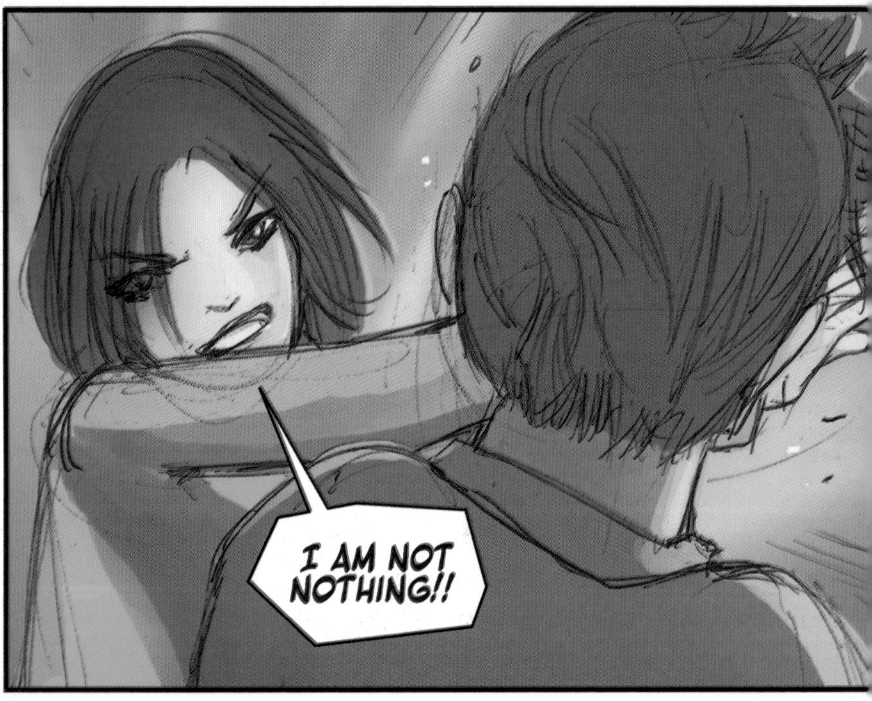
I AM NOT NOTHING!!

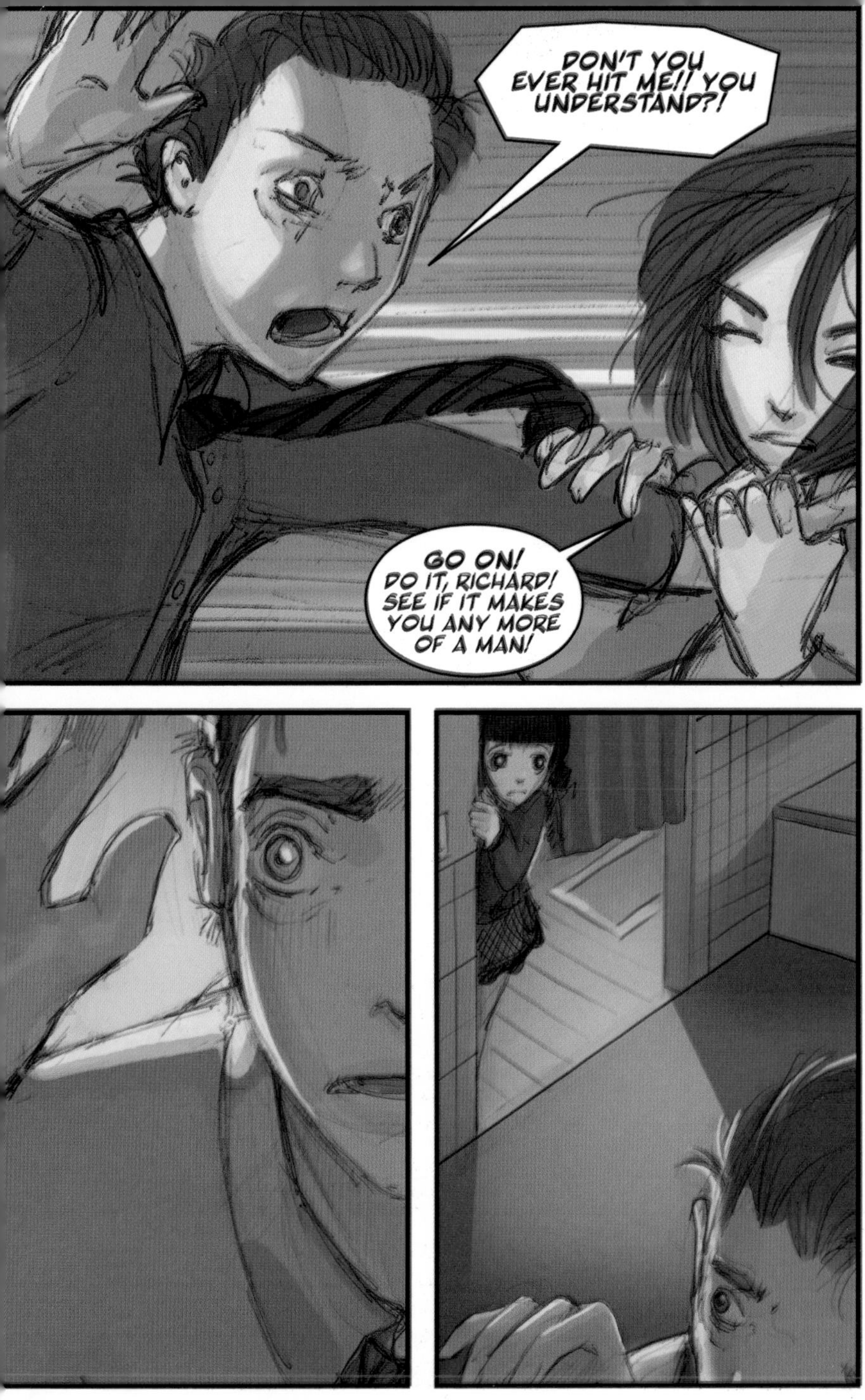
DON'T YOU EVER HIT ME!! YOU UNDERSTAND?!
GO ON! DO IT, RICHARD! SEE IF IT MAKES YOU ANY MORE OF A MAN!

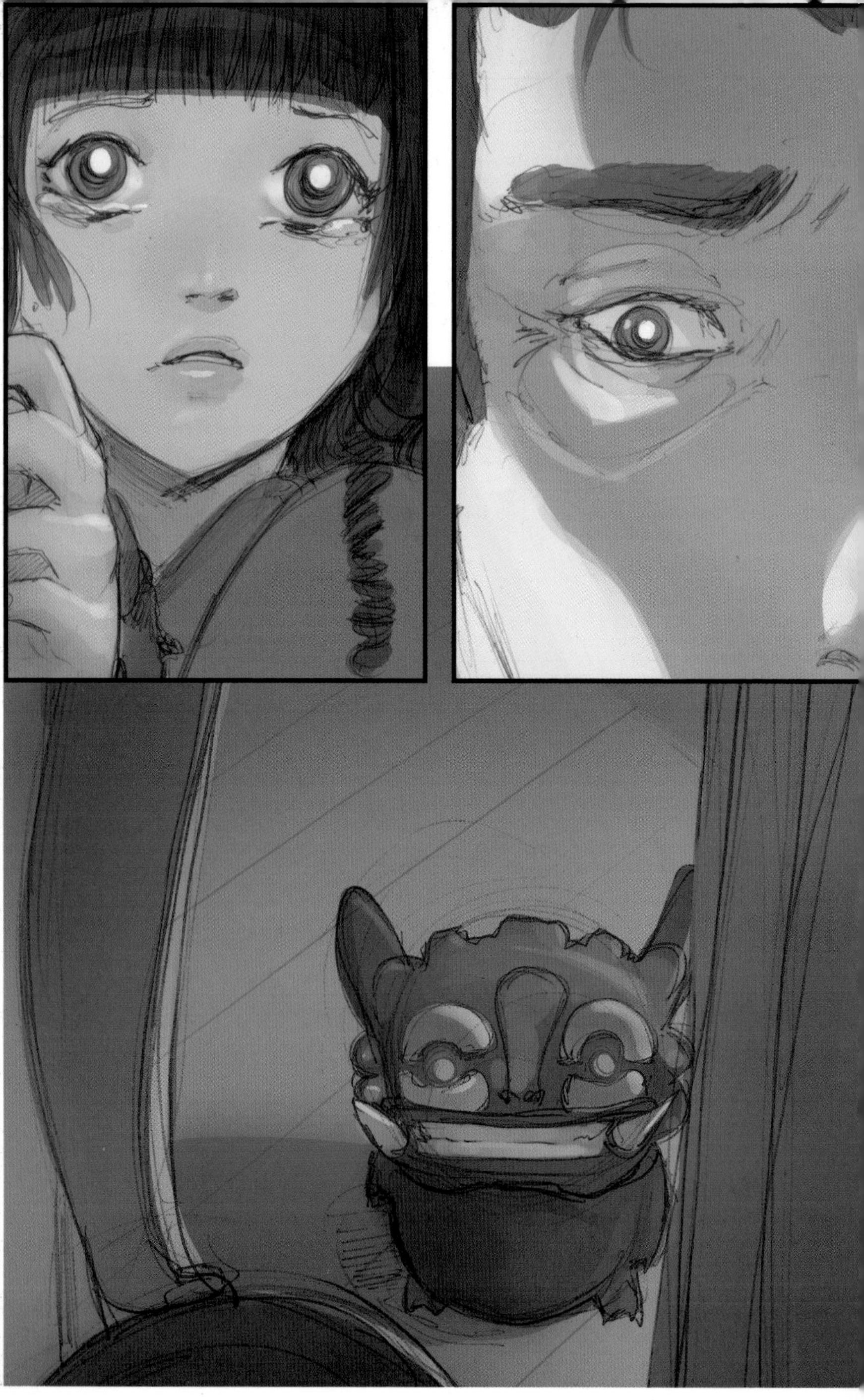

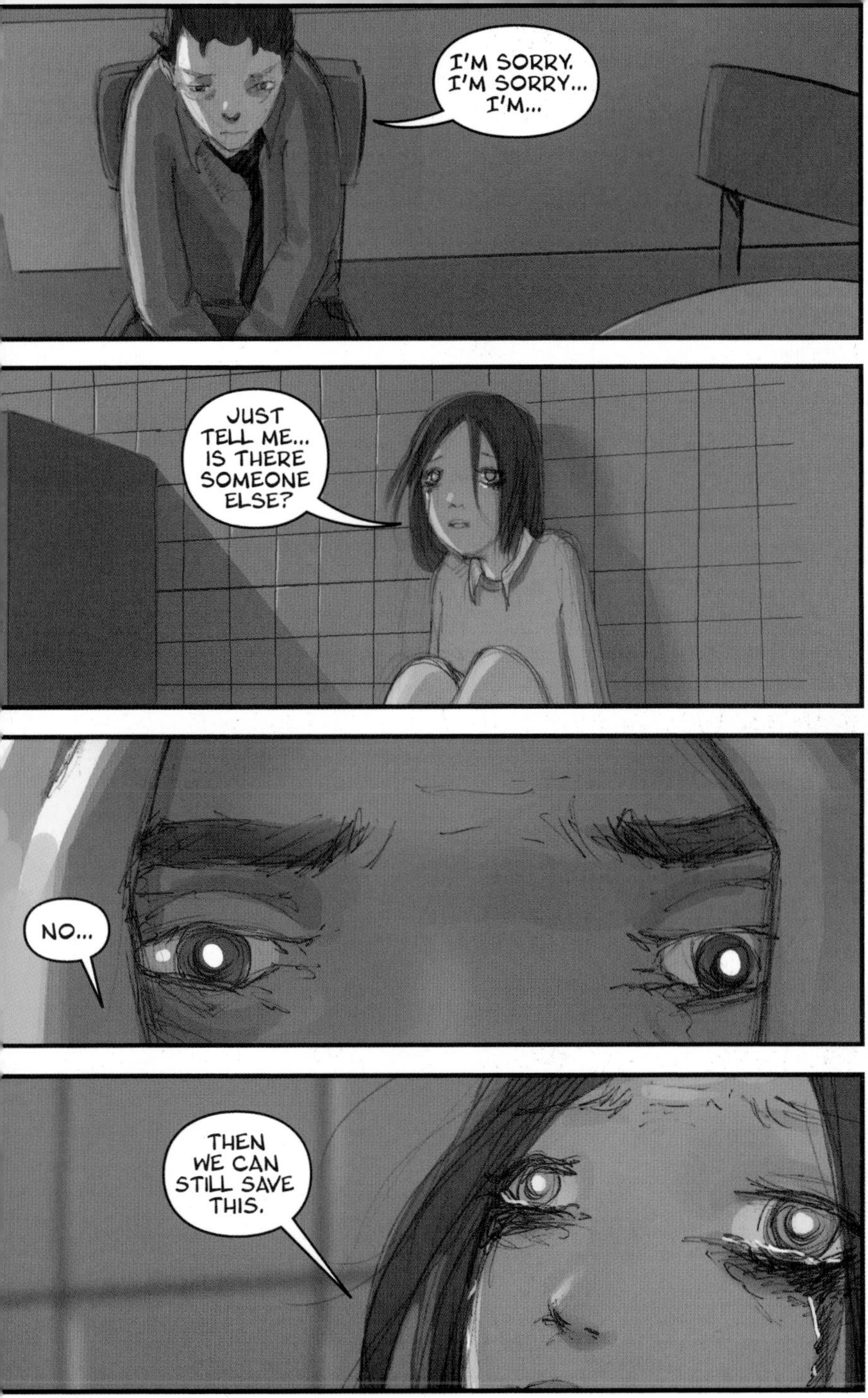
I'M SORRY. I'M SORRY... I'M...
JUST TELL ME... IS THERE SOMEONE ELSE?
NO...
THEN WE CAN STILL SAVE THIS.

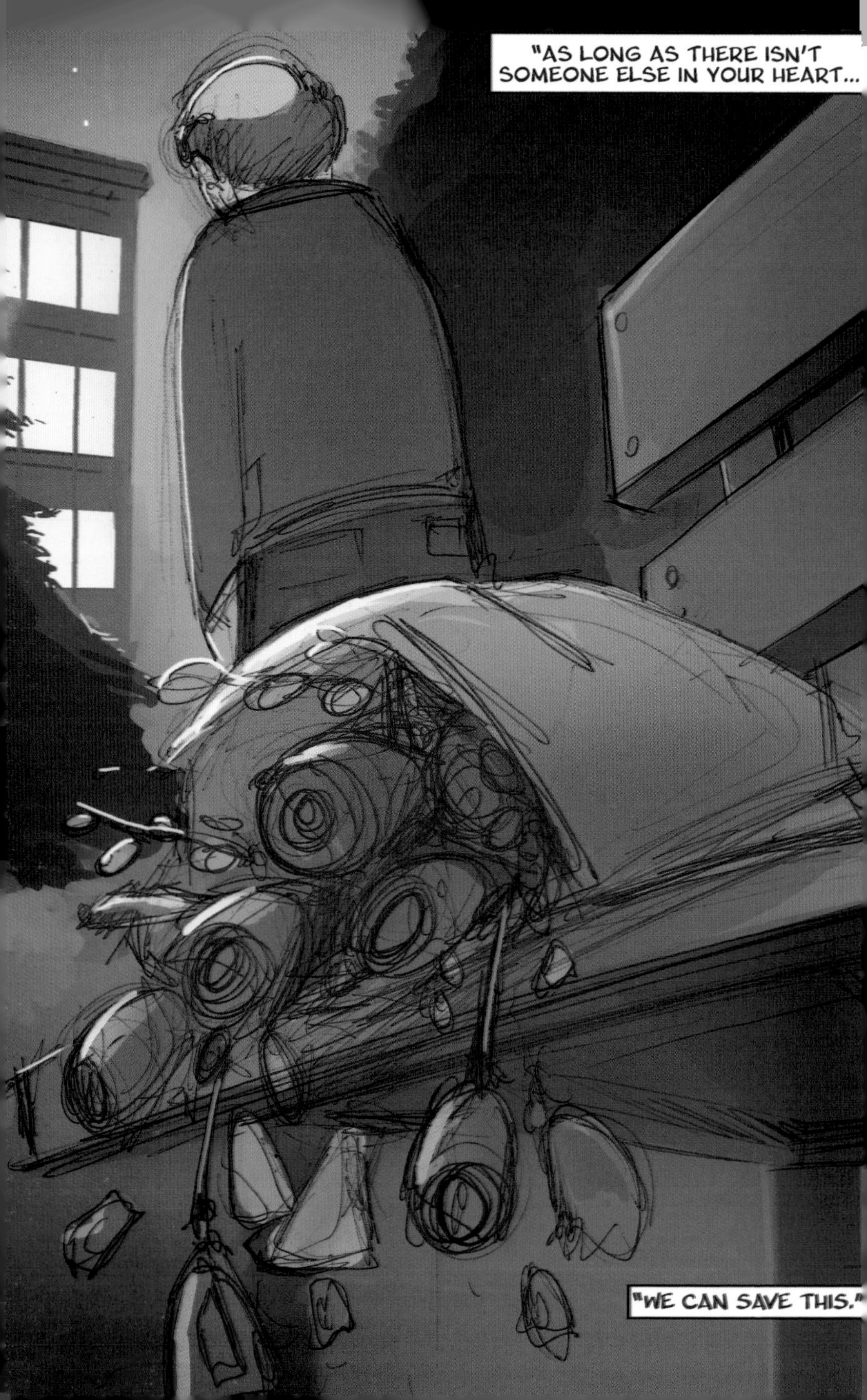
"AS LONG AS THERE ISN'T SOMEONE ELSE IN YOUR HEART...
"WE CAN SAVE THIS."

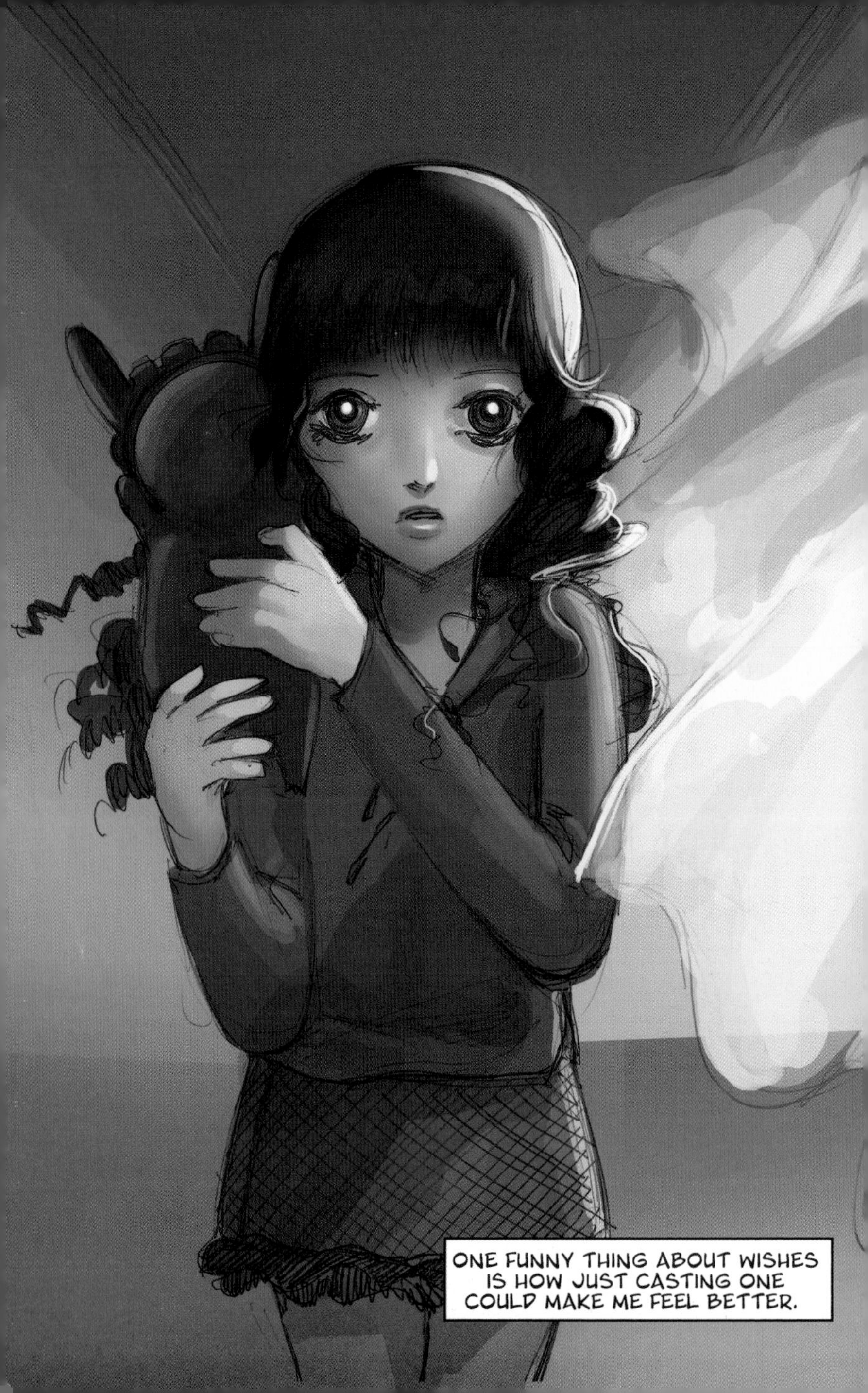
ONE FUNNY THING ABOUT WISHES IS HOW JUST CASTING ONE COULD MAKE ME FEEL BETTER.

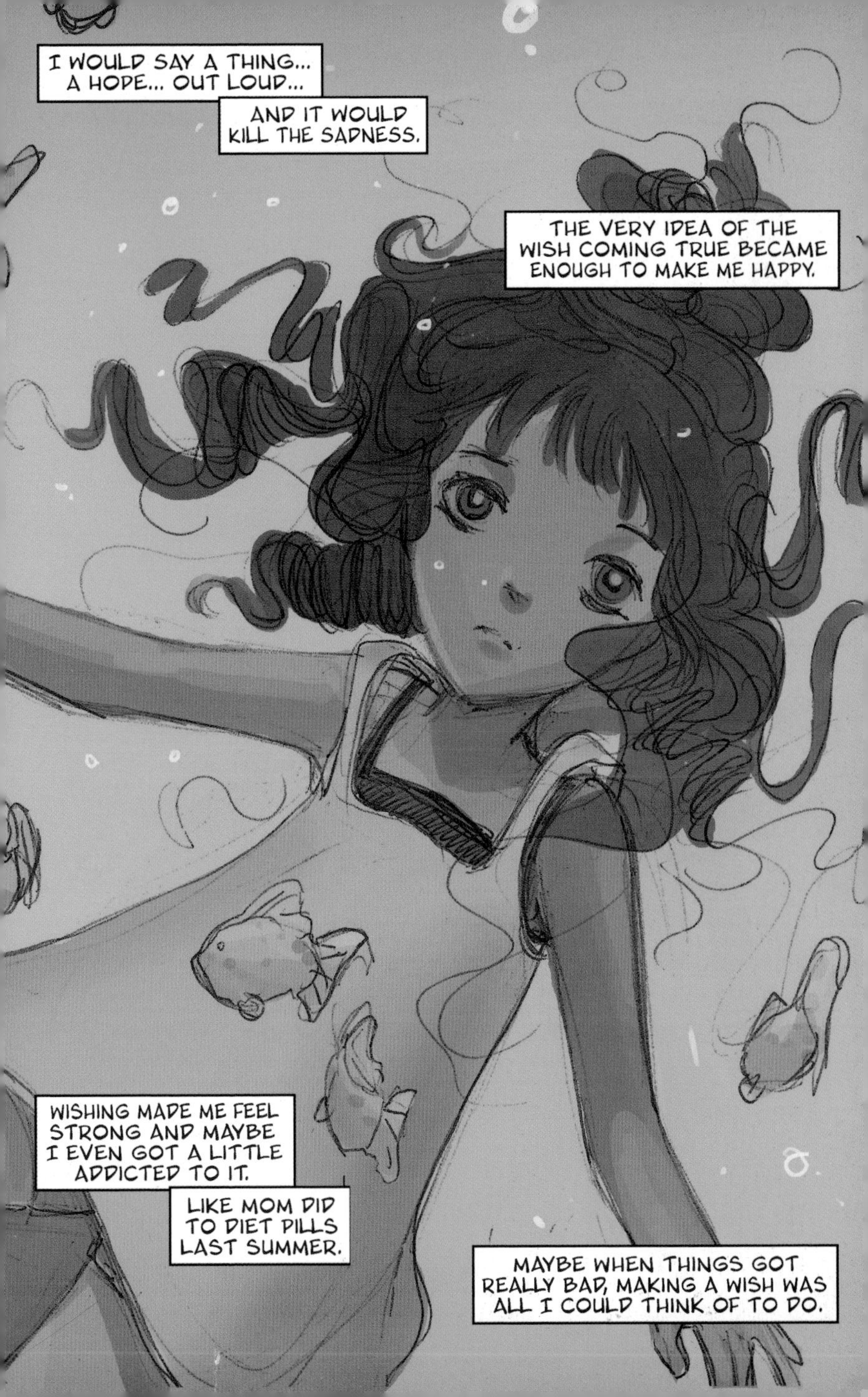
I WOULD SAY A THING... A HOPE... OUT LOUD...
AND IT WOULD KILL THE SADNESS.
THE VERY IDEA OF THE WISH COMING TRUE BECAME ENOUGH TO MAKE ME HAPPY.
WISHING MADE ME FEEL STRONG AND MAYBE I EVEN GOT A LITTLE ADDICTED TO IT.
LIKE MOM DID TO DIET PILLS LAST SUMMER.
MAYBE WHEN THINGS GOT REALLY BAD, MAKING A WISH WAS ALL I COULD THINK OF TO DO.

I THINK THAT'S HOW I FELT THAT NIGHT AFTER SEEING MY MOM AND DAD HAVE THEIR WORST FIGHT EVER.

AND SO, JUST LIKE THAT, I WAS COMMITTED TO MAKING MY FOURTH WISH.

EVEN THOUGH I'D MADE THREE ALREADY AND ONLY ONE HAD COME TRUE SO FAR.

I WANT MOM AND DAD TO BE HAPPY.

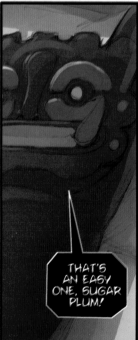

THAT'S AN EASY ONE, SUGAR PLUM!

I HAD ONE WISH LEFT, BUT I WANTED TO SIT ON IT.

TO THINK ABOUT IT.

SEE HOW THE OTHERS TURNED OUT.

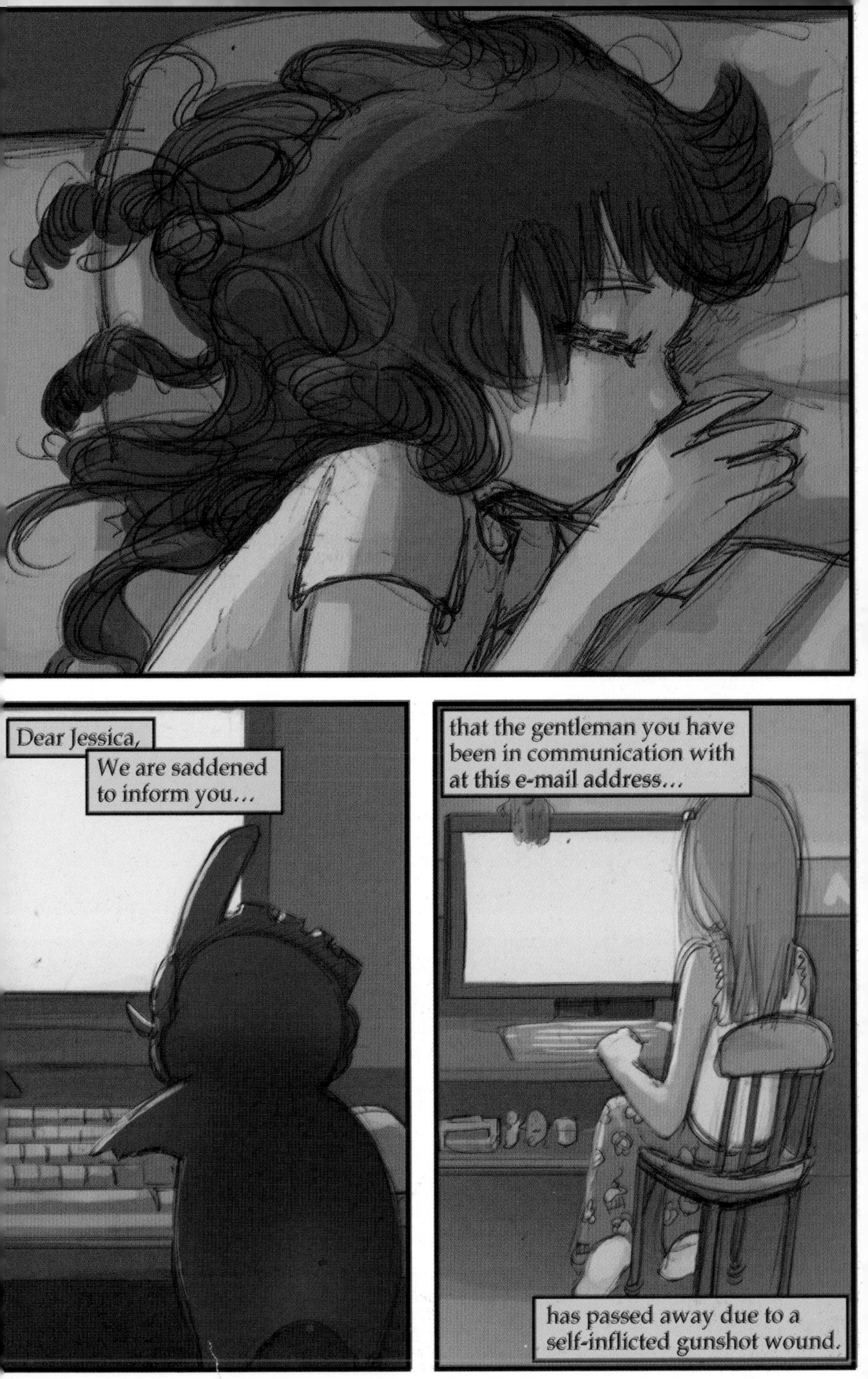
Dear Jessica,
We are saddened to inform you...
that the gentleman you have been in communication with at this e-mail address...
has passed away due to a self-inflicted gunshot wound.

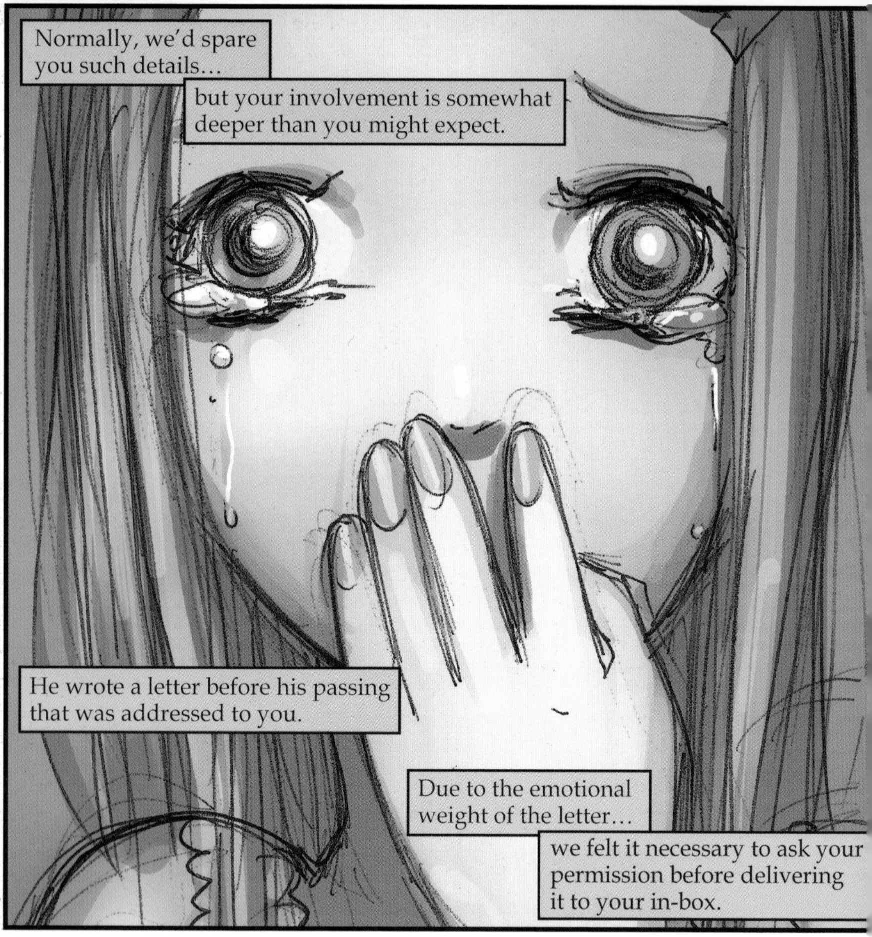
Normally, we'd spare you such details...
but your involvement is somewhat deeper than you might expect.
He wrote a letter before his passing that was addressed to you.
Due to the emotional weight of the letter...
we felt it necessary to ask your permission before delivering it to your in-box.

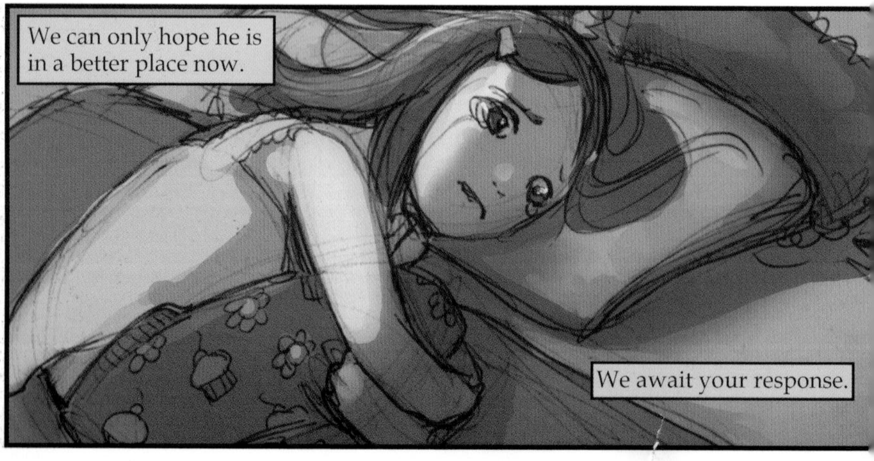
We can only hope he is in a better place now.
We await your response.

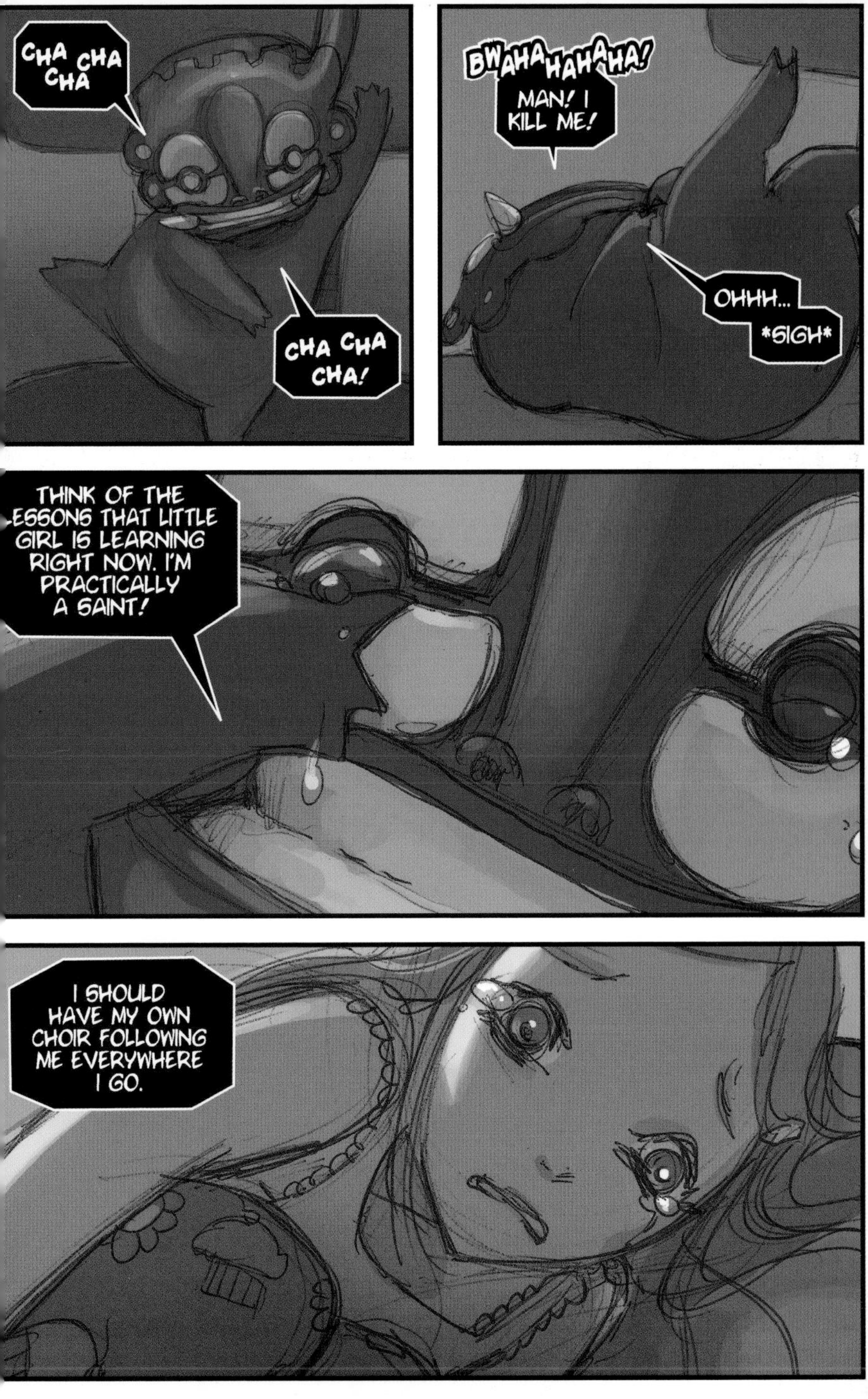
CHA CHA CHA
CHA CHA CHA!
BWAHAHAHAHAHA!
MAN! I KILL ME!
OHHH...
SIGH
THINK OF THE LESSONS THAT LITTLE GIRL IS LEARNING RIGHT NOW. I'M PRACTICALLY A SAINT!
I SHOULD HAVE MY OWN CHOIR FOLLOWING ME EVERYWHERE I GO.

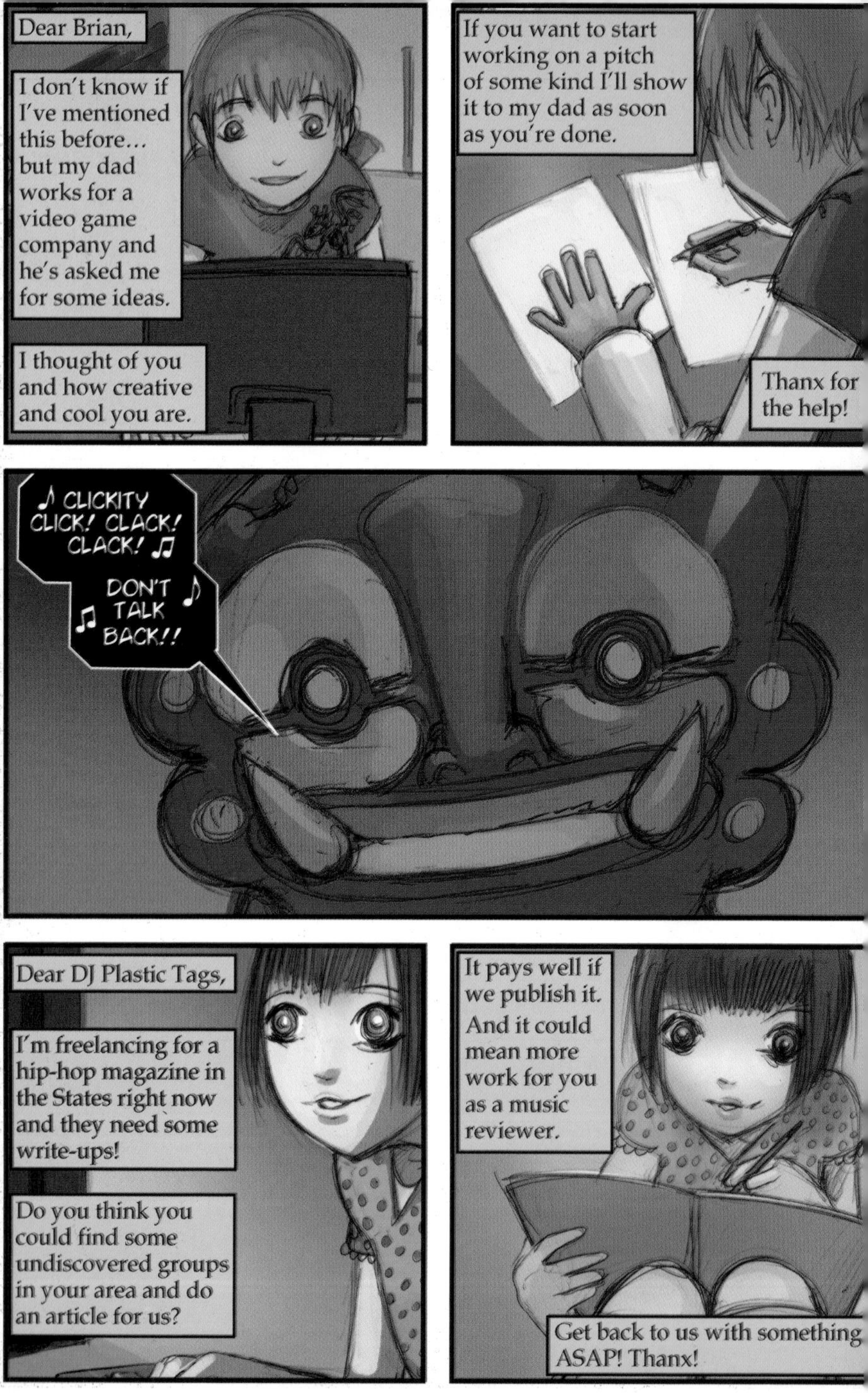
Dear Brian,
I don't know if I've mentioned this before... but my dad works for a video game company and he's asked me for some ideas.
I thought of you and how creative and cool you are.
If you want to start working on a pitch of some kind I'll show it to my dad as soon as you're done.
Thanx for the help!
♪ CLICKITY CLICK! CLACK! CLACK! ♫
DON'T TALK BACK!!
Dear DJ Plastic Tags,
I'm freelancing for a hip-hop magazine in the States right now and they need some write-ups!
Do you think you could find some undiscovered groups in your area and do an article for us?
It pays well if we publish it. And it could mean more work for you as a music reviewer.
Get back to us with something ASAP! Thanx!

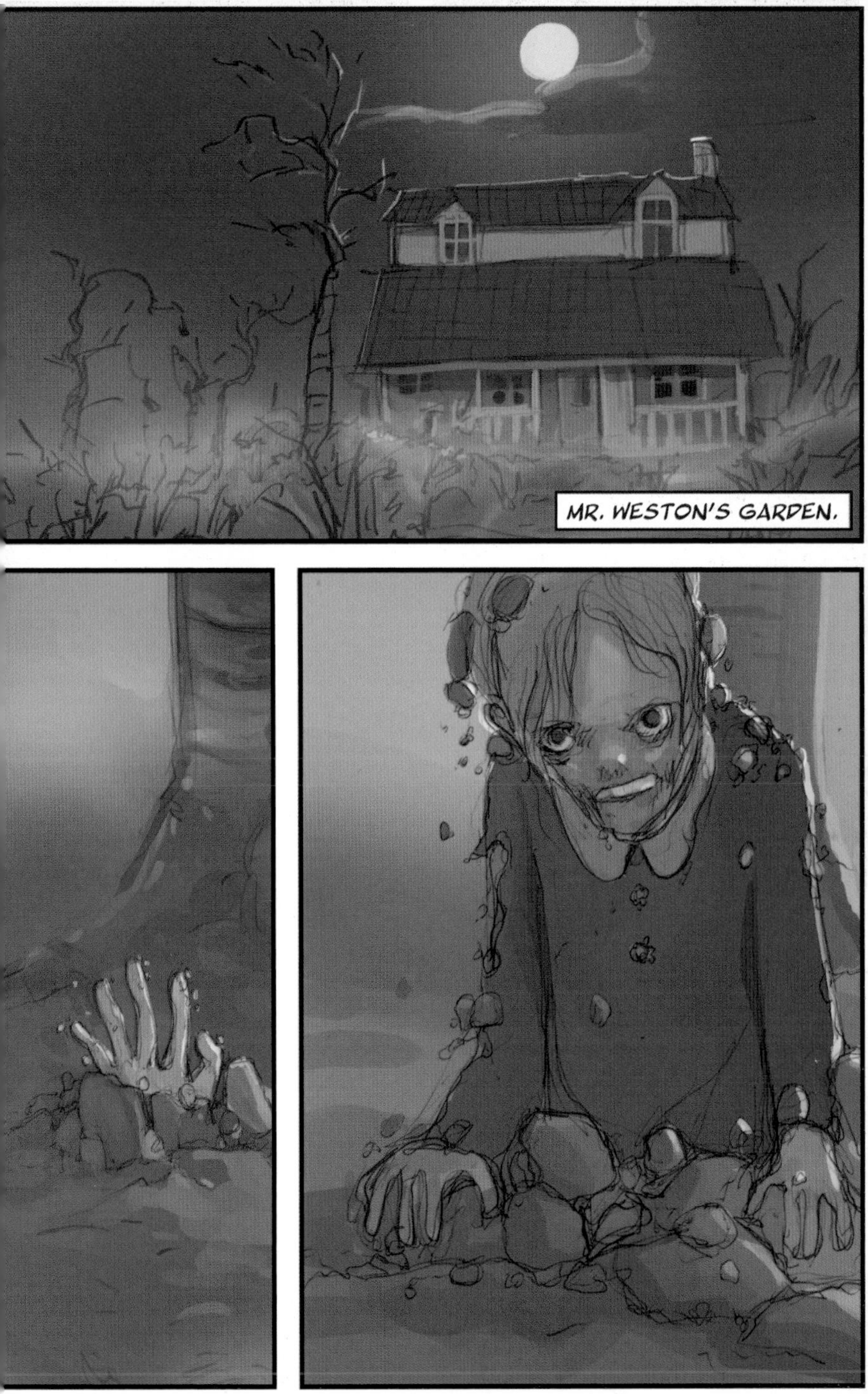
MR. WESTON'S GARDEN.

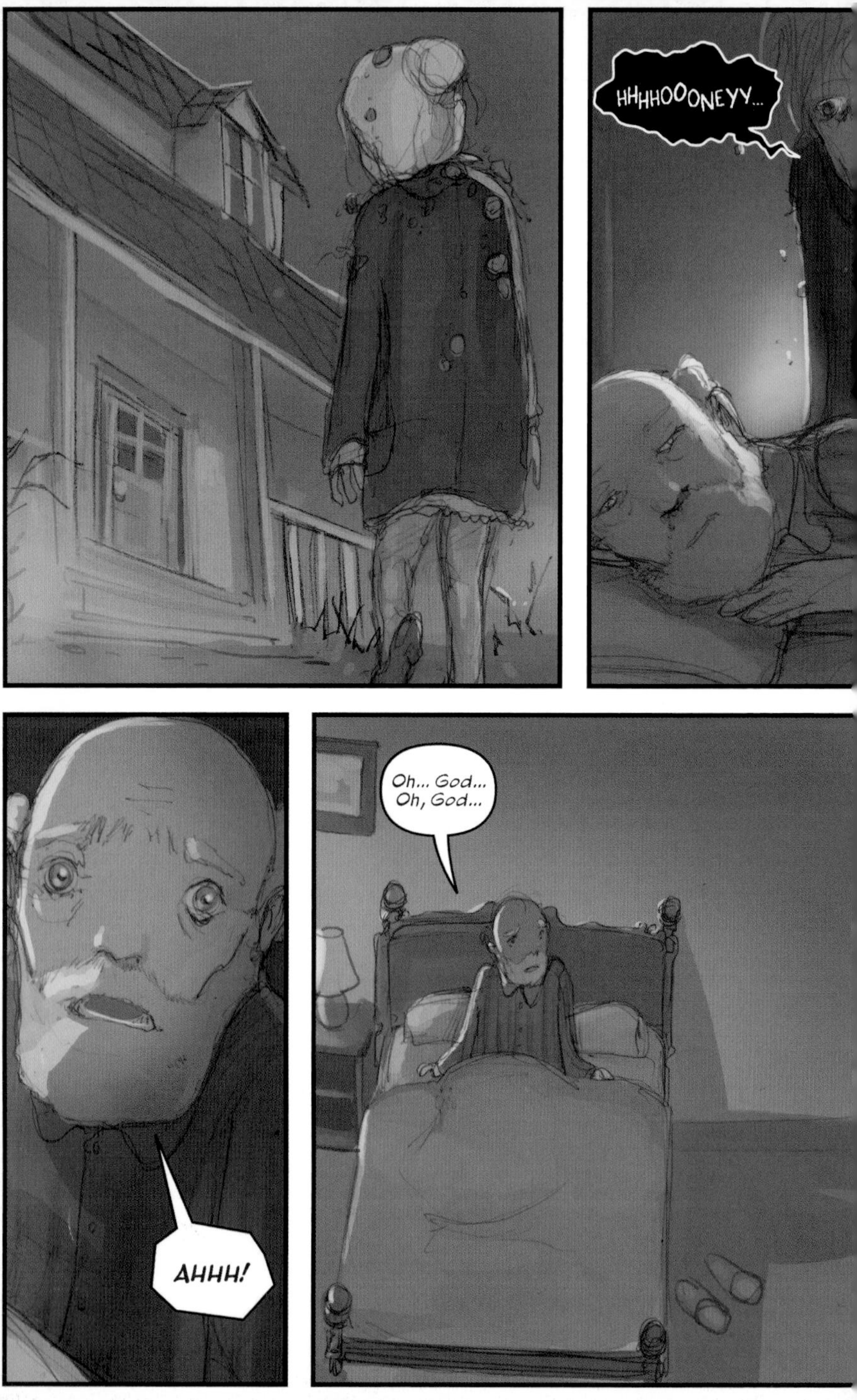
HHHHOOONEYY...
Oh... God...
Oh, God...
AHHH!

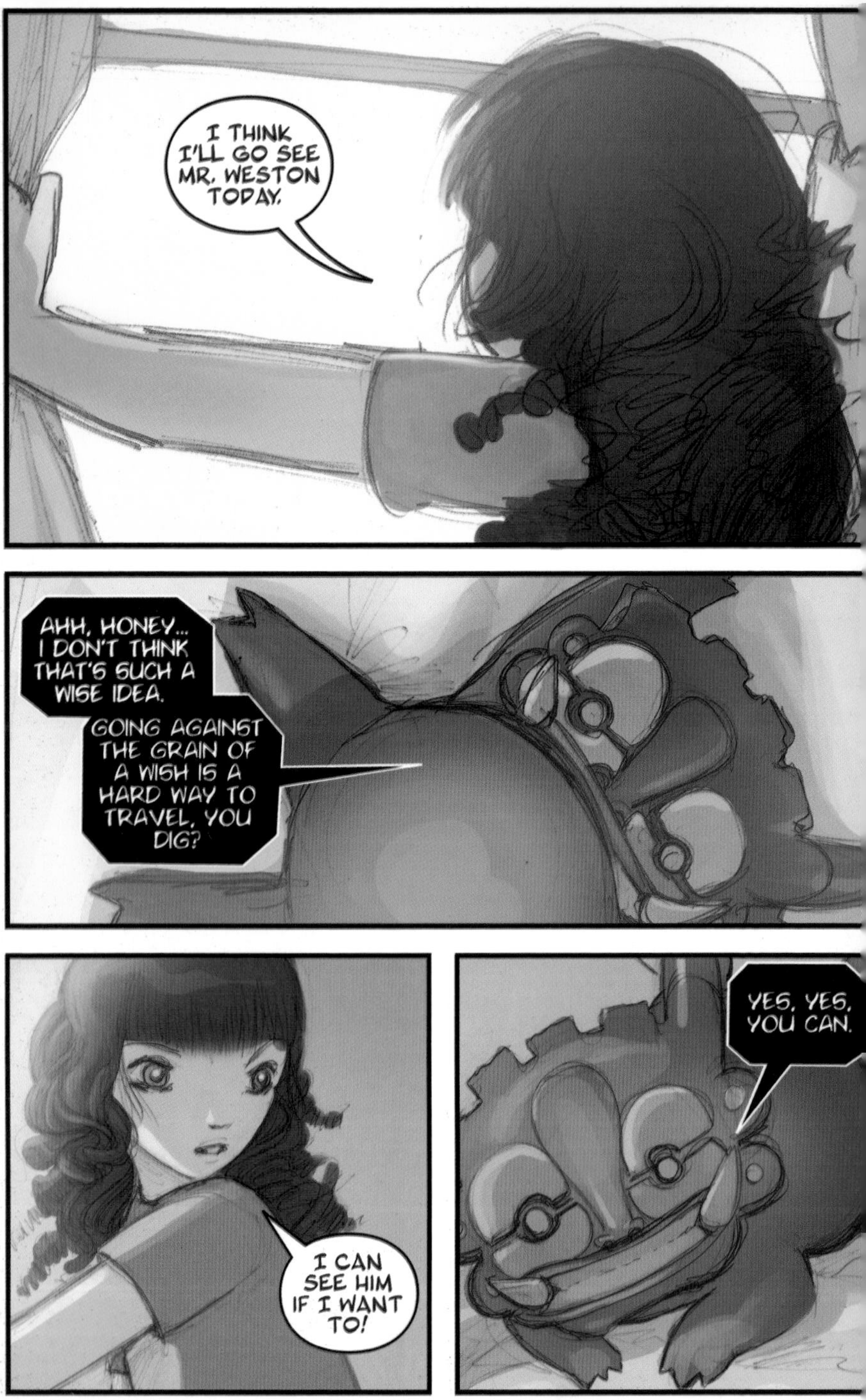
I THINK I'LL GO SEE MR. WESTON TODAY.
AHH, HONEY... I DON'T THINK THAT'S SUCH A WISE IDEA.
GOING AGAINST THE GRAIN OF A WISH IS A HARD WAY TO TRAVEL, YOU DIG?
I CAN SEE HIM IF I WANT TO!
YES, YES, YOU CAN.

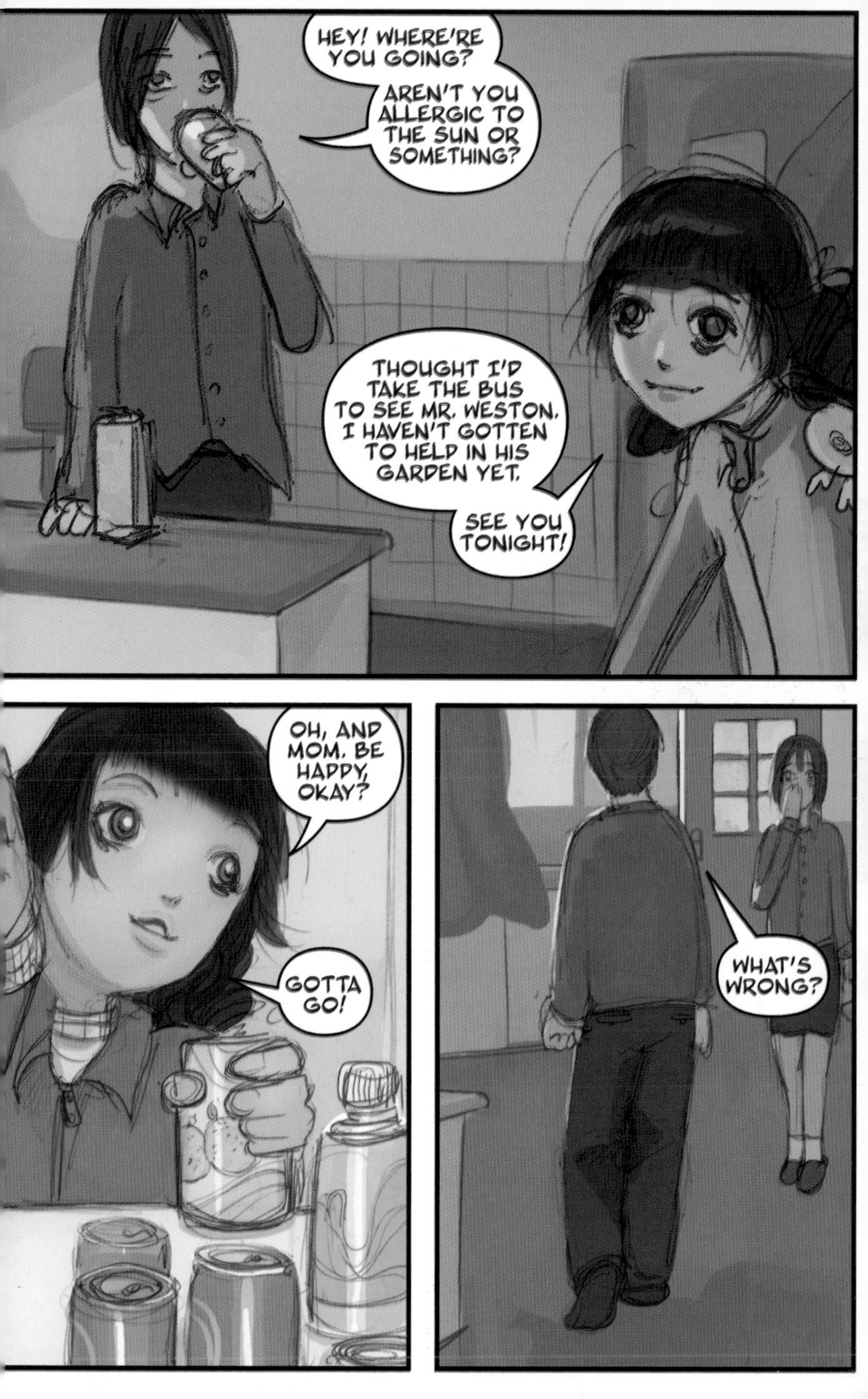
HEY! WHERE'RE YOU GOING?
AREN'T YOU ALLERGIC TO THE SUN OR SOMETHING?
THOUGHT I'D TAKE THE BUS TO SEE MR. WESTON. I HAVEN'T GOTTEN TO HELP IN HIS GARDEN YET.
SEE YOU TONIGHT!
OH, AND MOM. BE HAPPY, OKAY?
GOTTA GO!
WHAT'S WRONG?

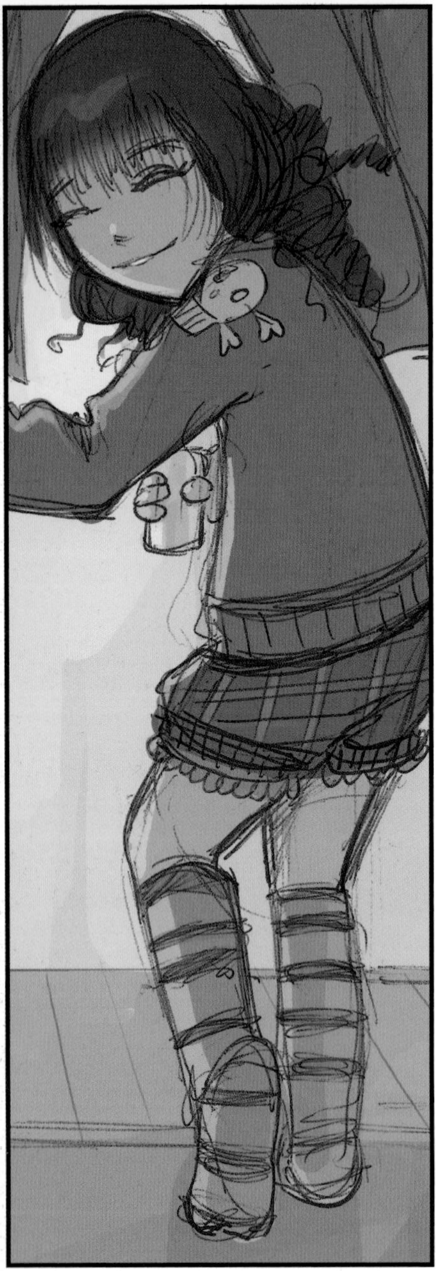

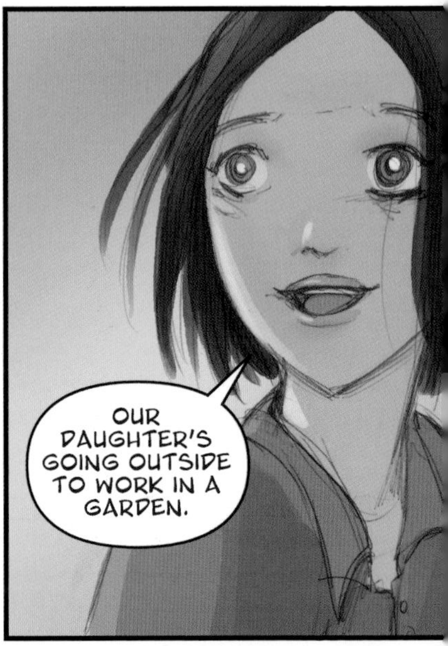
OUR DAUGHTER'S GOING OUTSIDE TO WORK IN A GARDEN.

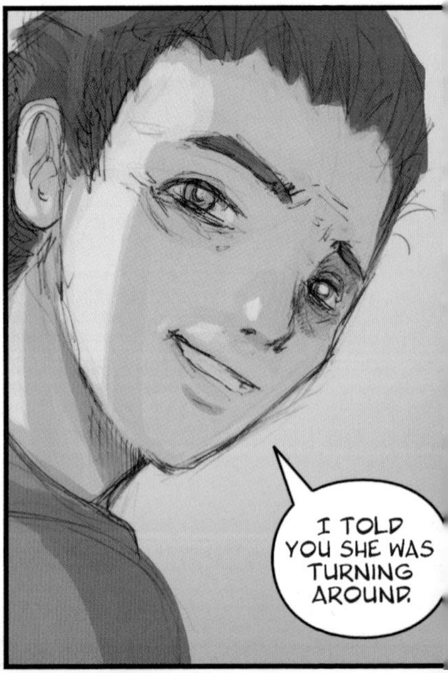
I TOLD YOU SHE WAS TURNING AROUND.

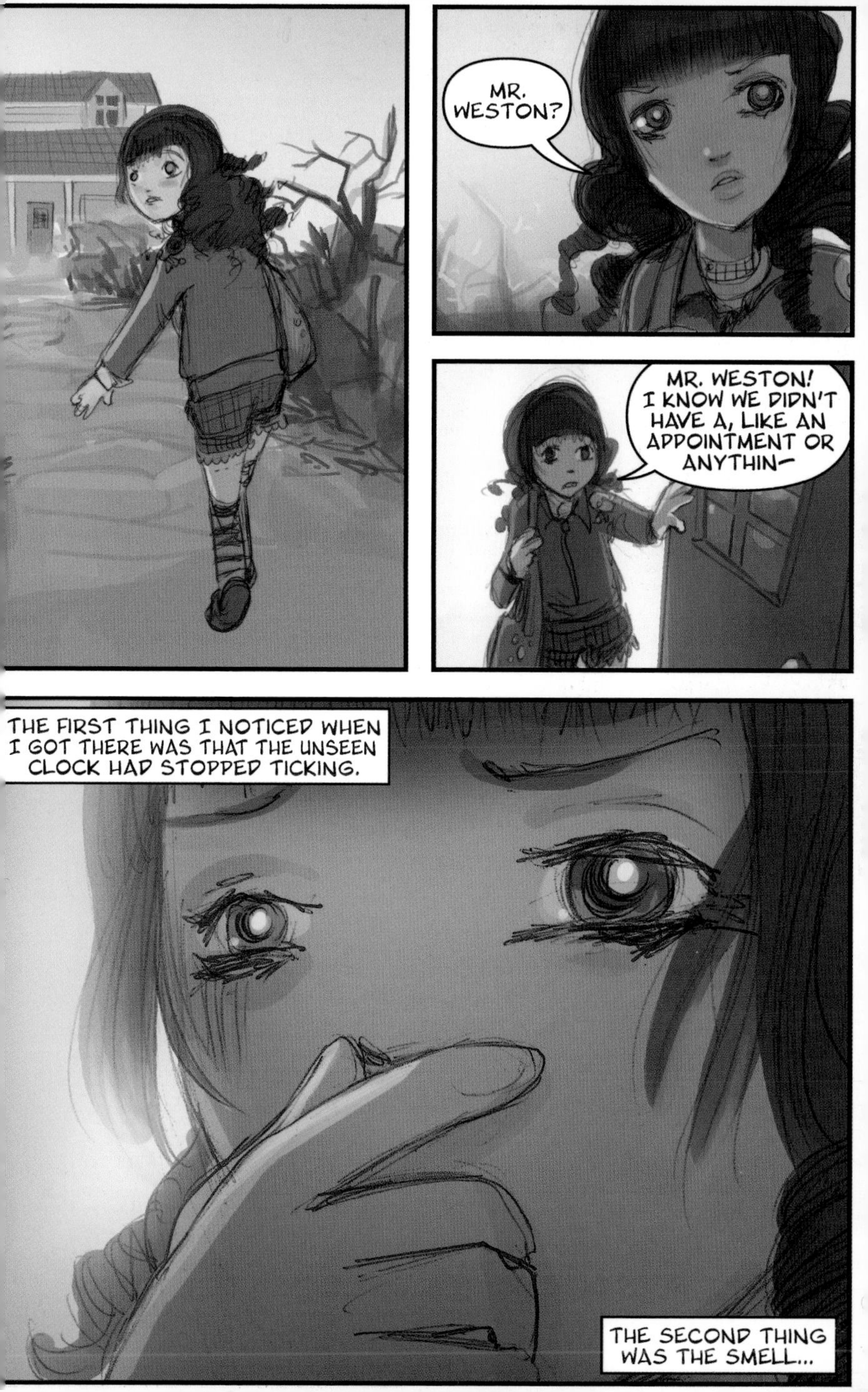
MR. WESTON?
MR. WESTON! I KNOW WE DIDN'T HAVE A, LIKE AN APPOINTMENT OR ANYTHIN—
THE FIRST THING I NOTICED WHEN I GOT THERE WAS THAT THE UNSEEN CLOCK HAD STOPPED TICKING.
THE SECOND THING WAS THE SMELL...

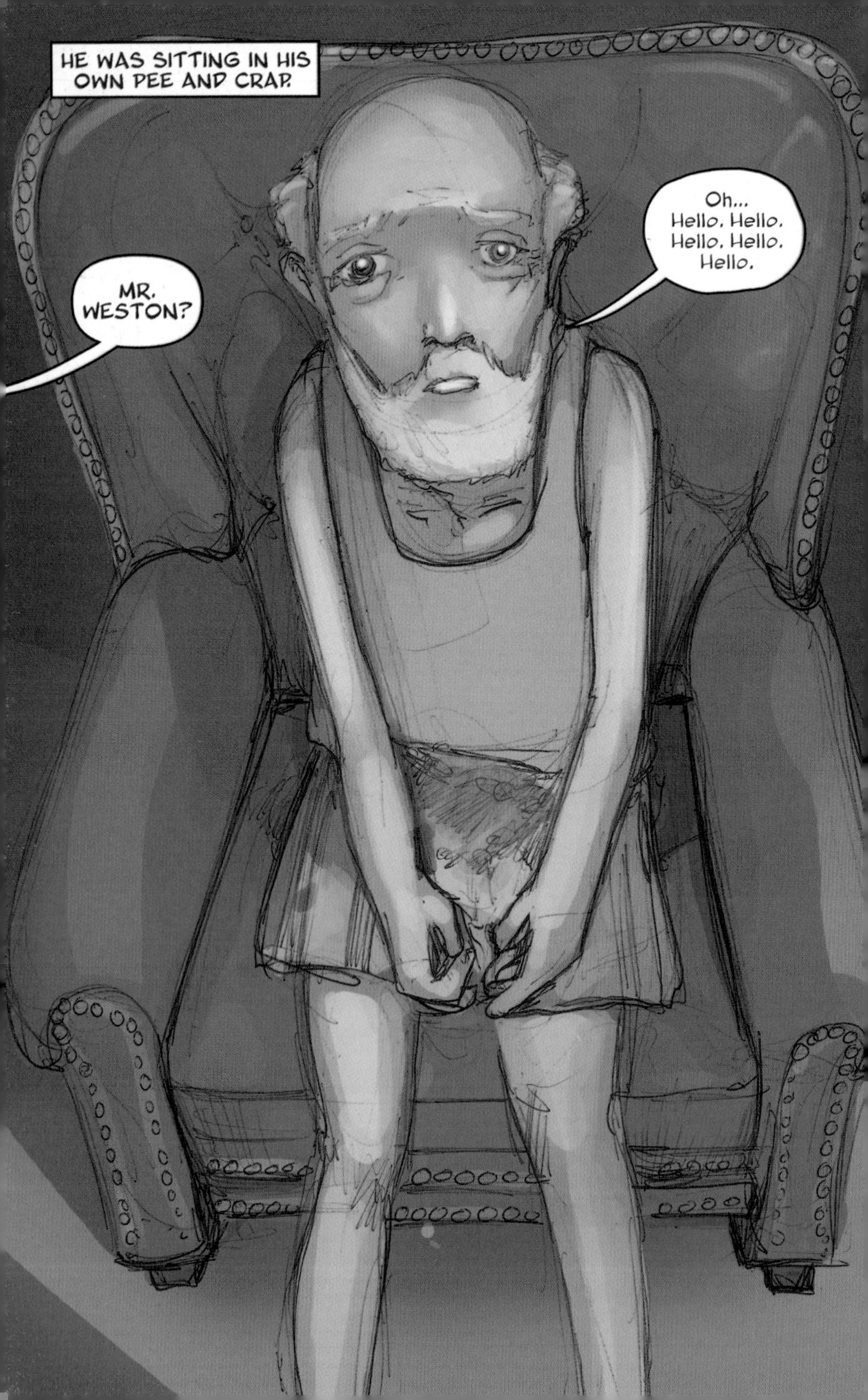
HE WAS SITTING IN HIS OWN PEE AND CRAP.
MR. WESTON?
Oh... Hello. Hello. Hello. Hello. Hello.

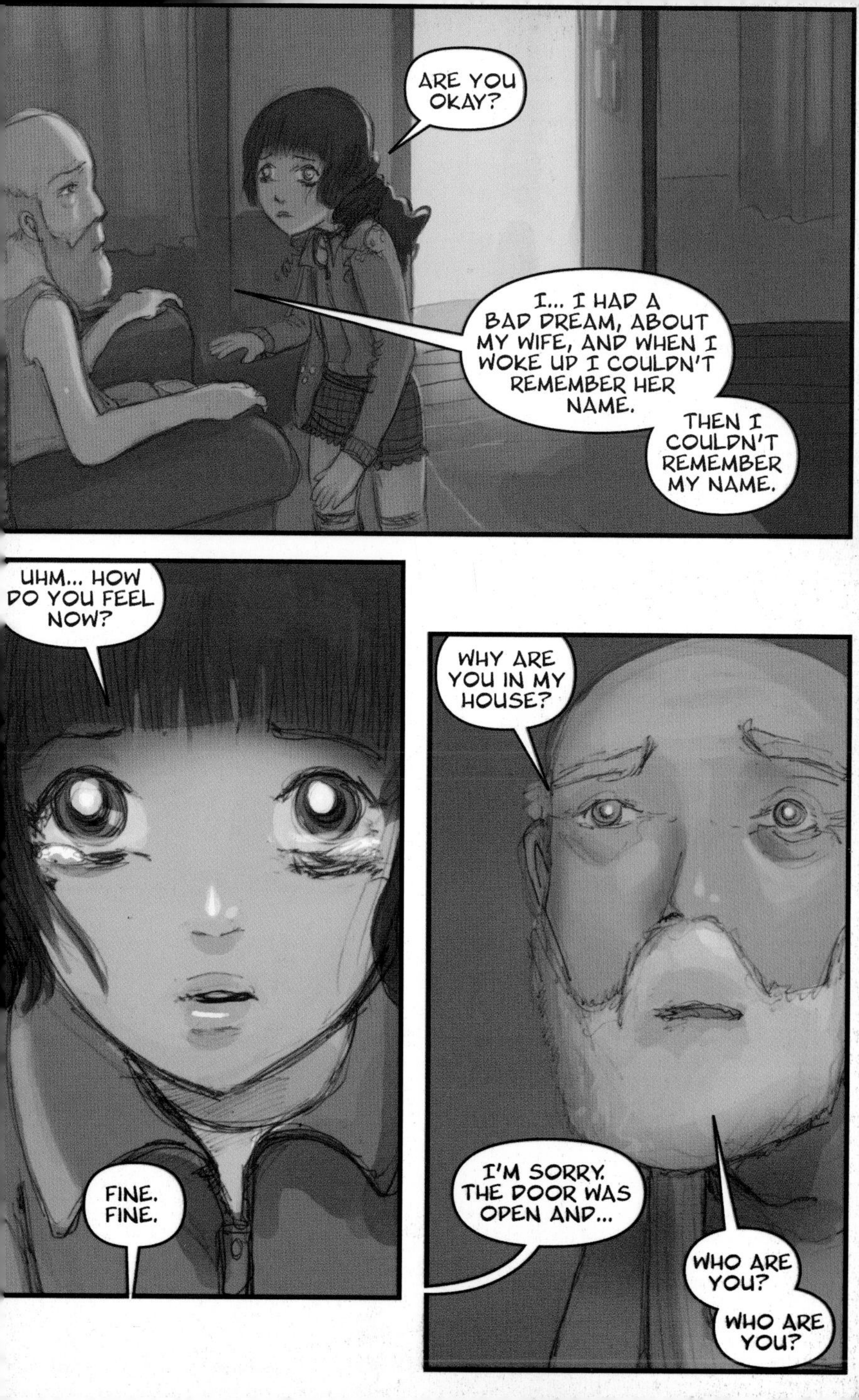
ARE YOU OKAY?
I... I HAD A BAD DREAM, ABOUT MY WIFE, AND WHEN I WOKE UP I COULDN'T REMEMBER HER NAME.
THEN I COULDN'T REMEMBER MY NAME.
UHM... HOW DO YOU FEEL NOW?
FINE. FINE.
WHY ARE YOU IN MY HOUSE?
I'M SORRY. THE DOOR WAS OPEN AND...
WHO ARE YOU?
WHO ARE YOU?

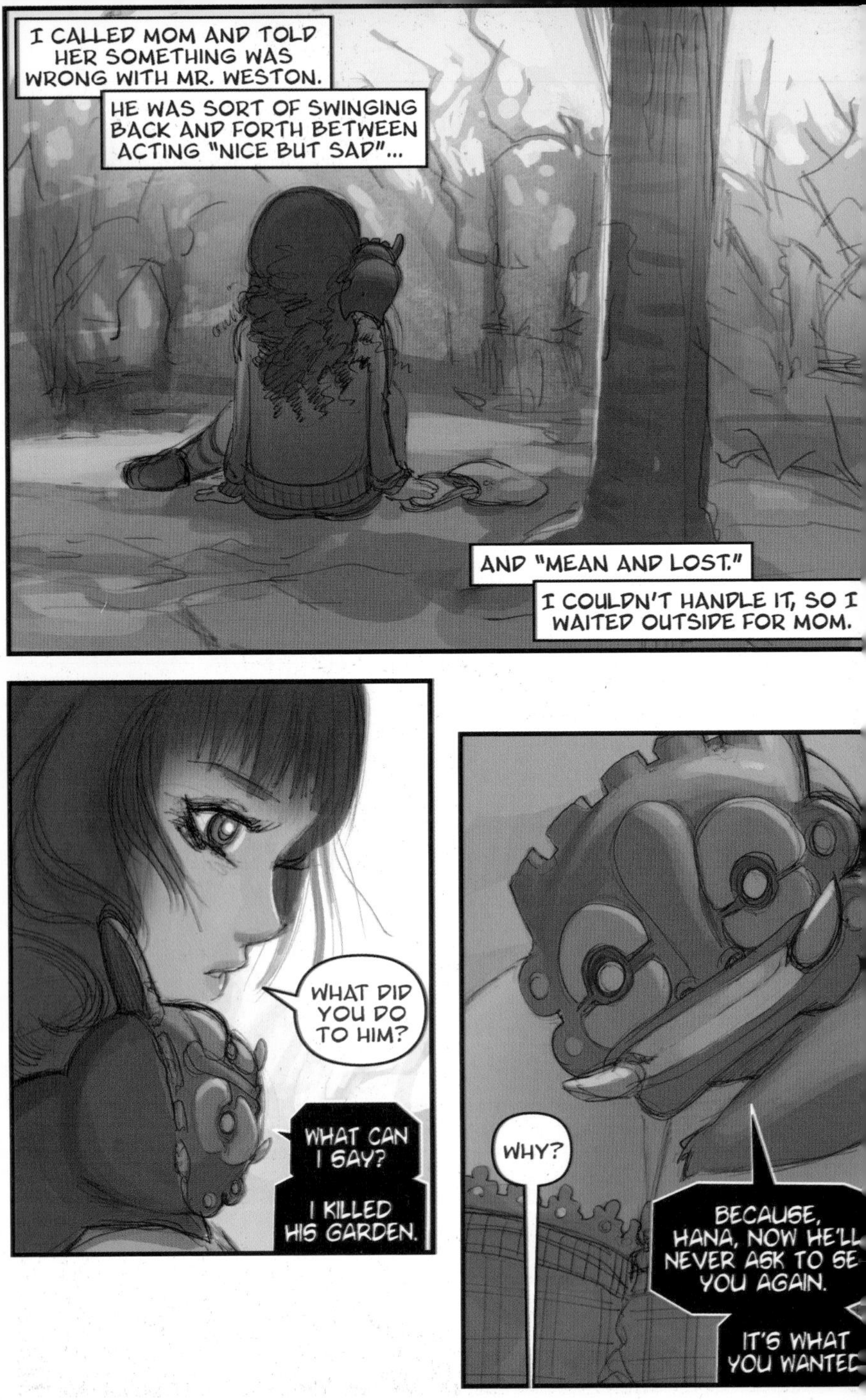
I CALLED MOM AND TOLD HER SOMETHING WAS WRONG WITH MR. WESTON.
HE WAS SORT OF SWINGING BACK AND FORTH BETWEEN ACTING "NICE BUT SAD"...
AND "MEAN AND LOST."
I COULDN'T HANDLE IT, SO I WAITED OUTSIDE FOR MOM.
WHAT DID YOU DO TO HIM?
WHAT CAN I SAY?
I KILLED HIS GARDEN.
WHY?
BECAUSE, HANA, NOW HE'LL NEVER ASK TO SE YOU AGAIN.
IT'S WHAT YOU WANTED

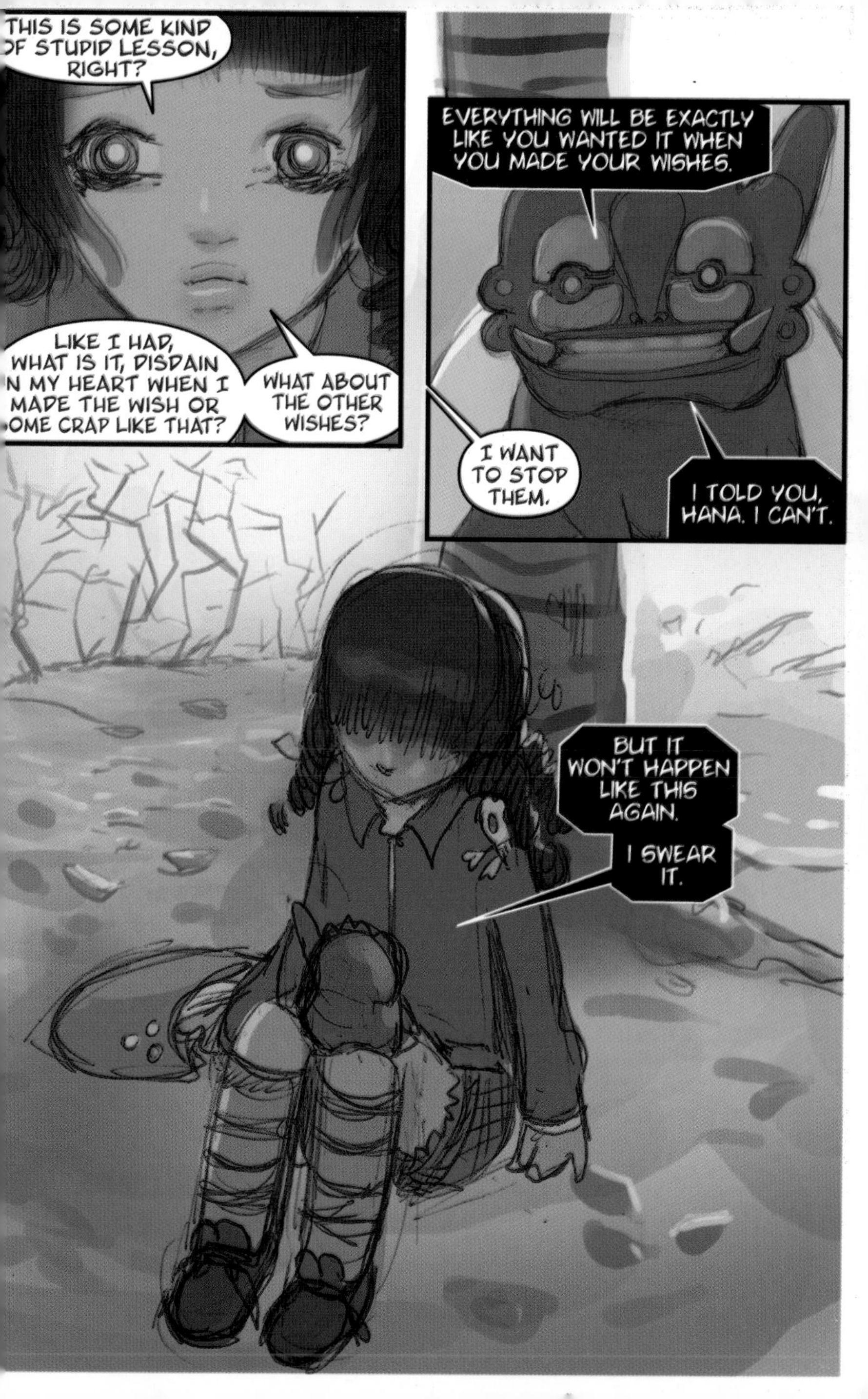

THIS IS SOME KIND OF STUPID LESSON, RIGHT?
LIKE I HAD, WHAT IS IT, DISDAIN IN MY HEART WHEN I MADE THE WISH OR SOME CRAP LIKE THAT?
WHAT ABOUT THE OTHER WISHES?
EVERYTHING WILL BE EXACTLY LIKE YOU WANTED IT WHEN YOU MADE YOUR WISHES.
I WANT TO STOP THEM.
I TOLD YOU, HANA. I CAN'T.
BUT IT WON'T HAPPEN LIKE THIS AGAIN.
I SWEAR IT.

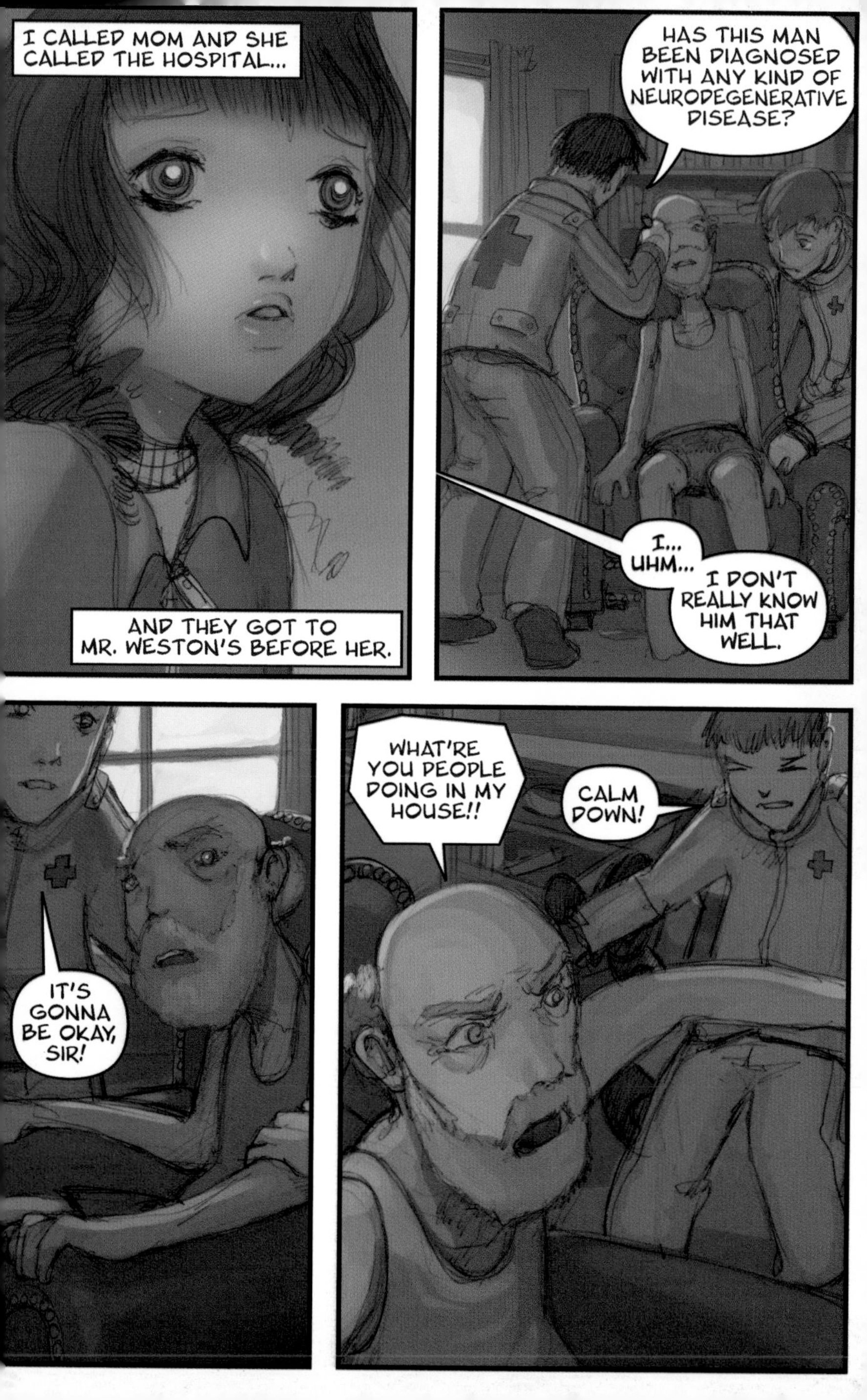
I CALLED MOM AND SHE CALLED THE HOSPITAL...
AND THEY GOT TO MR. WESTON'S BEFORE HER.
HAS THIS MAN BEEN DIAGNOSED WITH ANY KIND OF NEURODEGENERATIVE DISEASE?
I... UHM...
I DON'T REALLY KNOW HIM THAT WELL.
IT'S GONNA BE OKAY, SIR!
WHAT'RE YOU PEOPLE DOING IN MY HOUSE!!
CALM DOWN!

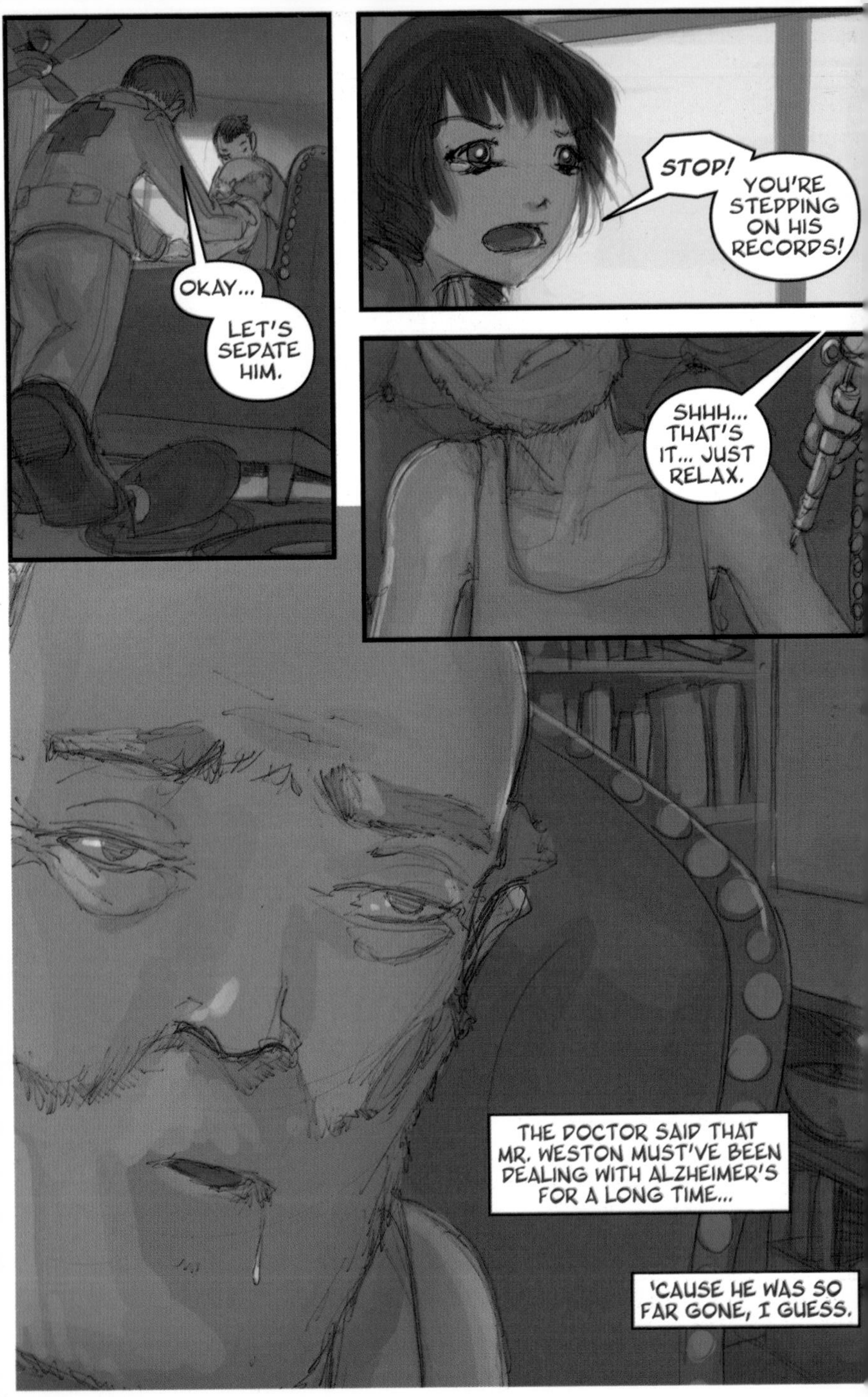
OKAY...
LET'S SEDATE HIM.
STOP!
YOU'RE STEPPING ON HIS RECORDS!
SHHH... THAT'S IT... JUST RELAX.
THE DOCTOR SAID THAT MR. WESTON MUST'VE BEEN DEALING WITH ALZHEIMER'S FOR A LONG TIME...
'CAUSE HE WAS SO FAR GONE, I GUESS.

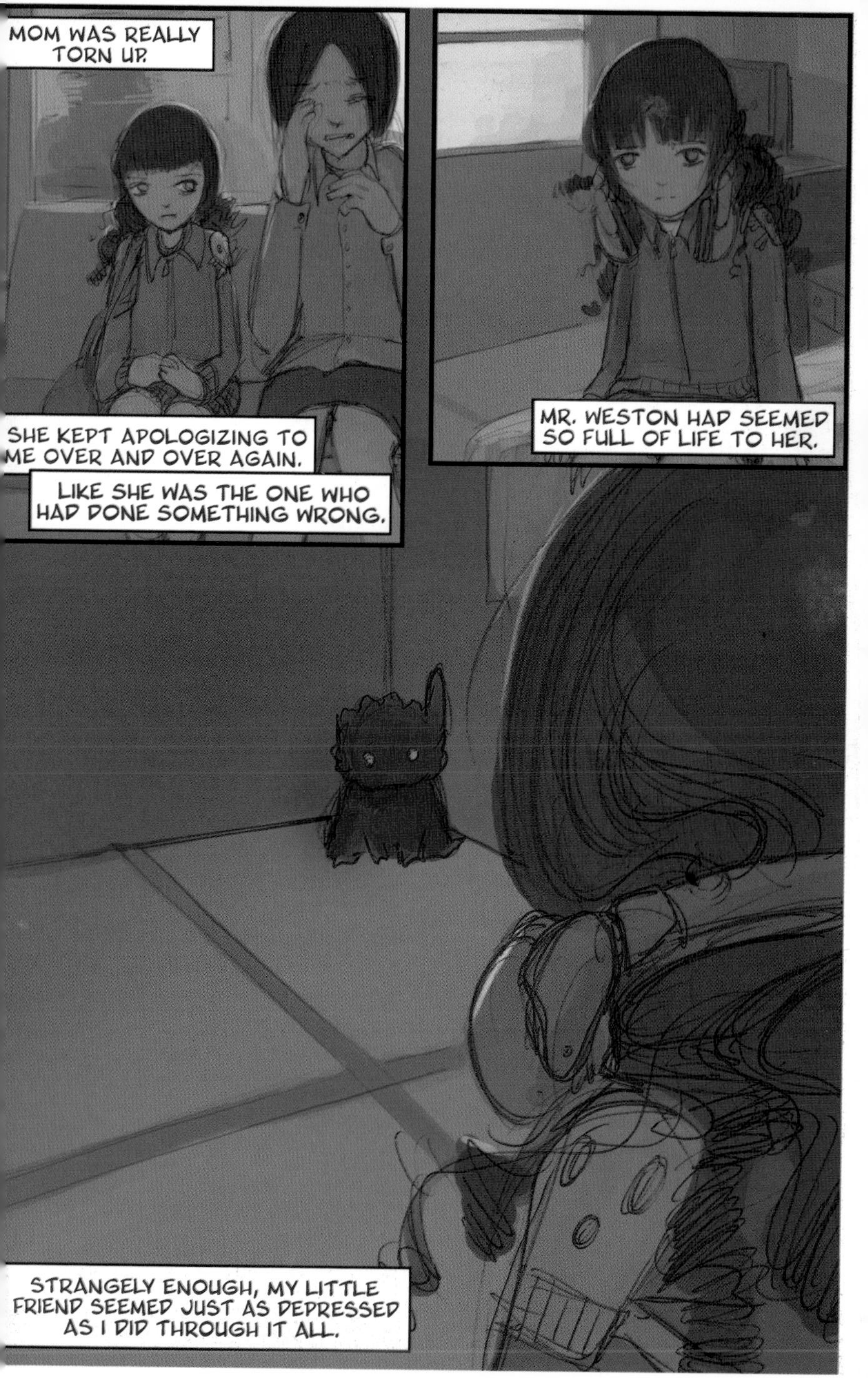
MOM WAS REALLY TORN UP.
SHE KEPT APOLOGIZING TO ME OVER AND OVER AGAIN.
LIKE SHE WAS THE ONE WHO HAD DONE SOMETHING WRONG.
MR. WESTON HAD SEEMED SO FULL OF LIFE TO HER.
STRANGELY ENOUGH, MY LITTLE FRIEND SEEMED JUST AS DEPRESSED AS I DID THROUGH IT ALL.

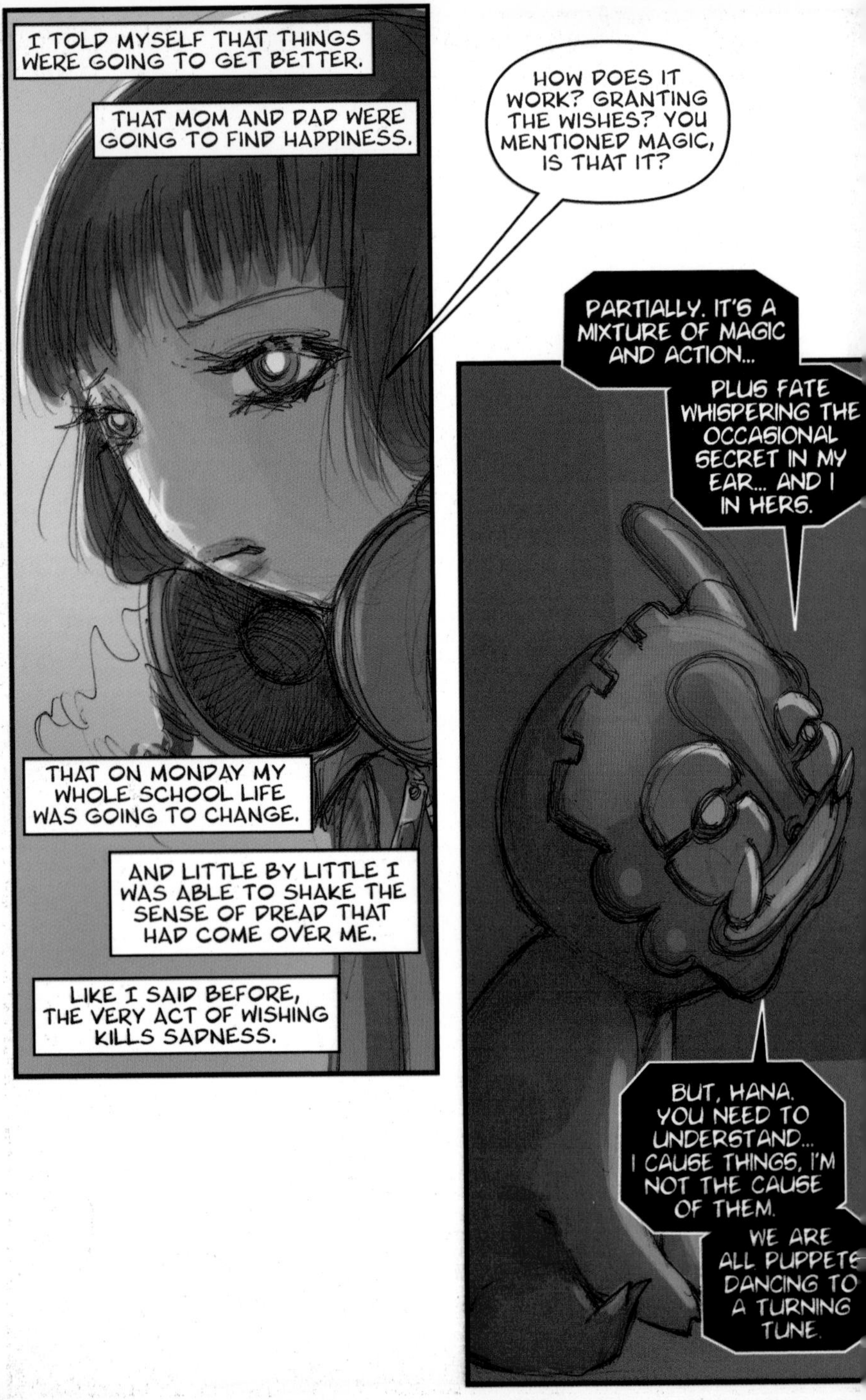
I TOLD MYSELF THAT THINGS WERE GOING TO GET BETTER.
THAT MOM AND DAD WERE GOING TO FIND HAPPINESS.
HOW DOES IT WORK? GRANTING THE WISHES? YOU MENTIONED MAGIC, IS THAT IT?
THAT ON MONDAY MY WHOLE SCHOOL LIFE WAS GOING TO CHANGE.
AND LITTLE BY LITTLE I WAS ABLE TO SHAKE THE SENSE OF DREAD THAT HAD COME OVER ME.
LIKE I SAID BEFORE, THE VERY ACT OF WISHING KILLS SADNESS.
PARTIALLY. IT'S A MIXTURE OF MAGIC AND ACTION...
PLUS FATE WHISPERING THE OCCASIONAL SECRET IN MY EAR... AND I IN HERS.
BUT, HANA. YOU NEED TO UNDERSTAND... I CAUSE THINGS, I'M NOT THE CAUSE OF THEM.
WE ARE ALL PUPPETS DANCING TO A TURNING TUNE.

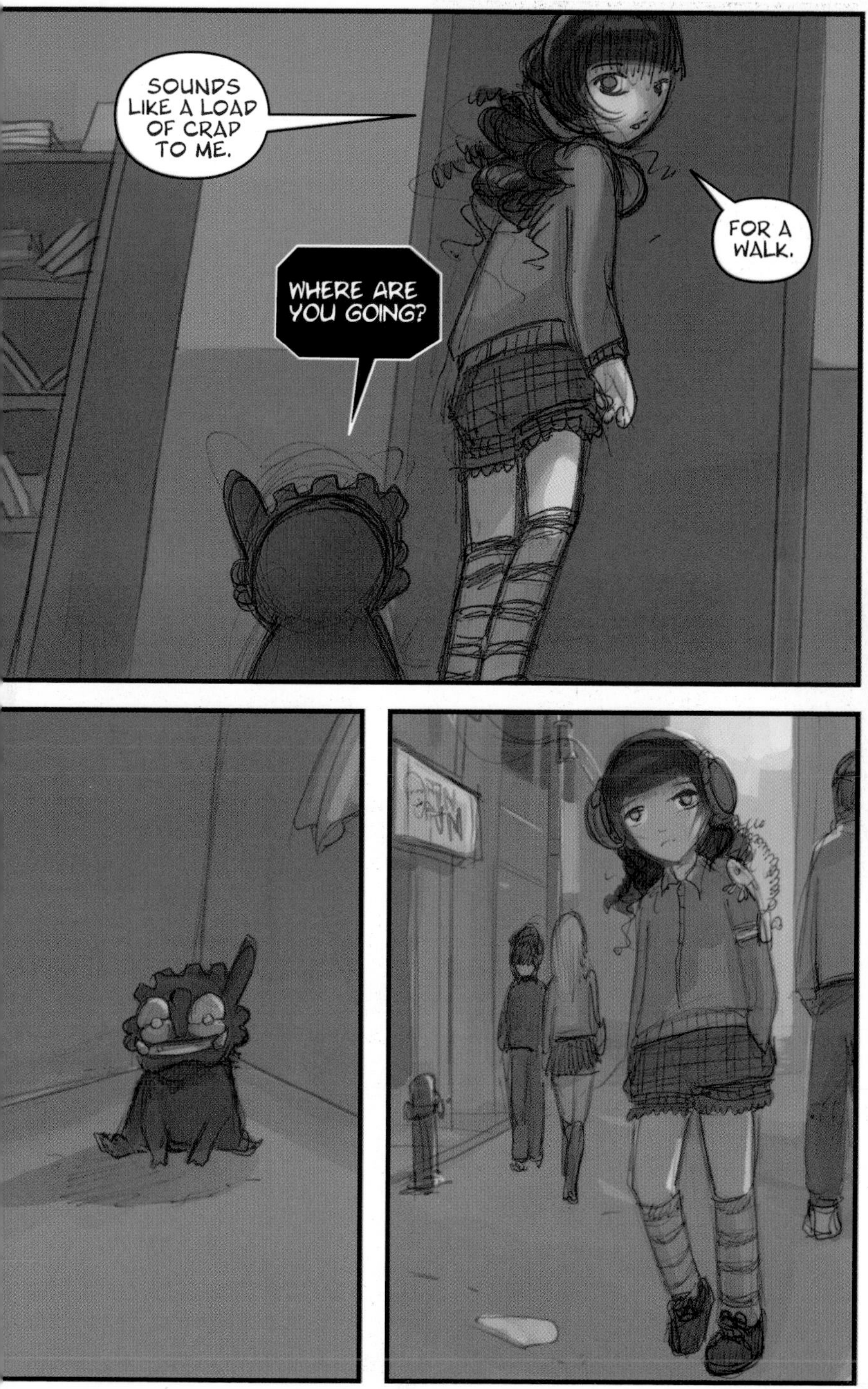
SOUNDS LIKE A LOAD OF CRAP TO ME.
WHERE ARE YOU GOING?
FOR A WALK.

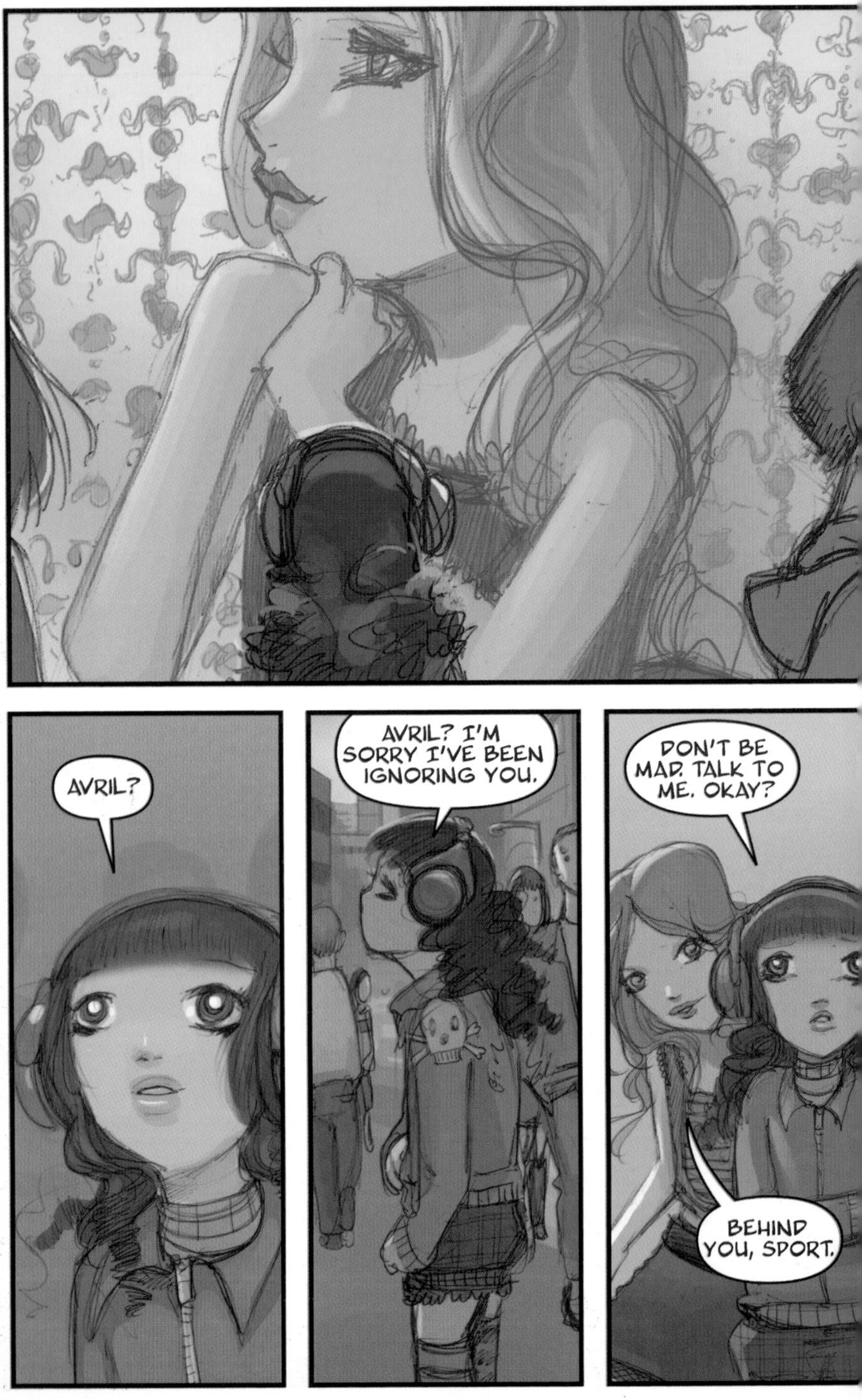
AVRIL?
AVRIL? I'M SORRY I'VE BEEN IGNORING YOU.
DON'T BE MAD. TALK TO ME. OKAY?
BEHIND YOU, SPORT.

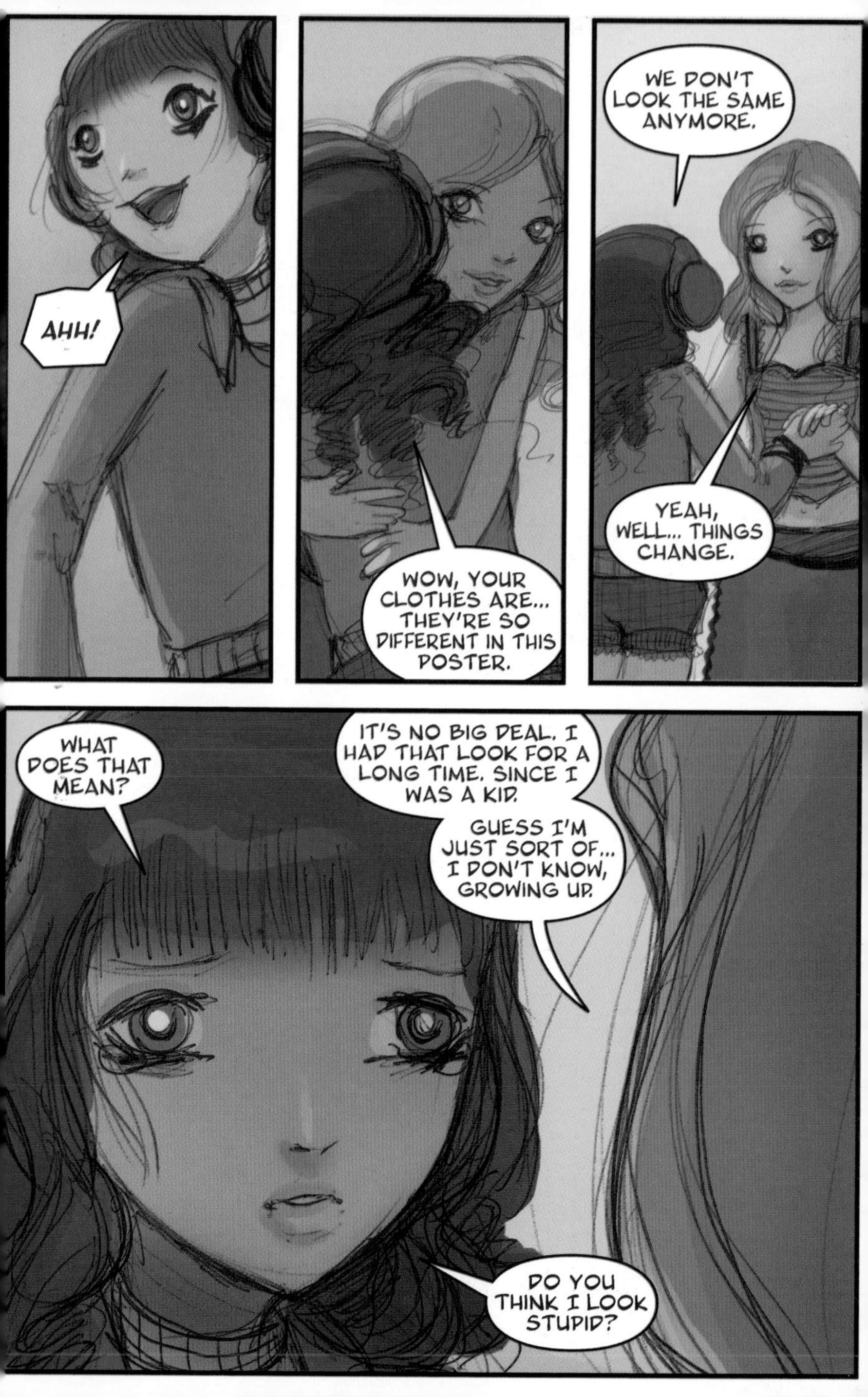
AHH!
WOW, YOUR CLOTHES ARE... THEY'RE SO DIFFERENT IN THIS POSTER.
WE DON'T LOOK THE SAME ANYMORE.
YEAH, WELL... THINGS CHANGE.
WHAT DOES THAT MEAN?
IT'S NO BIG DEAL. I HAD THAT LOOK FOR A LONG TIME. SINCE I WAS A KID.
GUESS I'M JUST SORT OF... I DON'T KNOW, GROWING UP.
DO YOU THINK I LOOK STUPID?

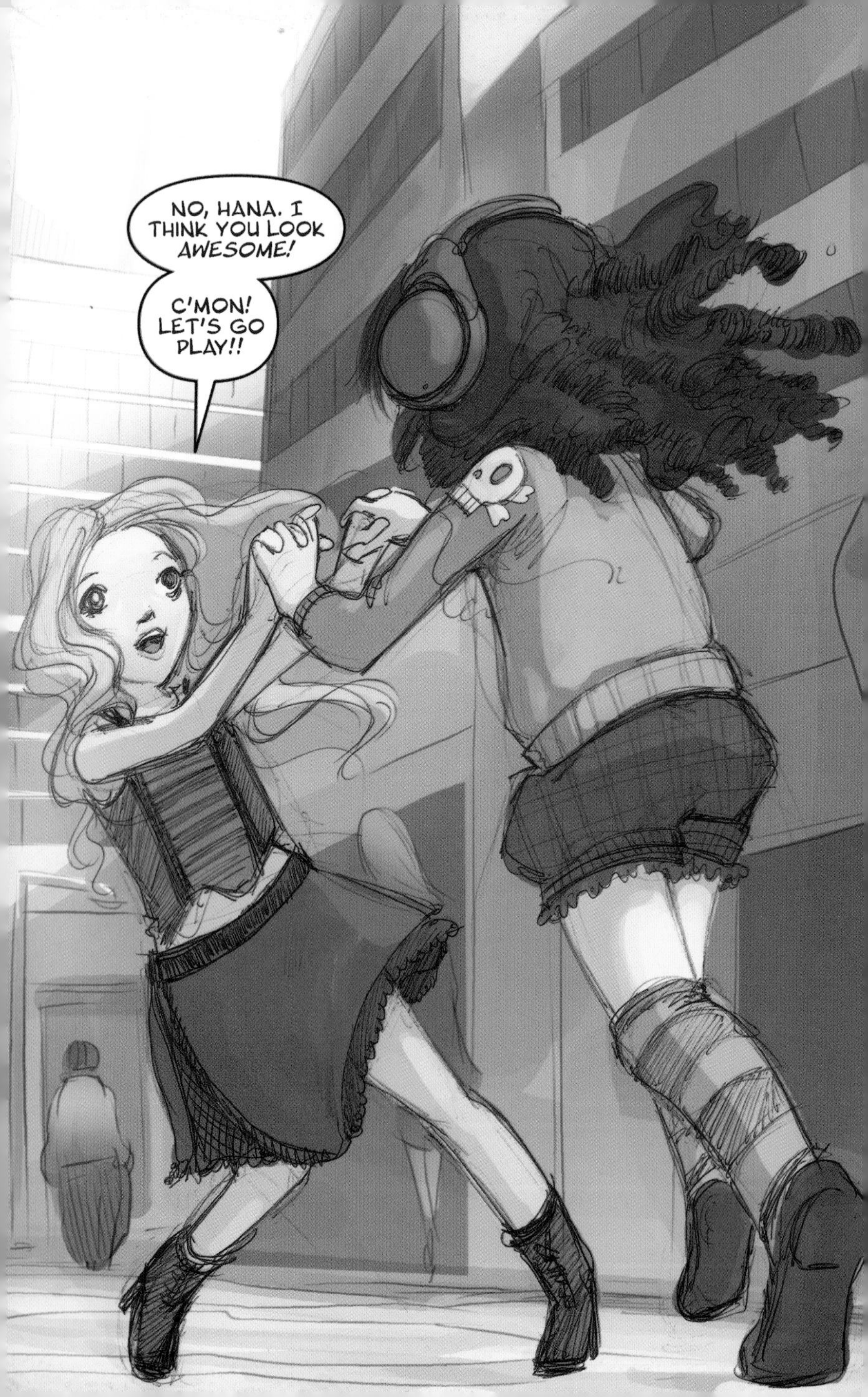
NO, HANA. I THINK YOU LOOK AWESOME!
C'MON! LET'S GO PLAY!!

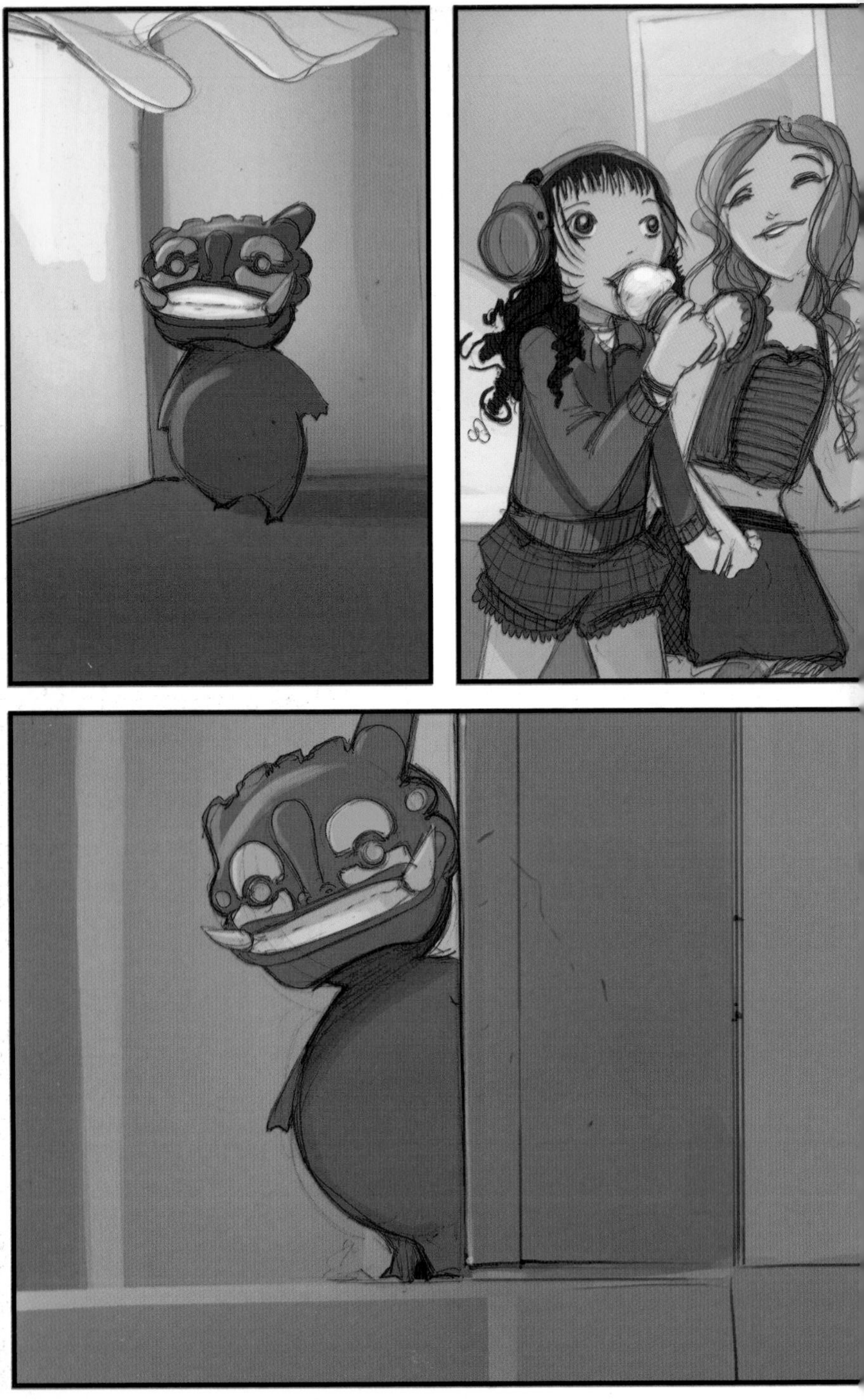

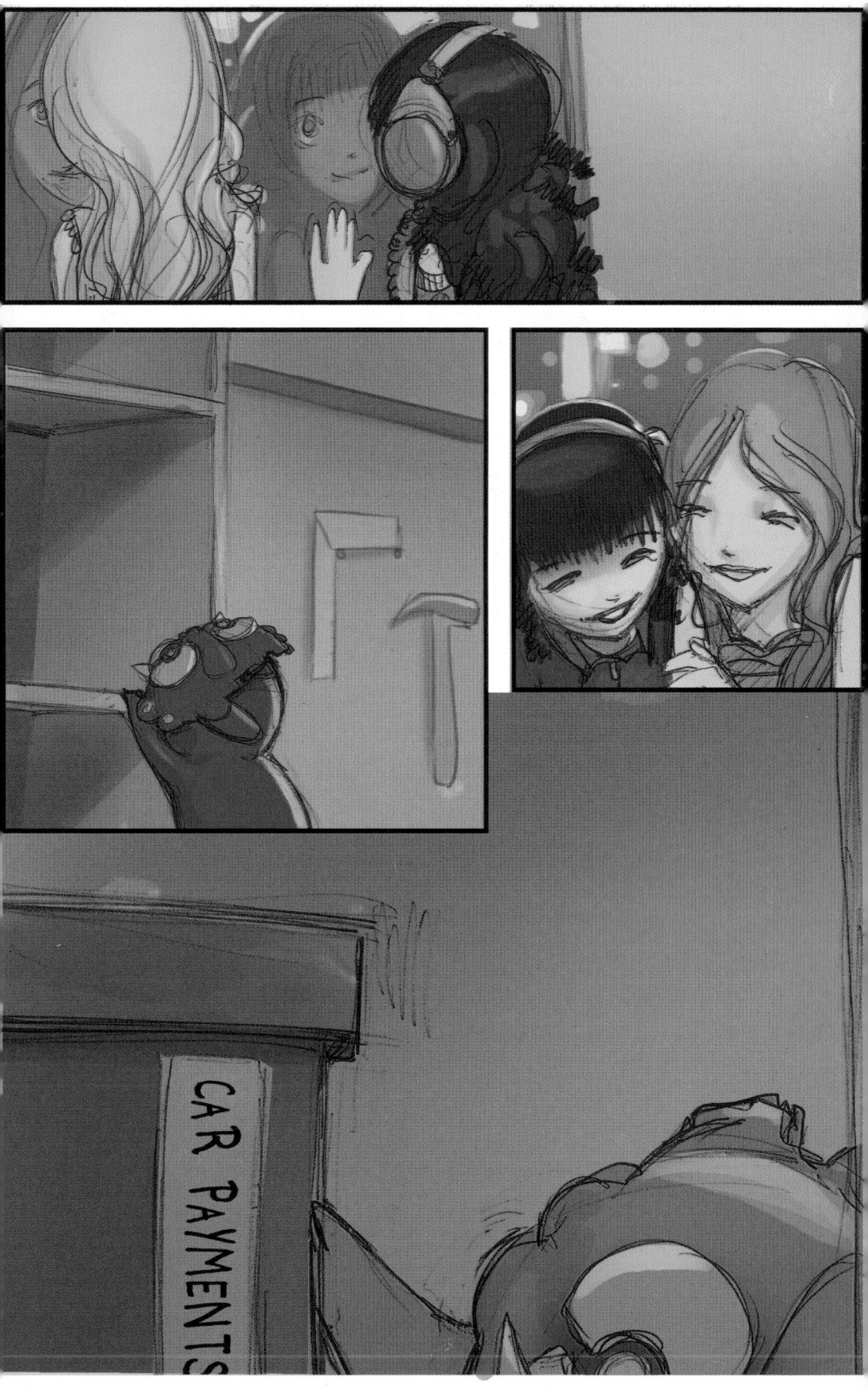
CAR PAYMENTS

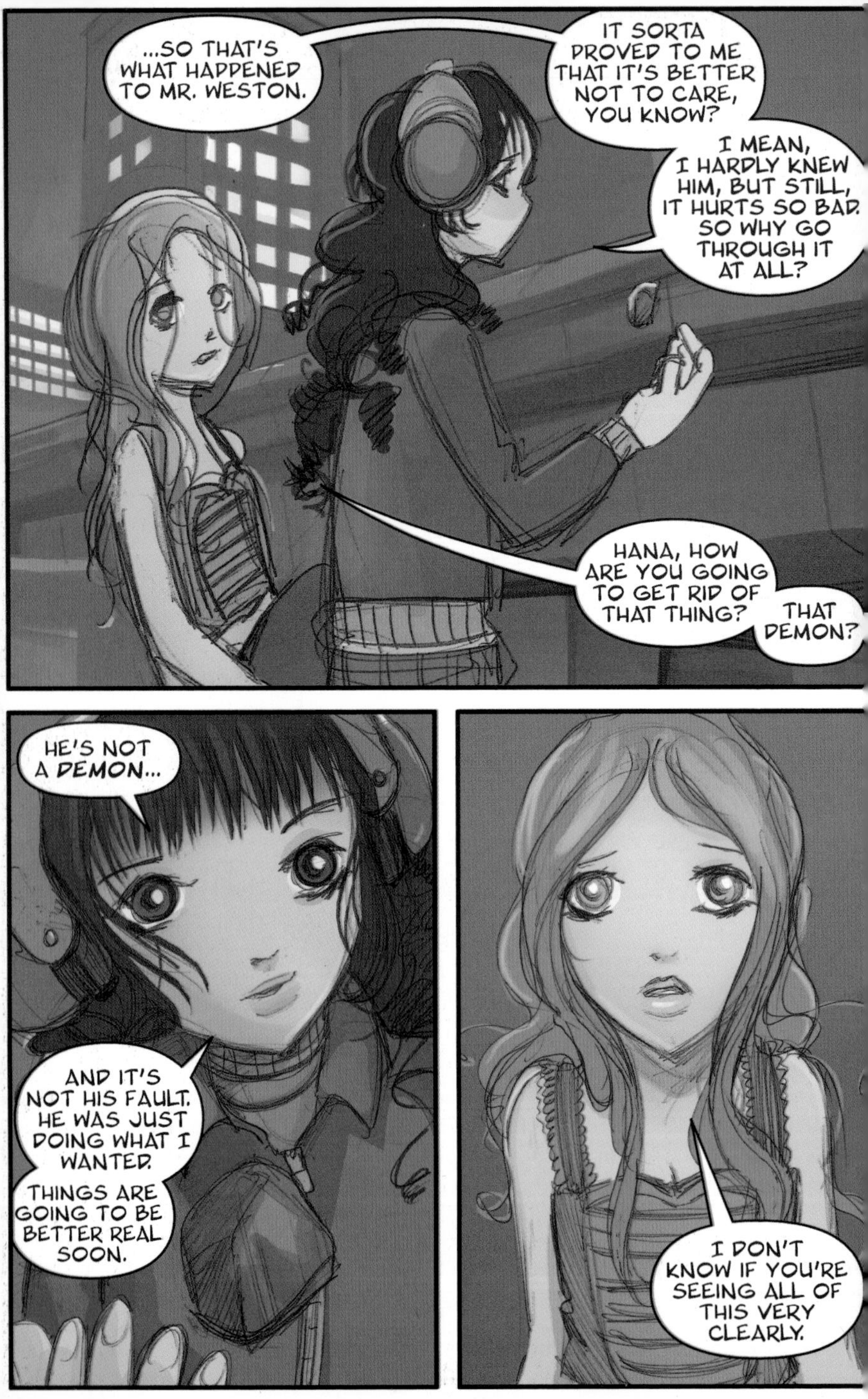
...SO THAT'S WHAT HAPPENED TO MR. WESTON.
IT SORTA PROVED TO ME THAT IT'S BETTER NOT TO CARE, YOU KNOW?
I MEAN, I HARDLY KNEW HIM, BUT STILL, IT HURTS SO BAD. SO WHY GO THROUGH IT AT ALL?
HANA, HOW ARE YOU GOING TO GET RID OF THAT THING?
THAT DEMON?
HE'S NOT A DEMON...
AND IT'S NOT HIS FAULT. HE WAS JUST DOING WHAT I WANTED.
THINGS ARE GOING TO BE BETTER REAL SOON.
I DON'T KNOW IF YOU'RE SEEING ALL OF THIS VERY CLEARLY.

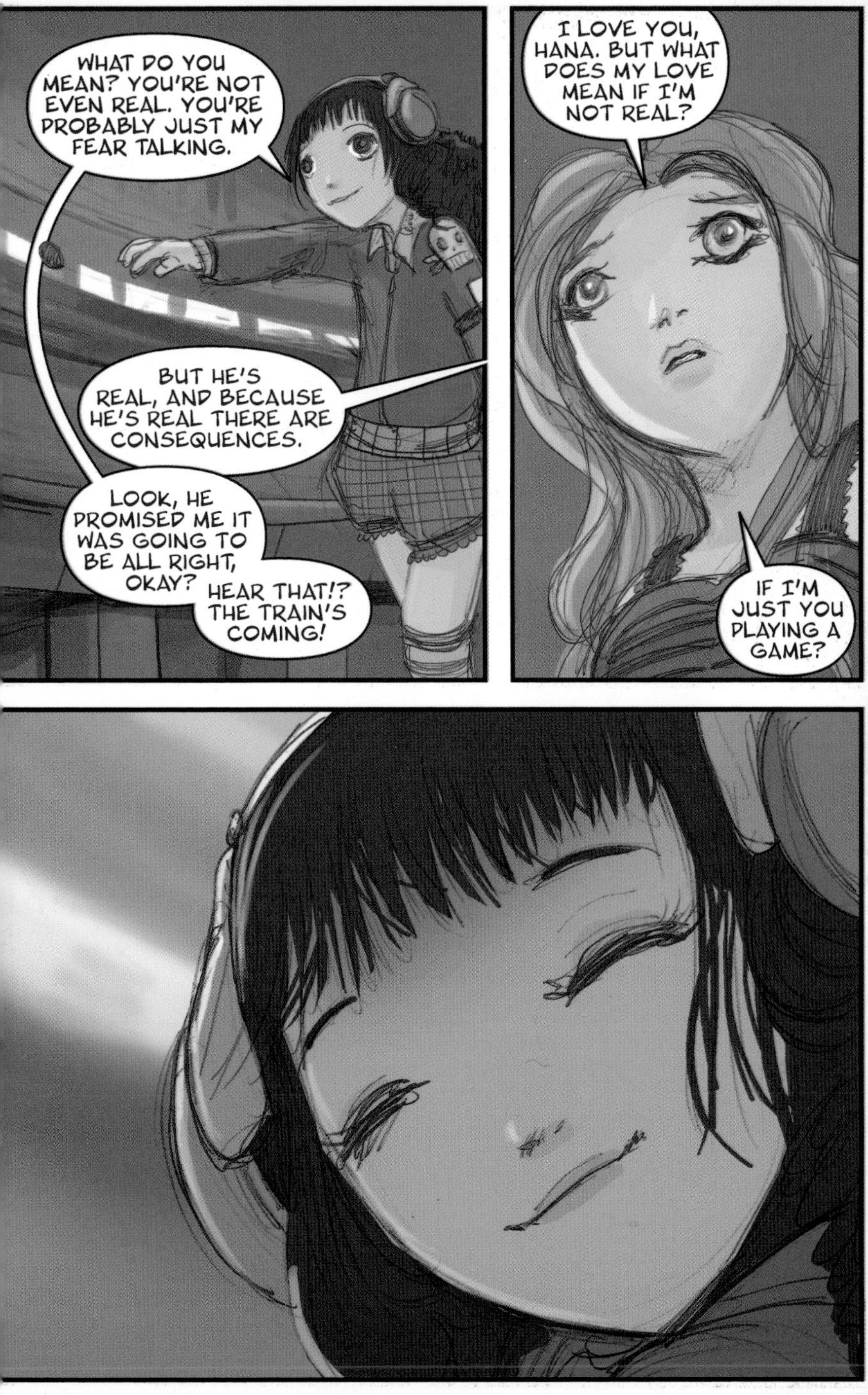
WHAT DO YOU MEAN? YOU'RE NOT EVEN REAL. YOU'RE PROBABLY JUST MY FEAR TALKING.
BUT HE'S REAL, AND BECAUSE HE'S REAL THERE ARE CONSEQUENCES.
LOOK, HE PROMISED ME IT WAS GOING TO BE ALL RIGHT, OKAY?
HEAR THAT!? THE TRAIN'S COMING!
I LOVE YOU, HANA. BUT WHAT DOES MY LOVE MEAN IF I'M NOT REAL?
IF I'M JUST YOU PLAYING A GAME?

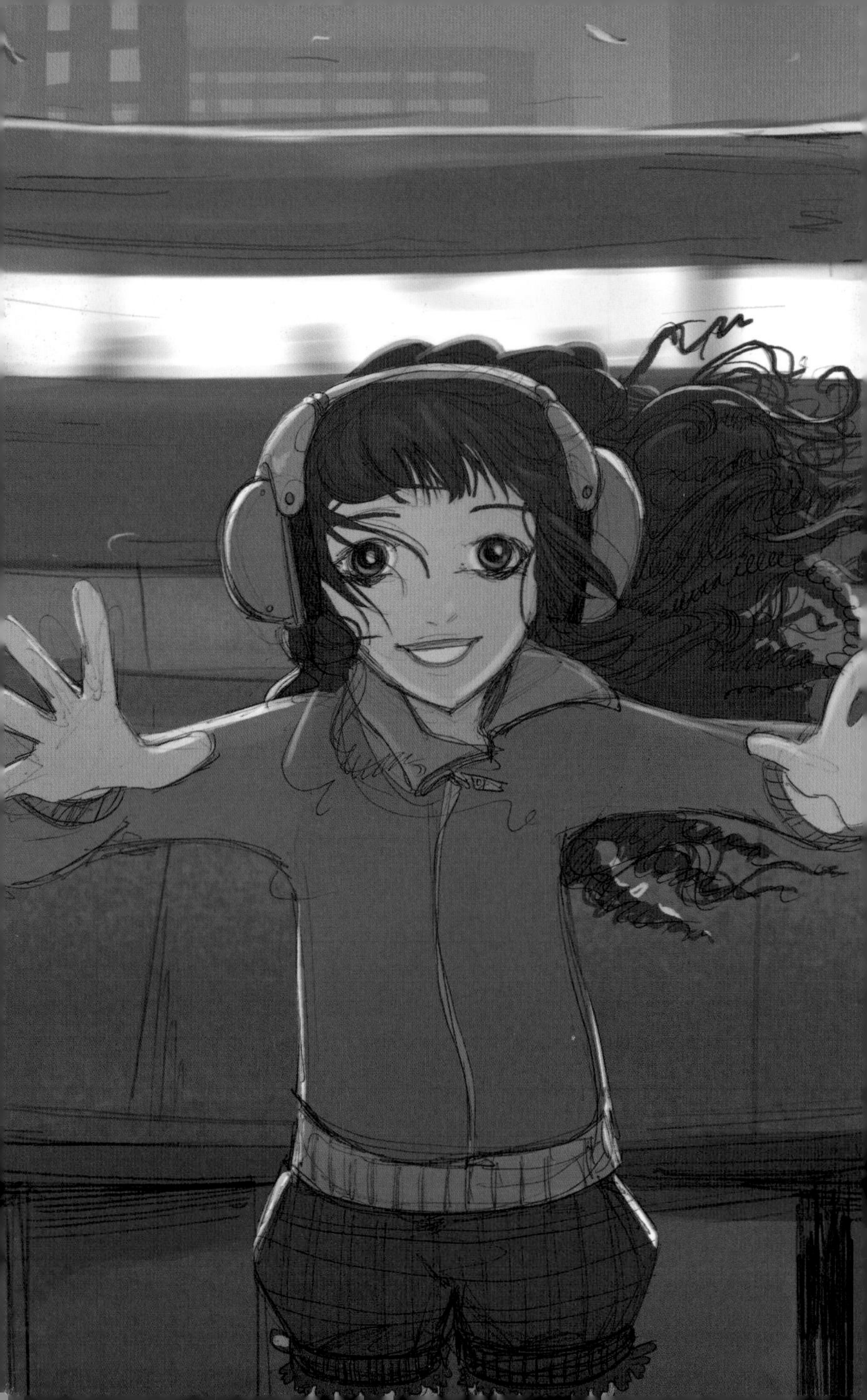

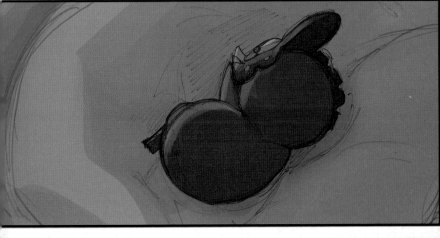

THE VISIT WITH AVRIL AND THE CUDDLY NIGHT'S SLEEP WITH MY LITTLE LIVING DOLL HAD HEALED ME SOME.

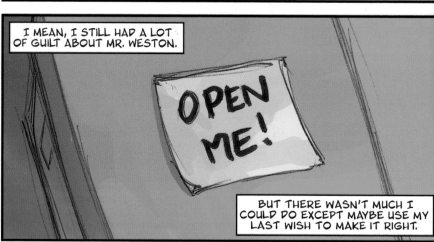

I MEAN, I STILL HAD A LOT OF GUILT ABOUT MR. WESTON.

OPEN ME!

BUT THERE WASN'T MUCH I COULD DO EXCEPT MAYBE USE MY LAST WISH TO MAKE IT RIGHT.

I'M OFF, MOM!

SEE YOU LATER, HON.

WHICH WAS SOMETHING I WAS CONSIDERING.

THING IS, THAT MORNING...

IT JUST FELT LIKE THINGS WERE ABOUT TO CHANGE FOR THE BETTER.

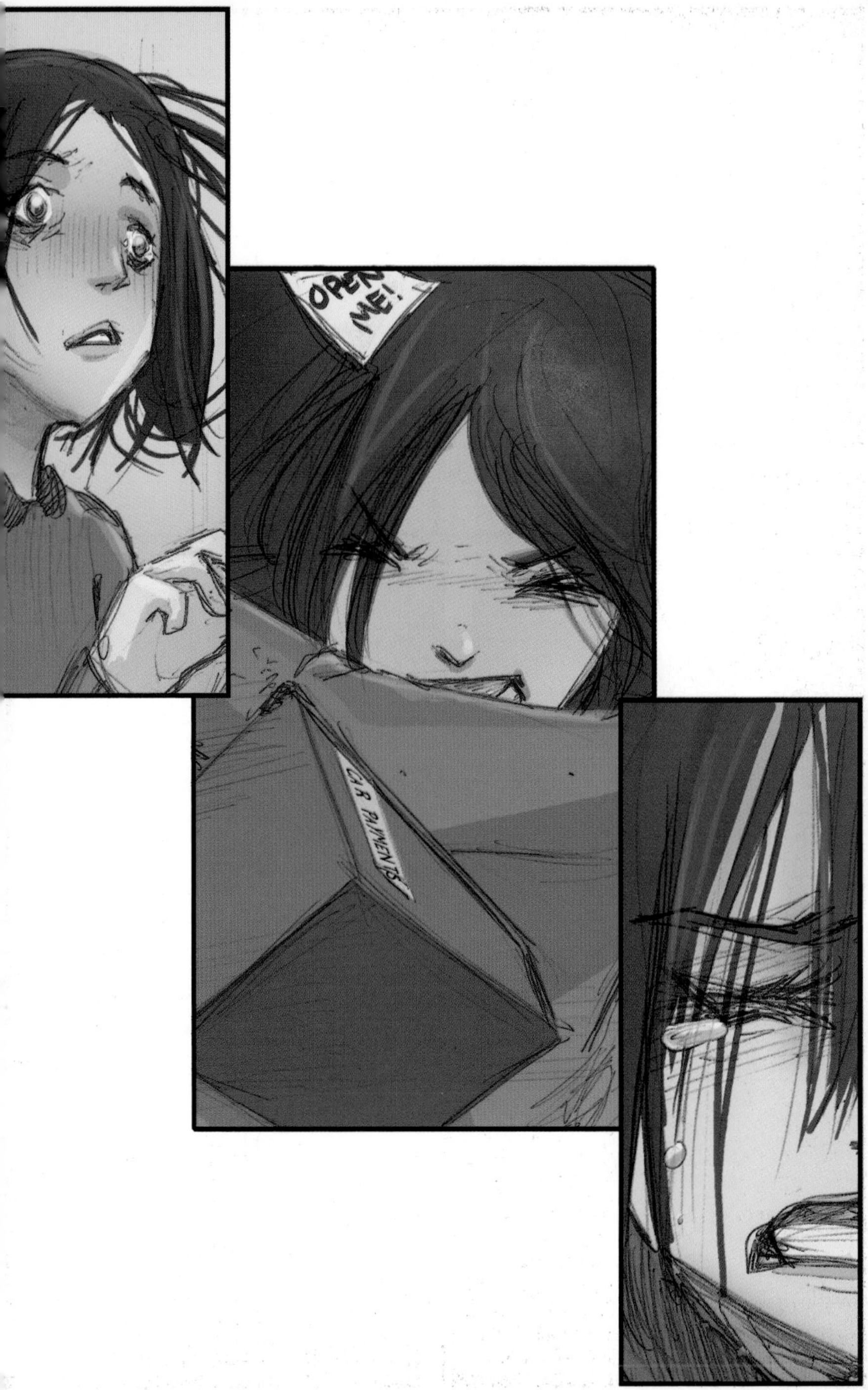
OPEN ME!
CAR PAYMENTS

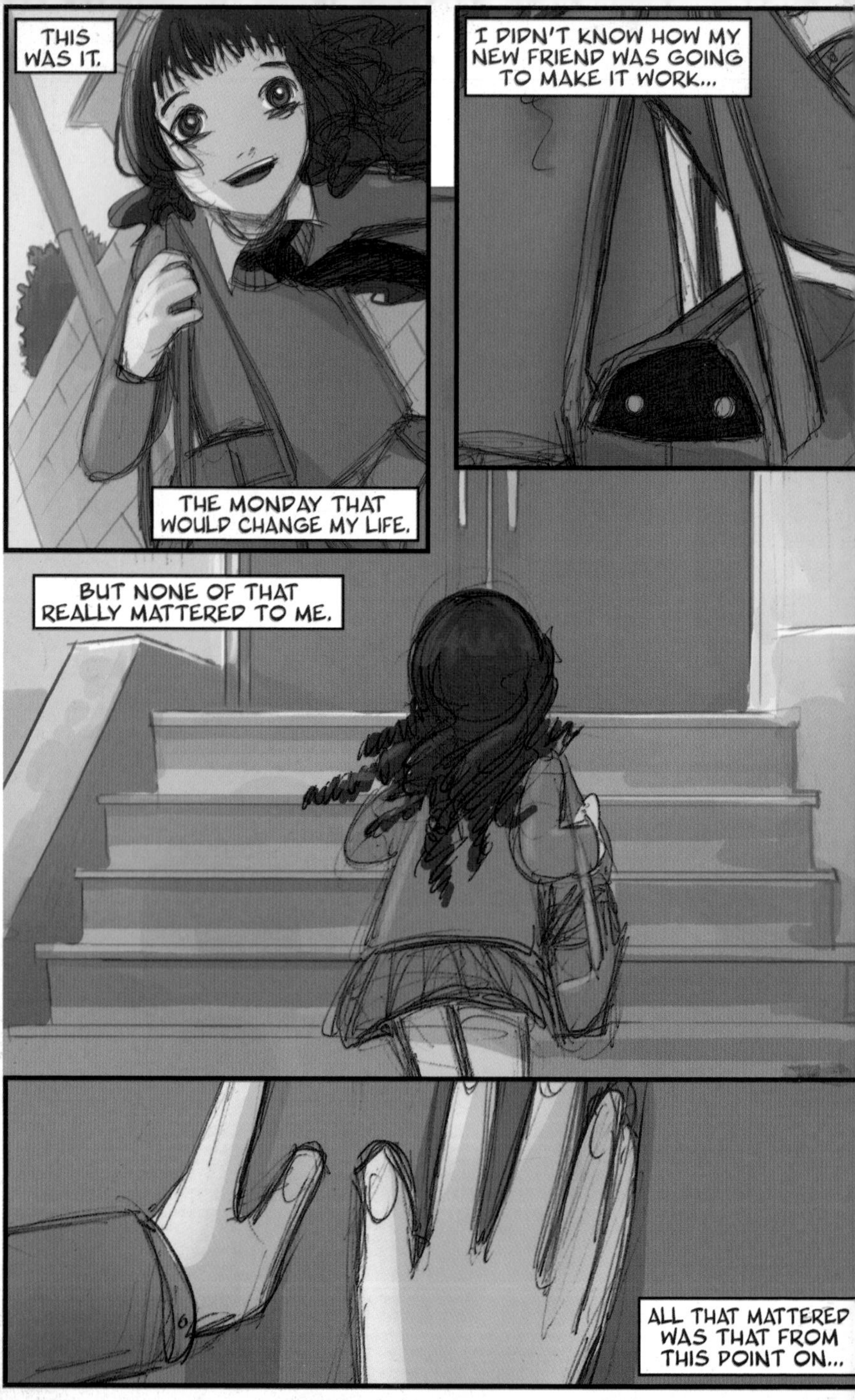
THIS WAS IT.
THE MONDAY THAT WOULD CHANGE MY LIFE.
I DIDN'T KNOW HOW MY NEW FRIEND WAS GOING TO MAKE IT WORK...
BUT NONE OF THAT REALLY MATTERED TO ME.
ALL THAT MATTERED WAS THAT FROM THIS POINT ON...

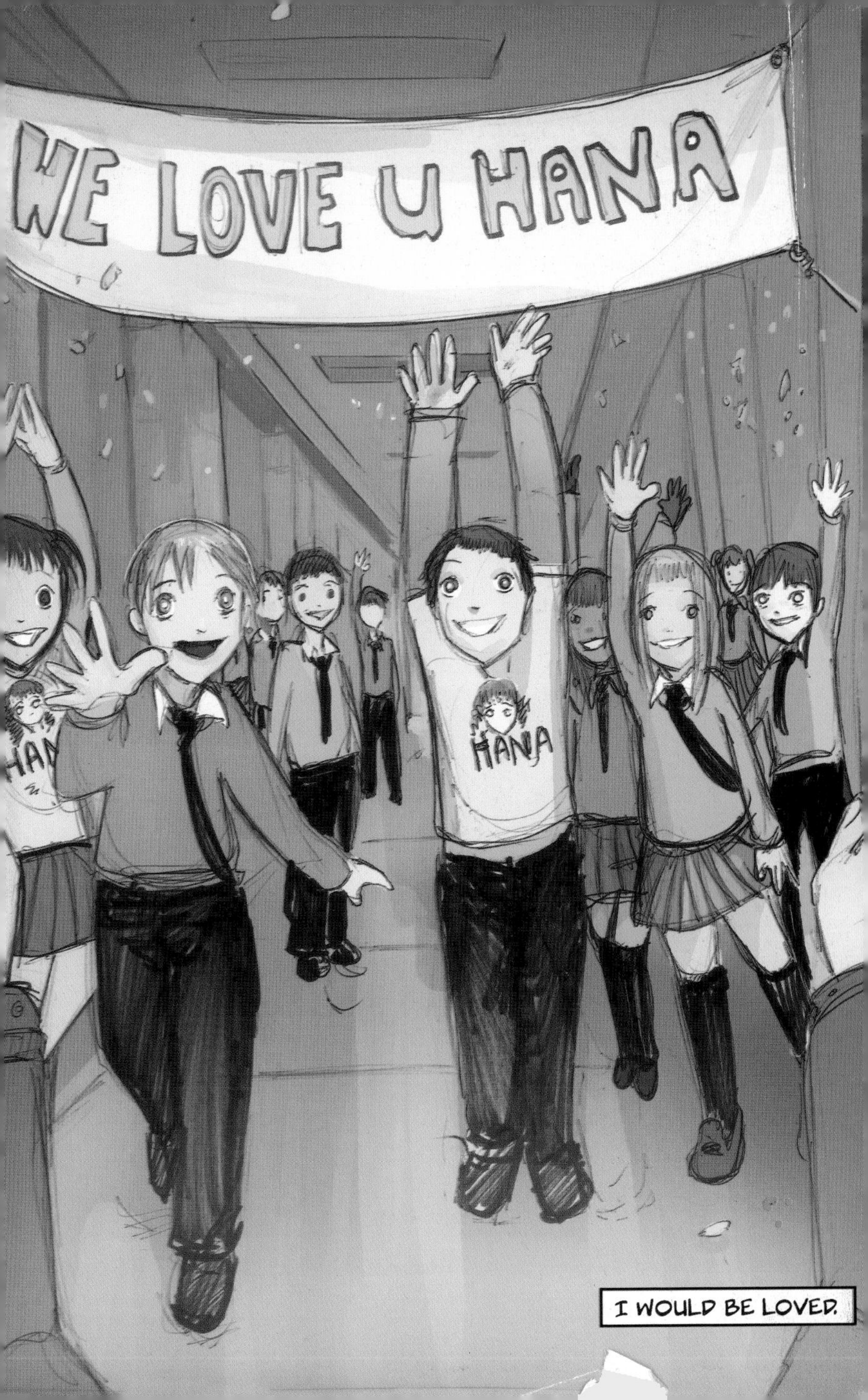
WE LOVE U HANA
HANA
HANA
I WOULD BE LOVED.

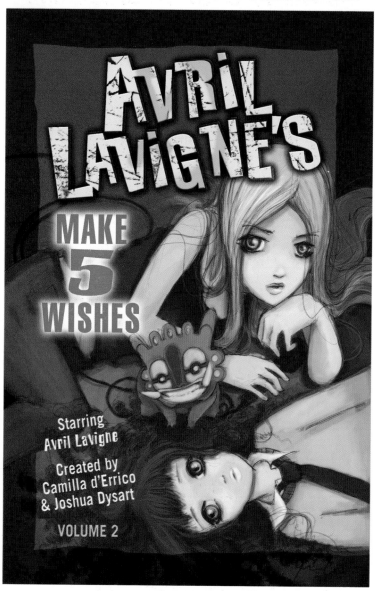

ARTIST'S SKETCHBOOK
Camilla d'Errico

AVRIL

When I started to design the Avril character, I referenced a lot of her old pictures to see how she dressed. It occurred to me that Avril has a few different personas now, so drawing her as she was a few years ago at the height of her punk/rebel phase would have a different impact than if I was to draw her the way she looks now. I chose to picture Avril as she was early on because it made sense from a fan's perspective, especially Hana's, to want to idolize the rebellious Avril.

We all wish we could act out and be free to express who we are. I think that Avril really opens that up for kids. In the story you see that she does change. It was important to deal with that issue for Avril and for the story.

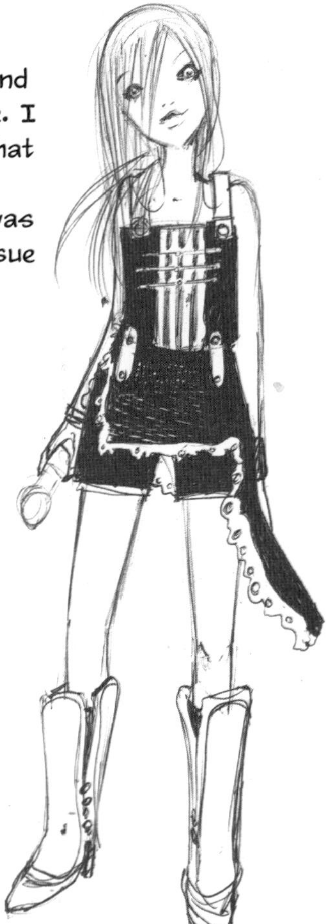

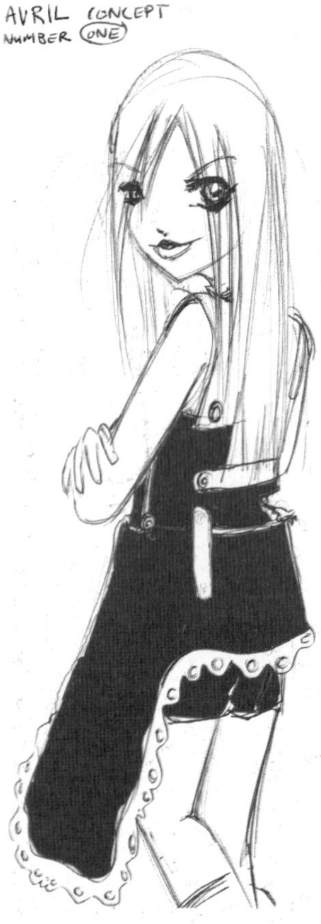
AVRIL CONCEPT
NUMBER ONE

Avril is always changing, as are we all, so I wanted to show her as she was and as she is. Hana also goes through a lot of growing up, and that is reflected in how we portray Avril (in my opinion, anyway!).

HANA

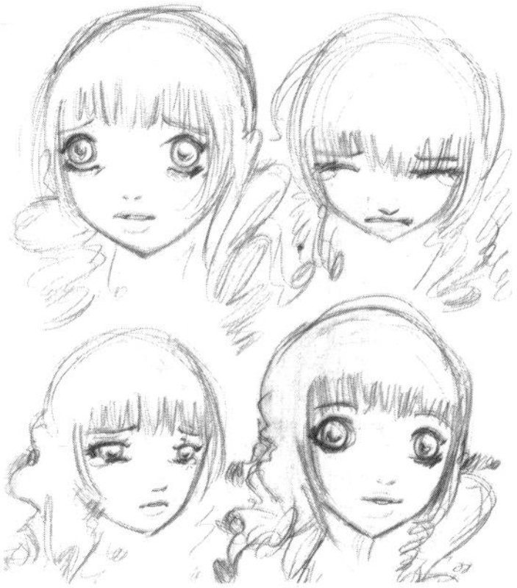

My dear little Hana! She has gone through quite a bit, actually. Her original name was Iku. I really liked that name, but we found out that it actually meant something quite unusual in Japanese, so we had to change it. Joshua came up with Hana, which is Japanese but still like a Western name.

I designed Hana to look like my younger sister. She has black, spiral hair that is quite long and really beautiful. As I started to draw her, she began to look a lot like I do. Hana's bangs, hair color, texture (my hair is also curly) . . . Suddenly someone who was supposed to be an homage to my sister became my twin. Personality was never an issue. She's a lot more like my sis than me—but we're sisters, so obviously we share some personality traits.

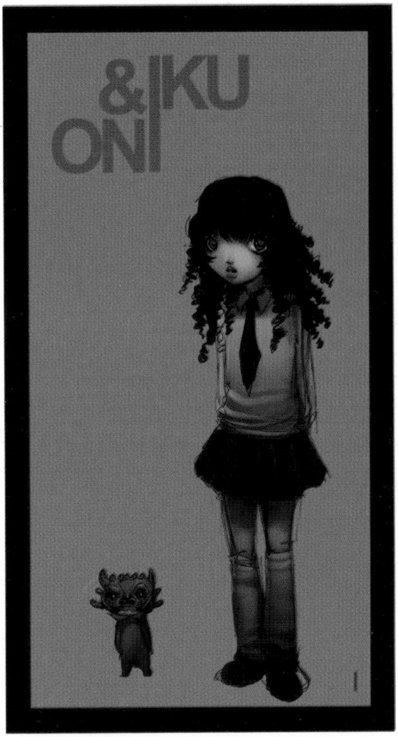
IKU
&
ONI

ROMEO

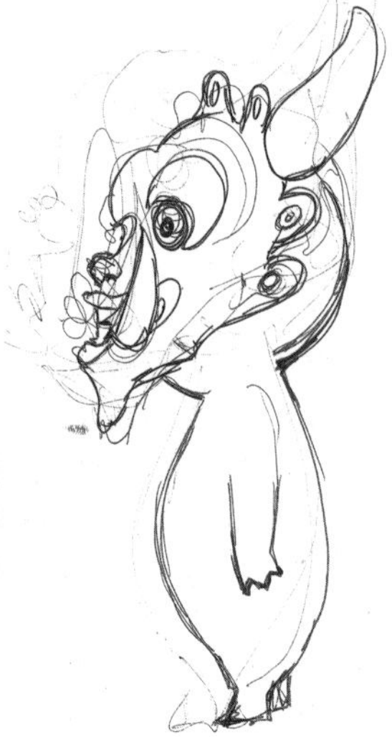

My original demon was very evil. He/it spoke only to Hana and no one else could see it, so it was with her constantly, whispering in her ear to keep her from talking to others and basically reinforcing Hana's insecurities. The demon in this story is cute and cuddly! He isn't evil; he just thinks differently than we do. Since he isn't human, why should he think like a human?

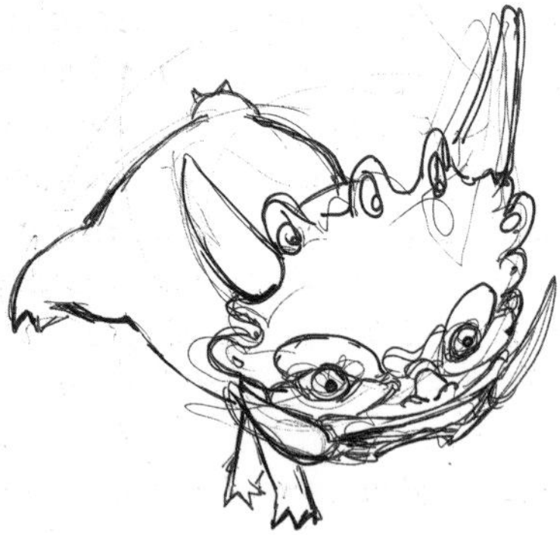

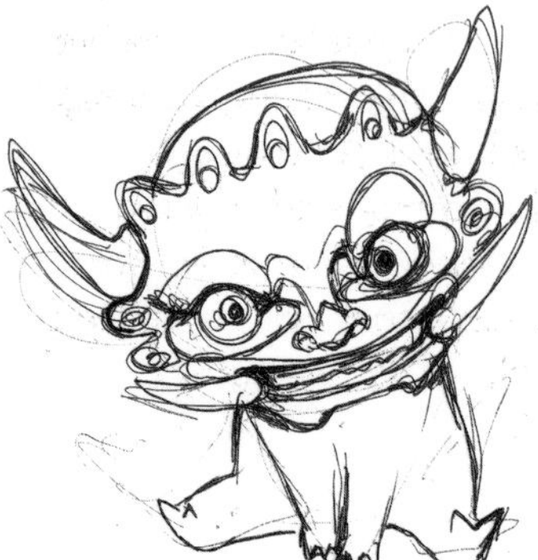

I always loved Mark Twain's story "The Mysterious Stranger." In a way, Romeo is a lot like Satan in that context. All that cute stuff is Joshua—I had nothing to do with it, that's all Joshua! And why shouldn't our demon enjoy himself? He is a wishing demon, after all.

ABOUT THE CREATORS

ABOUT AVRIL

AVRIL LAVIGNE was born in the small town of Napanee, Ontario, Canada, and stood out from the crowd at an early age. Her musical talents were noticeable by the age of two, and by the time she was in her early teens she was already writing songs and playing guitar. Singing in the church choir and local festivals allowed Lavigne to get her voice heard.

On a trip to New York at age 16, Lavigne was signed to Arista Records when she caught the attention of Antonio "LA" Reid. With her major label deal signed, Lavigne moved to New York City, but not long after moved on to Los Angeles to work on her record. By early 2002, her debut CD, *Let Go*, was released. With 15 million albums sold, 8 Grammy nominates, and three #1 singles—"Sk8ter Boi," "Complicated," and "I'm With You"—Lavigne gave young women a defiant voice.

In 2004, Lavigne returned with *Under My Skin*. This time the Canadian chanteuse took charge of her creative direction and reflected a more introspective Avril. The album debuted at No. 1 on charts worldwide and delivered her fourth #1 single, "My Happy Ending."

Twenty-six million albums later, and following numerous awards, multiple world tours, and myriad magazine covers and TV appearances, Lavigne is now finding time to concentrate on her other loves, acting and fashion. Her third CD, *The Best Damn Thing*, releases in the spring of 2007.

ABOUT THE ARTIST

CAMILLA D'ERRICO is an artist whose first love is the manga form. Her work will be featured by the underwear and lingerie company Ginch Gonch in their AIDS Awareness promotion scheduled for Fall 2007. In addition to the *Make 5 Wishes* series, she will have three comics published in 2007: *Burn*, a traditional manga series published by Arcana Studios in Canada; *Zevon-7*, a four-part miniseries published by AngelGate Press; and *Nightmares and Fairytales*, by Slave Labour Graphics.

ABOUT THE WRITER

JOSHUA DYSART has been writing comics and graphic novels for a decade. He's been published by DC, Vertigo, Dark Horse, Image Comics, IDW, and many more and translated into four languages. His work includes two years on the legendary *Swamp Thing*; the adaptation of *Crouching Tiger, Hidden Dragon*; *Van Helsing Beneath the Rue Morgue*, an original story featuring the character from the Universal film; *Monster House: A Skull and Bones Story* from Sony's animated kids' feature; and *Age of Conan*, a comic to be included in the forthcoming massive multiplayer online game package. He's currently working on the epic miniseries *Conan and the Midnight God* at Dark Horse.

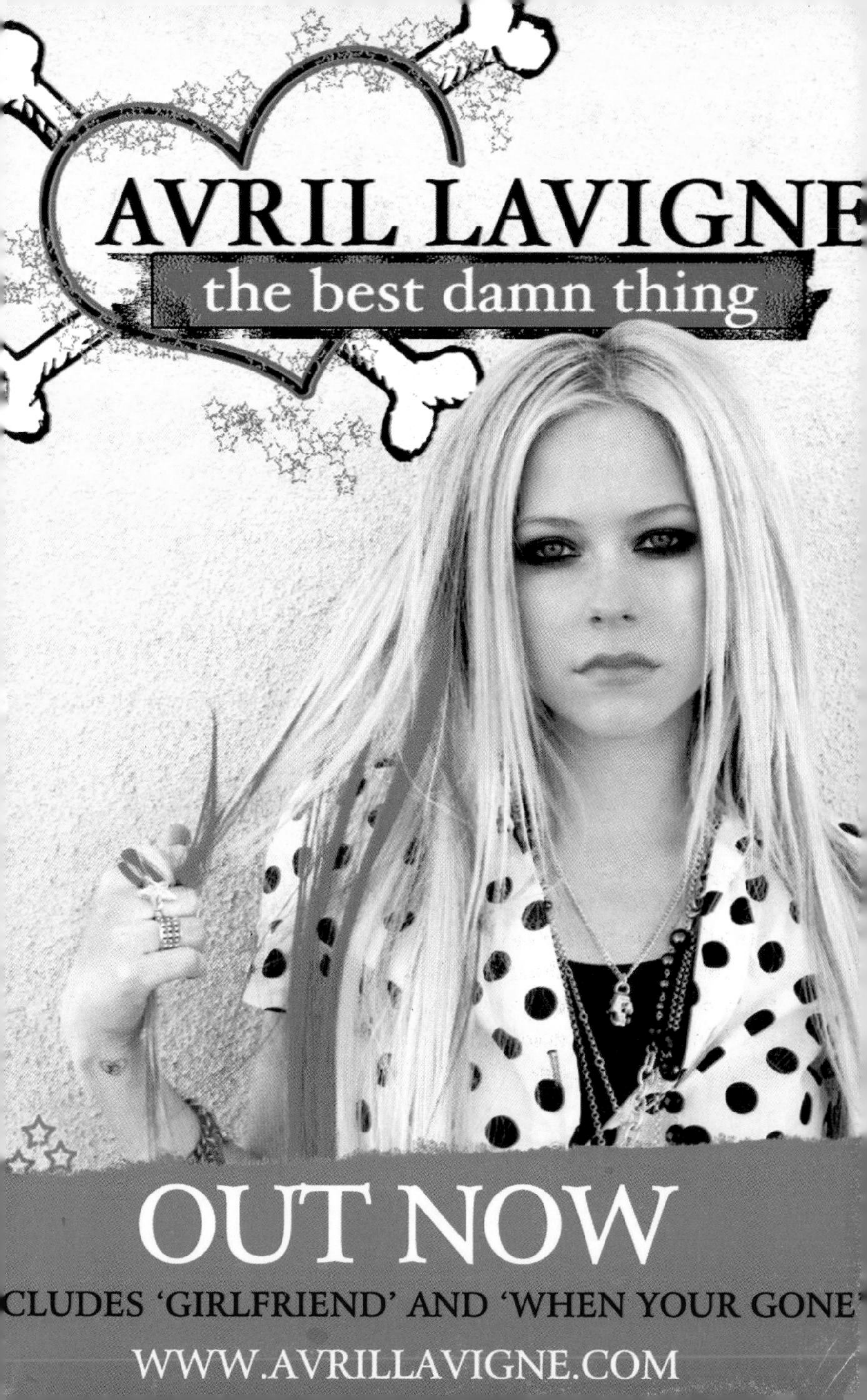
AVRIL LAVIGNE
the best damn thing
OUT NOW
CLUDES ‘GIRLFRIEND’ AND ‘WHEN YOUR GONE’
WWW.AVRILLAVIGNE.COM

VISIT AVRIL'S OFFICIAL WEBSITE:
www.AvrilLavigne.com

KILL YOUR DEMONS:
Make5Wishes.com

GET THE HOTTEST OFFICIAL AVRIL GEAR HERE:
www.AvrilMerch.com

JOIN AVRIL'S OFFICIAL MYSPACE PAGE:
www.MySpace.com/AvrilLavigne